Researching Black Communities

Researching Black Communities

A METHODOLOGICAL GUIDE

Edited by James S. Jackson,
Cleopatra Howard Caldwell,
and Sherrill L. Sellers

UNIVERSITY OF MICHIGAN PRESS | ANN ARBOR

First paperback edition 2015
Copyright © by the University of Michigan 2012
All rights reserved

Published in the United States of America by the
University of Michigan Press
Manufactured in the United States of America
⊗ Printed on acid-free paper

2018   2017   2016   2015   5   4   3   2

A CIP catalog record for this book is available from the British Library.

Library of Congress Cataloging-in-Publication Data

Researching black communities : a methodological guide / edited by
    James S. Jackson, Cleopatra Howard Caldwell, and Sherrill L.
    Sellers.
        p.   cm.
    Includes bibliographical references.
    ISBN 978-0-472-11750-5 (cloth : alk. paper) —
    ISBN 978-0-472-02618-0 (e-book)
    1. Blacks—Social conditions—Research.   2. Blacks—Research.
3. Ethnology—Methodology.   I. Jackson, James S.   II. Caldwell,
Cleopatra Howard.   III. Sellers, Sherrill L.
    HT1581.R47   2012
    305.896'073—dc23
                                                    2011043632
    ISBN 978-0-472-03477-2 (pbk. : alk. paper)

Acknowledgments

This book is dedicated to professionals and students conducting empirical research on black populations. The idea for this book on methodological issues and lessons learned grew over the last three decades as a part of our attempts to develop conceptually and methodologically sound studies of black populations. Over this period we have conducted 30 national, regional, and international studies on black populations focused on substantive issues related to health, mental health, and political behavior.

Much of this research was conducted under the auspices of the Institute for Social Research's Program for Research on Black Americans (PRBA). Established in 1976, PRBA has among its major objectives the collection, analysis, and interpretation of empirical data, and the dissemination of findings based upon national and international studies of peoples of African American and African descent. The program was founded upon the premise that data of this nature are essential for advances in basic social science knowledge and for public policy formulation. A related and equally important purpose is to provide research and training opportunities for black social scientists and students.

Thirty years ago high-quality national social science data with a sociocultural focus sensitive to black life did not exist. Thus, in addition to the substantive contribution of the empirical studies, it was necessary for the PRBA to develop novel and unique methods. These methods are of general utility and have made important contributions to several national and regional surveys, particularly the sampling of racial and ethnic minorities and other high-visibility, geographically clustered groups. Procedures developed in one of PRBA's flagship studies, the National Survey of Black Americans (NSBA), permitted blacks to be sampled for the first time in a way that ensured that individuals in each and every black household in the continental United States had a known probability of selection.

The application of multiplicity sampling procedures produced, for the first time in *any* population group, a three-generation family lineage national probability sample (National Three-Generational Family Study). We also developed novel telephone sampling procedures to conduct the

1984 National Black Election Study (NBES) and, more recently, methods and procedures to follow up the 1980 NSBA and the 1984 NBES samples. These large national probability samples coupled with detailed, culturally relevant and extensive questionnaires make this research unique in the social and behavioral science study of black Americans.

PRBA researchers have also been leaders in the use of back-translation procedures, focus groups, random probe procedures, cognitive interviewing assessments, and "concept mapping," the consolidation of thematic material in oral respondent reports ("chunking"), new analytic procedures with this data, and the integration of qualitative data and quantitative data into scientific presentation. For example, the Adolescent Transition Network of the Macarthur Foundation provided funding for support of a pilot project to assess the feasibility of developing quantitative instruments and qualitative procedures to study the intergenerational context of teenage pregnancy. We continue to refine our techniques in the integration of qualitative instrument development and data collection, and the analysis and interpretation of qualitative data.

We have been fortunate over the years to have received research support from a wide variety of funding sources. Grants from the National Institute of Mental Health, the National Institute on Aging, the Office of Behavioral and Social Science Research, and the National Science Foundation provided much of the research infrastructure for PRBA success. Additional grants from the Rockefeller, Ford, Robert Wood Johnson, Macarthur, and Annie Casey Foundations, along with the Carnegie Corporation, have also provided support. Without their support the research and this book would not have been possible.

We owe this book to the members of the PRBA who have contributed so much to the development of empirical studies of black populations. Many of them began as students in the early days, and today they provide important scientific leadership. Notable among these people are Dr. Harold Neighbors, current director of PRBA, and Drs. Robert Taylor and Linda Chatters, as well as the long-term contributions of Ms. Myriam Torres in her role as senior research associate.

We want to thank the anonymous reviewers for their feedback. Your comments and suggestions strengthened each chapter. We must also acknowledge the authors included in this volume for their patience, professionalism, and enthusiasm for the project. Ms. Phyllis Stillman played a major role in the original editing and feedback to the authors during the early part of the process. We would like to acknowledge and thank her for this critical contribution to the completed book.

Finally, we want to sincerely thank Ms. Antoinette Booze-Battle whose hard work and correspondence and interactions with the authors in preparing the final manuscripts were invaluable to the completed book. We would also like to thank Ms. Katie Muldowney who provided considerable help with editing and formatting in the early stages of the book and Ms. Karen Spirl who provided critical administrative assistance during the final stages of the process.

Contents

PART I | Theoretical Issues: Race,
Ethnicity, Culture, Gender, Class,
and Intersectionality

1 | Conceptual and Methodological Challenges in Studies of Black Populations

James S. Jackson, Cleopatra Howard Caldwell, and Sherrill L. Sellers

Recent census data indicate that blacks are the second largest racial group in the United States (U.S. Census Bureau 2007). The black population is also increasingly diverse, with a rising middle class and a surge in the number of black immigrants coming to this country since 1965. Over the past two decades, there have been noticeable efforts by the National Institutes of Health (NIH) and other funding agencies to require the inclusion of racial and ethnic minority groups in agency-sponsored studies in an effort to increase scientific knowledge in an ever-diversifying society. We applaud these efforts and hope this volume will assist researchers, especially young scholars, who study racial and ethnic minority populations by offering insights from a group of social science researchers experienced in conducting research within black communities.

One important dimension of the research task, community resistance, has not been the object of enough systematic study (Caldwell et al. 1999; Copeland-Linder, chap. 7, this volume; Israel, Eng, Schulz, and Parker 2005). It is a problem that is well known to researchers who have worked in black and other racial and ethnic minority communities. This resistance to research appears to be appreciably greater in minority than in white communities (Caldwell et al. 1999). There are several reasons for this greater resistance. Among these are the poor reputations that previous researchers have in conducting studies in these communities and beliefs that such research can have negative and damaging effects on the community through changes in public policies (Caldwell et al. 1999). At a more personal level there may be a greater tendency to mistrust the basic intent of the research and researchers and to believe that it is directed at ascertaining personal information about the individual that will have deleterious consequences (e.g., social welfare office checking on household composition; see Norton, Vincson, and Wilhelm, chap. 5, this volume). Thus, proportionately fewer blacks participate in empirical investigations than whites, resulting in limited scientific knowledge about this population.

The purpose of this volume is to examine conceptual and methodological issues that are critical to the study of black people in different settings and across diverse black ethnic populations, both within the United States and abroad. A number of issues addressed have implications for research generally. We have purposely limited our focus to a single racial group in order to capture more within-group complexity due to immigrant status and ethnic group differences. For example, research findings reinforce the significance of understanding cultural influences in the research process. Specifically, early research on language revealed that blacks had a well-developed language form distinctly different from that of white Americans (e.g., Labov 1972). In the highly language-dependent methodology of survey research, culturally based language differences can have significant effects. This is particularly true for older cohorts of blacks reared in the South as well as among non-native-born Caribbean blacks (Williams, Haile, Gonzalez, Neighbors, Baser, and Jackson 2007) and Africans (Arthur 2000) who may assign different meanings to study concepts based on their life experiences. Similarly, a great deal of research points to cultural differences in style and expression (both behavioral and verbal) that can affect responding in research situations (Caldwell et al. 1999). These style differences are heavily influenced by the nature of the life experiences of racial and ethnic minority populations. We believe, however, that many of the methodological strategies presented and lessons learned that are offered here are applicable when conducting research with other racial and ethnic minority populations.

Numerous complex challenges continue to confront scholars interested in conducting effective research with racially and ethnically diverse populations, especially in areas such as health disparities (Mays, Cochran, and Barnes 2007). The chapters in this volume address substantive research areas each contributor has been investigating for a number of years. Collectively they examine the distinct phases of the research process, including conceptualizing, designing, and collecting and analyzing data, as well as interpreting results. Practical examples are provided to share how challenges were approached. We hope that the examples will serve as catalysts for others to find creative ways of overcoming some of the obstacles to conducting culturally competent research within black communities and contributing to more blacks participating in empirical studies that could have benefits for improving their quality of life.

In this volume, some chapters focus on a specific group of black people (e.g., black men or black women); others use a race-comparative or an ethnic-differences approach (e.g., black-white; African American–Caribbean black). Study settings range from New York City to South Africa, and institutional issues related to conducting research involving the mental health system and media are critically assessed. Although most studies rely on regional data and cross-sectional study designs, issues related to conducting national studies and effectively implementing studies with longitudinal designs are also discussed. The strengths of both qualitative and quantitative approaches to research are considered, and diverse analysis strategies, including specific ethnographic, multivariate, and mixed-methods approaches, are described as they relate to research with black populations.

The breadth of research settings and approaches offered are important strengths of the volume; however, we were unable to include some social institutions that are salient in the lives of blacks in contemporary society. Specifically, we have not included research conducted within the adult criminal justice system. As the incarnation rates of blacks, particularly black men, have soared (Harrison and Beck 2006; Sampson and Wilson 1995), we acknowledge this limitation and refer readers to Megargee (1995) for a valuable account of how to conduct research in correctional settings. We also have not dedicated a chapter to the advantages or disadvantages of specific data analysis approaches or data analysis techniques (e.g., hierarchical regression, structural equation modeling, hierarchical linear models) when working with diverse populations. Rather, individual authors address these issues based on their own experiences with illustrations of the outcome of their approach (for examples, see Veroff and Orbuch, chap. 6, and Snowden, chap. 14, this volume). Nevertheless, we believe that the research experiences and exemplary knowledge of methodological literature throughout will make this volume a useful tool.

Scholarly Discourse on Conducting Research in Black Communities: Why This Volume, Now?

Perhaps the single most pressing question is why this volume now, particularly in light of recent events with the election of the first black American president of the United States. We address this question and provide examples of past research involving minorities that produced misleading or inaccurate results because the researchers did not employ proper methods or lacked proper sensitivity. We suggest that these new historically important national events are precisely the reason for a book now on methodological challenges in conducting research in black communities. The rapidly changing demographic landscape of America reflecting new areas of immigration and differential birth rates among ethnic minority groups prompt a renewed sense of urgency in conducting research with communities of color. This is especially true when a major political barrier has been hurdled in the election of the first black American president, which may lead many to a sense of complacency in the areas of concern to social and behavioral science research. Regardless of the important political changes that are occurring, there remains limited research conducted within black communities that reflects both conceptual and methodological clarity and rigor (Caldwell et al. 1999; Manly 2006; Smith 1993).

To illustrate these ideas, we focus on research on black Americans' mental health. However, similar arguments can be made for a diverse set of areas of scientific inquiry, including marital relationships (see Veroff and Orbuch, chap. 6, this volume), education (see O'Connor, Lewis, and Mueller, chap. 2, this volume), and media consumption (see Haggins and Squires, chap. 16, this volume).

The mental health status of black Americans continues to be a controversial issue. It has been used to justify slavery, enforce racial segregation, and reinforce the idea that blacks were inferior to whites (Washington 2006). The question of the mental health status of black Americans has been complicated by a number of methodological and conceptual problems. These include racial biases, small sample sizes, and widely varying definitions of mental health and illness.

Sellers and colleagues (2002) suggested that the history of mental health research on blacks in America can be divided into four historical periods marked by changing methodological approaches. The first period encompasses slavery and early pseudoscientific studies of the mental health status of black Americans. This research had racist overtones that shaped diagnoses, prevention efforts, and treatment strategies. For instance, researchers coined the phrase *escape disorder* and labeled the flight for freedom a mental health problem among enslaved Africans. The second period considers early hospital admissions studies. These efforts were aimed at estimating the prevalence of mental health problems by examining hospital admissions records. The studies indicated that black Americans had higher rates of psychopathology than whites based on hospital data (Neighbors 1989). One flaw of these early studies was that blacks tended to disproportionately use public agencies while whites more often entered private treatment facilities, yet admissions rates were computed from public, not private, facilities. The third period describes the advent of epidemiologic community surveys. Rather than reviewing admissions rates, researchers used household surveys based upon probability sampling methods. Based upon this interview data they would assess "caseness" using clinical judgments. The aim was to develop more accurate estimates of psychopathology within entire populations. Unfortunately, researchers often lacked awareness of cultural differences among blacks and whites and did not account for differences in socioeconomic status that may influence presentation, language styles, and openness to personal interviews. The final period presents the symptoms checklist approach, which allows nonclinical interviewers to gather data on mental disorder. The checklist approach received substantial support in the early 1970s from the National Institute of Mental Health when it funded the Epidemiological Catchment Area Study (ECA). This multisite study used the Diagnostic and Statistical Manual criteria, the Diagnostic Interview Schedule (DIS) and nonclinical lay interviewers to gather data on psychiatric disorders in noninstitutionalized populations.

Although many studies had been conducted on local and regional convenience samples of blacks (Jackson et al. 1982; Stanfield 1993), until the 1980 National Survey of Black Americans (NSBA), most of these studies were severely limited by methodological and conceptual problems. Gerald Gurin places the NSBA in a larger psychiatric epidemiology context.

> To truly appreciate what a monumental and historic feat the NSBA was, one has to think back to the tenor of the 1970s (in the US). This was a time still heavily influenced by the radicalism of the 1960s. In 1977, when planning for the original NSBA began, we were not that distant from the urban civil disorders and subsequent federally funded research attempts to understand and control these protests. Nor were we far removed from publication of the Moynihan Report (which described the "pathology" of black American families). These and other forces combined to create a pessimistic atmosphere for social science research on African Americans during the 1970s. (Neighbors and Jackson 1996)

The original NSBA was a face-to-face interview conducted by a predominantly black research team. The focus was on establishing a sampling procedure to ensure equal probability of selection and resulted in a sample of 2,107 adult black Americans (Jackson 1991; see Caldwell, this volume). The original NSBA did not attempt to assess clinical disorders, rather the study aimed to consider how black Americans coped with everyday life, using a stress and coping framework. The methodological strengths of the NSBA are numerous, including use of focus groups to develop questions, race matching of interviewers, and innovative sampling and interviewing methodologies. The next step in this landmark study was the 2003 National Survey of American Life, which continues the tradition of innovative, high-quality research with black communities (see Jackson et al., chap. 9, and Hastings et al., chap. 10, this volume).

Drawing from the history of research on mental health and black Americans, several lessons can be learned that prompt and shape this volume. Research is not conducted in a vacuum. Researchers are embedded in a sociocultural milieu that shapes the questions we ask, the methods we choose, and the conclusions we draw. This does not suggest, however, that objective social science research is impossible; rather, we argue that awareness is a central feature of high-quality research with diverse populations. Researchers must be aware of assumptions the researcher and society make about racial groups. The meaning of race is a social and political construction that changes over time and across space. It is a fluid categorization that permeates our social, political, and cultural milieu. Historically, social science research has struggled to deal with race in an objective fashion (Zuberi and Bonilla-Silva 2008). Epistemological issues include the assumptions that society and the researchers make about race and the meaning of racial categories in research (Stanfield 1993).

Race, particularly the divide between blacks and whites, has been a central concern of social policy, economic strategies, and research agendas. The idea that phenotypical racial differences were associated with variations in personal traits and biological differences was part of mainstream scientific thinking of the late nineteenth and early twentieth centuries (Washington 2006). Perhaps the most notorious twentieth-century study involving blacks that indicated the prevailing view of scientific inquiry of this period is the Tuskegee Syphilis study (Katz et al. 2008). In 1927, the U.S. Public Health Service conducted a study that tested a hypothesis that syphilis was a different disease in blacks than in whites and determined that it was important to observe and document the impact of the disease on blacks. The study lasted four decades, and when effective treatment for the disease became available during the study, the participants in this longitudinal study did not receive it (Jones 1993).

America's racial legacy continues to influence the language used to describe group differences and the methodological approaches used to study these differences. For instance, racial classifications, though largely determined by social and political pressures, are in many areas of scientific inquiry being made problematic (Zuberi and Bonilla-Silva 2008). Researchers are asked to define these terms and explain why race-comparative analysis is appropriate. We applaud such efforts and believe the present volume will aid researchers as they continue to deepen their understanding of the role of race in scientific inquiry.

Implicit in this volume is a view about the role of research and the researcher. Vulnerable populations may be the subject of considerable research (consider what many have referred to as "the poverty research industry"). We suggest that prior to conducting the study, considerations such as whether participants have some ownership of the data, if the research can be conducted in a participatory fashion, and what purpose racial comparisons serve are key questions to address before engaging in research with diverse populations.

Similarly, an awareness of the researchers' own identities may facilitate entry into communities of color, the questions that are investigated, and the presentation of findings. Identity is perhaps more salient when researching black communities; often the researcher is an outsider in terms of race, class, or gender. Our authors are themselves diverse—men and women, blacks and whites, new scholars and seasoned veterans of the academy. Negotiating the racial dynamics may be a challenge for any researcher but may be especially salient for researchers conducting studies with ethnic groups different from their own. Researchers must confront issues of trust and the usefulness of the research for those being researched (Alvarez et al. 2006). Further, if differences among groups are found, strong theory and careful discussion are paramount. A danger of portraying black people as "different" is that difference may then be associated with negative, stereotypical connotations. Being sensitive to these issues enhances the quality of the research (Johnson-Bailey 1999).

Historically, culturally reliable and valid tools have been lacking (Prelow et al. 2000). The use of particular conceptual frameworks, measurement tools, and instruments could promote bias. Further, recent efforts at inclusive research have had an unintended consequence of uncritically "controlling for race," with limited discussion of whether or how race should be included in the research. How scientists construct and explain race and racial differences is subject to considerable debate. As noted earlier, race has been defined as a social construct whose meaning changes dependent upon historical era and location (e.g., Omi and Winant 1994). This social-construction definition of race is the predominant view in the social sciences. Although these scientists view race as historically variable and contingent on social, economic, and political practices of the time, because the meaning of race is built upon biological, phenotypical characteristics of people, it is far from inconsequential (Krieger 2000; Williams, Neighbors, and Jackson 2003).

A second definition of race suggests that it serves as a proxy for other social dimensions, such as socioeconomic status and particular historical processes. A third definition suggests that race is probably biologically meaningful (Satel 2002). The rise in the view of a biological base for race has met with considerable consternation among social scientists, in large measure because of the history of eugenics, racial discrimination, and the portrayal of blacks as deviant (Duster 2005). A central concern is that genetic differences may be used to justify social inequalities in health and health services (Jackson 2004).

Comparative research is essential to the advancement of social scientific knowledge. We suggest however, that researchers must consider how and why the comparisons are made. Shim (2005), in a study of epidemiologists, writes, "While there may have been rationalizations previously, the practice is now so common that 'controlling' or adjusting for race is 'standard operating procedure'" (413). A more critical stance is necessary if we are to advance our knowledge. The chapters in this volume conceptualize research to be sensitive to race, ethnicity, and culture. For scholars conducting research within communities of color, we suggest the nuanced use of both mainstream and culturally specific conceptual frameworks and research questions.

At every stage in the research process, it is critical to assess possible bias. For instance, inattention to the systematic nature of survey research has been particularly apparent in research with racial and ethnic minority populations. Violating critical elements of survey research methodology can lead to faulty analysis and biased interpretations of research results. Perhaps the research tools and instruments need to be adapted for different populations (Manly 2006). Perhaps data collection strategies need to be modified to collect data on a hard-to-reach population. Perhaps mixed quantitative and qualitative approaches will address some puzzling findings. An important aim of this volume is to describe how a group of scholars have addressed these and other methodological challenges over the last several decades.

In the remainder of this chapter we provide the theoretical orientation that guides the structure of the volume along with definitions of the commonly used terms *race, ethnicity, culture, gender,* and *class.* Then, using the survey research approach as an example, we offer a discussion of why it is vital to define these concepts. Finally, we present an overview of each chapter, ending with a general set of principles encompassing the cumulative perspective of the volume and expectations for what is necessary to conduct culturally competent research in black communities.

Race, Ethnicity, Culture, Gender, and Class: Using Intersectionality as a Framework for Conducting Research in Black Communities

Research on racial and ethnic minority populations will benefit from greater attention to the development of theoretical perspectives that are sensitive to the nature and lived experiences of racial and ethnic minority populations. Better definitions and classification of racial and ethnic statuses, as well as insightful and more complex research questions, should result from greater attention to these concerns. Although the widely used race-comparative research paradigm is valuable in doing this work when properly conducted (Jackson 2002), equally important is the need to better understand variability that exists within ethnic minority groups. Theoretical perspectives regarding within-group variations among black populations is limited at best. Regardless of the approach taken, as an initial step, researchers must provide conceptual clarity in studies involving the concepts of race, ethnicity, culture, gender, and class in order to advance scientific knowledge involving black people (Johnson-Bailey 1999).

Unfortunately, a substantial amount of empirical literature is based upon poorly designed studies that have not been attentive to providing definitions or making conceptual distinctions in the race/ethnicity/culture concepts. The terms *race, ethnicity,* and *culture* are often conflated, limiting opportunity for determining interactive influences on outcomes for these concepts. Providing clear definitions for each concept in research should facilitate better interpretations of study findings, as well as influence the type of research questions posed, allowing for more complexity and meaningfulness from the participants' perspective. Below we discuss the significance of defining these concepts in social science research.

Definitions of Terms: *Race, Ethnicity, Culture, Gender,* and *Class*

Some have argued that the term *race* refers to a sociobiological construct in which society places people in a social and value hierarchy depending on history, traditions, personal experiences, and genetic heritage based on physical characteristics, whereas *ethnicity* refers to perceived common ancestry and perceptions of a shared history, language, beliefs, norms, behaviors, and symbols of peoplehood (Brown et al. 1999; Phinney and Ong 2007; Sue 1999). Ethnicity is often considered the more inclusive concept because it includes both race and culture (Murry et al. 2004). Culture has been defined as a dynamic force of symbolic meanings that shapes how people see themselves as influenced by the social environment and functional experiences (Brown et al. 1999). It is boundless, encompassing and providing meaning for beliefs, rituals, values, and norms that dictate how a group of people live and act. Culture is transmitted from one generation to the next, with ethnicity as a key *content* component (Murry et al. 2004). Gender and class are often examined as individual-level variables measured by biological sex (i.e., male or female) and socioeconomic status (i.e., income, education, and/or occupation). Viewed from a structural or larger societal perspective, *gender* has been defined as a social construct that changes over time. It refers to the meaning societies give to the proper place and roles of men and women (Lindsey 1994). *Class* indicates a person's position in the larger political economy. Created by societies as a way of defining social relationships (e.g., employer vs. employee, owners vs. nonowners), *class* involves an element of economic exploitation that can "help explain generation, distribution, and persistence of . . . specific pathways leading to social inequalities in income, wealth, and health" (Krieger, Williams, and Moss 1997, 346). Structural definitions of *gender* and *class* allow for a better understanding of factors external to the individual, societal issues that contribute to gender discrimination and the socioeconomic position of a people faced with historical oppression. Conceptual clarity when using these terms has implications for every phase of the research process.

Emerging literature has called for the concept of race to be defined with regard to distinguishing between its biological, social, and political constructions in an effort to achieve a better understanding of social inequalities (Gabard and Cooper 1998; Mays et al. 2007). For example, applying a biological explanation to observed differences in violent behavior among black and white youth suggests that violence is genetically predetermined and not significantly influenced by environmental conditions that may facilitate or hinder specific expressions of violence (Anad 1999). This approach shifts responsibility for reducing or extinguishing violence to the individual while minimizing the role of social factors in explaining racial differences in youth violence.

Previous research has found that there is more genetic variation within race groups than between them (Jackson 2004). Consequently, it is impossible to ignore the social environment in determining the influence of race on outcomes of interest (Jones 1991; Mays et al. 2007; Williams, Lavizzo-Mourey, and Warren 1994). The vast majority of studies of race and ethnicity rely on self-identified group membership as the defining characteristic. Defining race and ethnicity solely as demographic variables limits the depth of understanding of the role that culture can play in shaping the lives and adaptation of racial and ethnic subgroups in a racist society. Gabard and Cooper (1998) suggest that "racial identifications serve as frameworks of personal identifications with the groups' accomplishments, histories, political power bases, struggles, and victories" (343). Since racial and ethnic categorizations can be used for purposes of inclusion or exclusion, research that only controls for race or ethnic differences in data analysis limits our understanding of other factors that may facilitate or prevent specific outcomes based on cultural experiences (LaVeist 1996).

Race as a proxy for socioeconomic status has been used extensively in the research literature despite studies challenging the usefulness of such an approach (Williams et al. 1994). While the effects of race on health outcomes, for example, appear to be reduced when socioeconomic status is introduced, race most often remains an important independent predictor in such analyses. This suggests that other factors may be involved. For example, neighborhood characteristics (e.g., poverty, violence, social organization, residential mobility) represent critical indicators of socioeconomic status (SES) that may be especially relevant when examining the relation between race or ethnicity and social class on outcomes in black communities (see Mays et al. 2007 for a review related to health disparities).

The inclusion of factors such as neighborhood characteristics, the structure of employment, or wage discrimination rather than individual SES alone in research broadens our understanding of environmental conditions that contribute to outcomes for black people. This type of an approach allows the impact of structural and historical experiences to be assessed and should result in efforts to reduce or prevent problems that are not limited to what Silver (2000) characterized as the "individualistic fallacy." The individualistic fallacy assumes that outcomes for individuals can be explained by only individual characteristics. Treating race, ethnicity, gender, and class as demographic variables excludes the cumulative, interlocking, and historically embedded influences that they can have in shaping the lives, adaptation, and social identities of black people.

An Intersectionality Framework

One theoretical perspective that considers the effects of the multiple influences of race, ethnicity, gender, and class as social identities is the intersectionality framework (Collins 1991). Intersectionality refers to the fluid processes inherent in holding two or more social identities that are situated within a historical context (Collins 1991; Crenshaw 1995). Social identities, such as race, ethnicity, gender, and class, are defined as attributes that societies use to stratify or to place individuals in a social hierarchy that can in turn lead to the creation of different meanings for life experiences (Harding 2004).

An intersectional perspective provides the theoretical framework for this book. All of the chapters highlight the role of multiple social identities (e.g., race, ethnicity, gender, and class) and historical experiences that have implications for the need to be cognizant of specific issues when conducting research within black communities. Shields writes, "Intersectionality is urgent because it gets us as researchers to go beyond the individually informed perspective that we each inevitably bring to our scholarship and science . . . the intersectionality perspective is thus an invitation to move beyond one's own research comfort zone" (309). We believe that a reflective researcher is an important safeguard against potential bias.

Further, the chapters are grouped into four sections that build on this framework by (1) discussing theoretical issues that address race, ethnicity, culture, gender, and/or class; (2) focusing on domestic and international research emphasizing the role of historical experiences in the lives of specific black groups; (3) presenting challenges and solutions to obtaining national data with ethnically diverse or clearly defined black populations and black churches that consider cultural issues; and (4) identifying structural issues involving families, the mental health system, and media that should be considered when conducting research with blacks.

Research on Race, Ethnicity, Gender, and Class Using Survey Research as an Example

The critical elements of a rigorous sample survey can be briefly summarized as including (1) a known population; (2) a sample drawn in a systematic and statistically appropriate manner; (3) a well-designed, rigorous questionnaire; (4) well-trained competent interviewers (or self-administered); (5) responses that are coded in a standard and replicable way; and (6) analyses and interpretations of data that are conducted appropriately with sensitivity to the nuances of the population and topic under investigation. It is probability sampling and the standardization of data collection and data preparation that distinguishes the scientifically rigorous surveys from "questionnaire studies" (Tanur 1983).

In practice, much of what is labeled as survey research lacks the systematic and replicable features noted above. Inattention to the systematic nature of survey research has been particularly apparent in research with racial and ethnic minority populations, even in many surveys performed by large survey organizations. Frequently, many of the critical elements of survey research methodology are violated; there may be a lack of defined populations, poorly constructed stimulus materials (questionnaires), inappropriate conceptual and coding schemes, and inaccurate analysis and interpretation of data. Since the sample survey and use of questionnaires (either self- or other-administered) have become the major data collection procedure in many social science disciplines, especially when studying ethnic minority populations (Caldwell et al. 1999), designing reliable and valid survey studies is particularly important.

Researchers also face numerous methodological problems in attempting to employ other research approaches when studying racial and ethnic groups (Smith 1993). Many of the observations about sampling, measurement, and analysis will be appropriate to the breadth of methodologies employed in the social sciences. These include ethnographic procedures, experimental and quasi-experimental procedures, and biographical methods, as well as quasi-survey research methods (Jackson 1988). Regardless of the methodology employed, the potential for error in research with racial and ethnic groups is magnified by cultural factors (Knauper 1996). Disentangling these factors and assessing their influence are critical to a better understanding of outcomes for black populations.

Methodological and substantive problems, especially in nonexperimental methods, are of long-standing scientific interest. The problem that faces social scientists today is that conducting research involving racial and ethnic minority populations has not received the same scrutiny. Specifically, general sources of error, as well as sources of error unique to race and ethnicity in research planning, execution, and interpretation of findings may all contribute to variations in outcomes in research involving blacks (Caldwell et al. 1999; Jackson, Tucker, and Bowman 1982). Cultural differences among racial and ethnic groups are considered by some researchers to contribute substantial and significant variability to findings. Support for this perspective, however, has been noticeably absent in the empirical literature.

Finifter (1977) labels the general orientation to research on race and ethnicity as "agnostic," since it often seeks to determine the existence of cross-cultural differences without making errors of a Type I (specific) or Type II (universalistic) nature. Levine (1982) suggests the need to consider race and ethnic characteristics of a sample as more than mere sources of error. Failure to do so runs the risk of missing important sources of variation. The concepts of race, ethnicity, culture, gender, and class are all essential aspects of human development and should be fully considered scientifically in the research process with black populations.

In sum, most research conducted in the United States has neglected to provide definitions for the concepts of race, ethnicity, culture, gender, and class. Further, previous research often has not distinguished between the concepts of race, ethnicity, and culture (Brown et al. 1999; Murry et al. 2004). Race and ethnicity are frequently treated as nuisance factors to be ignored or statistically controlled rather than as important independent variables that offer explanatory power for outcomes of interest (LaVeist 1999). In general, research on racial and ethnic minority populations is characterized by problems at all stages of the research process, including conceptualization, execution, analysis, and interpretation (Smith 1993) due, in part, to lack of a clear definition of the population in the study.

For the most part, conclusions in the present chapter and the overall volume draw heavily upon research experiences with black populations. The impetus for our narrow focus is that there is a relatively restricted pool of research that has been conducted within black communities that reflects both conceptual and methodological clarity and rigor (Caldwell et al. 1999; Smith 1993). We believe, however, that the principles, practices, and lessons learned can be applied to research with other racial and ethnic populations, and hope that the issues discussed in this chapter will sensitize other researchers to ideas that can be addressed in future studies that include racial and ethnic minority participants.

Overview of the Volume

The chapters in this volume provide examples of a wide variety of methodological and substantive challenges that confront researchers working with black populations. Part I includes this introductory chapter and three theoretical chapters that exemplify aspects of the intersectional framework. O'Connor, Lewis, and Mueller provide a fuller discussion of the meaning of race, ethnicity, culture, and class in research with blacks focusing specifically on the educational system; Hamilton and Darity examine a gap in economic theory that fails to consider the historical context of black workers; and Chadiha and Brazelton consider the utility of a linked gender and life-course perspective when conducting health disparities research involving black women.

Part II focuses on heterogeneity across black populations, emphasizing meanings that blacks assign to their lived experiences observed through a gendered or political lens. The four chapters address issues that arise in studying children at risk in impoverished neighborhoods (Norton, Vincson, and Wilhelm), marital relationships involving both black and white husbands and wives as couples (Veroff and Orbuch), the challenges of conducting contextually sensitive research in an African setting with political overtones (Copeland-Linder), and research with black immigrant female domestic workers facing challenges in a gendered labor position (Sellers, Wilson, and Harris).

Part III introduces lessons learned based on nationally representative samples of blacks and includes four chapters. Jackson, Caldwell, Torres, and Sweetman describe the challenges faced and overcome when conducting specific components of the groundbreaking National Survey of American Life (NSAL) that includes samples of African Americans and Caribbean blacks. This is followed by a chapter that describes the interviewer training process for the NSAL in which mistrust of the initial training staff was rooted in cultural differences with interviewers (Hastings, Kromrei, and Caldwell). Using the precursor to NSAL, the seminal

National Survey of Black Americans, Wolford and Torres consider culturally specific strategies for handling the nonresponse issue in longitudinal studies. This part concludes with a chapter by Caldwell that implemented a community-based participatory research (CBPR; Israel et al. 2005; Minkler and Wallerstein 2003) approach in conducting a national study of black churches to understand how to work with religious communities in the research process. The NSBA sampling framework was used in the design of this study.

The fourth and final part of the volume focuses on structural issues: studying black families through multiple lenses (Hunter and Johnson), the mental health service system through an economic lens (Snowden), and two chapters that focus a cultural lens on media research—media and sexuality in black adolescents (Ward) and media and black audiences (Haggins and Squires). In the next section we describe each chapter in more detail.

Overview of Individual Chapters

Part I: Theoretical Issues: Race, Ethnicity, Culture, Gender, Class, and Intersectionality

O'Connor, Lewis, and Mueller note in chapter 2 that the subject of race is regularly invoked in educational research on African Americans, particularly as part of "naming" or identifying racial groups, and in the heightened exploration of how the educational experiences of those marked as black differ from those of other racial groups. They argue that researchers have not adequately conceptualized race as a social phenomenon and that the failure to attend to race with greater conceptual and methodological precision impinges upon the ability to develop more exact interpretations of how and why black students fare in school as they do. They assess how race has been employed as a social category in the contemporary educational literature. Focusing on research produced within the last 40 years, they provide examples from research concerned with the elementary and secondary schooling of black children and youth. They identify several limitations that effectively cloud the ability to interpret when and how race is implicated in the educational experiences, achievement, and outcomes of black students. Similar analyses are made for gender and class issues, and an intersectional framework is discussed as a useful lens for addressing current research limitations. They also suggest that future studies of the educational experiences of black students should account for specific limitations at different stages in the research process. The authors note that an emerging area, race as capital, is one of several fruitful starting points for a reorientation, and they elaborate upon ways in which this reorientation can be supported by using ethnographic and mixed-methods research approaches.

In chapter 3, Hamilton and Darity focus on the ways in which race might influence labor market conditions. They are especially concerned with providing an updated estimate of black male occupational classifications based on a more extensive list of occupations and discussing a stratified test of the relationship between occupational crowding and earnings for black males that is theoretically determined. They note that standard economic theory has not been very successful in explaining persistent inequality between blacks and whites. They describe two broad possibilities for the existence of persistent black-white disparities in occupation and earnings. First, there may be something inherent about blacks that inhibits their ability to achieve economic rewards. This inherent inaptitude may take the form of a biological or a cultural deficiency. The second explanation is related to social structures that privilege whites over blacks in two ways: the structures may favor one group's ability to accumulate characteristics (e.g., education) that lead to desired economic outcomes, or the structures may provide greater economic returns to the accumulated characteristics of one group. Both mechanisms can be termed discrimination—"pre-market discrimination" for disparities in acquired productivity-linked characteristics, and "in-market discrimination" for disparities in the returns to characteristics. Using a measure developed to assess occupation crowding, Hamilton and Darity find considerable evidence in support of the theory, finding that blacks are systematically crowded into lower earning occupations. They challenge economists and other social scientists to devise a theory of persistent inequality and appropriate measures that account for "pre-market" and "in-market" transactions simultaneously.

The last chapter in this section, chapter 4 by Chadiha and Brazelton, focuses on the status and quality of black women's physical health, work, marriage, and caregiving roles within an aging context. The chapter provides an overview of a gender and life-course model that is appropriate for understanding how the experiences of black women as they age impact their health. Similarly, the authors use the gender and life-course perspective in a discussion of evidence bearing on the need to consider the multiple roles that black women historically have assumed (e.g., work, marriage, and caregiving) and how this contributes to observed health disparities in heart disease and cancer. The chapter concludes with strategies for conducting life-course research with black women, emphasizing the need for a gendered life-course perspective with an emphasis on the heterogeneity of black women's roles. Broad use of qualitative methods and the need for flexible, responsive research designs also are supported by this chapter.

Part II: Research with U.S. and International Populations involving Children, Couples, and Women

The fifth chapter, by Norton, Vincson, and Wilhelm, directs its attention to research issues of specific relevance in studying African American infants and children born to young mothers residing in impoverished urban neighborhoods. The chapter draws on the experiences the authors gained in conducting a longitudinal study following a small sample of African American infants from birth to age 18 called Children at Risk: The Infant and Child Development Research Project (ICDP) (Norton 1990, 1993, 1996). In keeping with the overall goals of this volume, the authors focus on issues in four research areas with their population of young African American children and their families: (1) research conceptualization and design; (2) sample criteria and recruitment; (3) data collection methods and appropriate assessment measures; and (4) maintenance of the sample. They conclude with a number of specific recommendations, including having a strong focus on sample criteria.

In chapter 6, Veroff and Orbuch share their experiences in conducting a large-scale project of the progressive development of marriage during the early years. The aims of the project were to delineate both the processes that generally underlie positive development of marital relationships in the early years and the processes that are specific to such development in black couples in comparison to white couples. The research is unique in its capacity to provide a black-white American cultural analysis within a longitudinal investigation of marriage. They reasoned that any methods used to examine marital processes over time should incorporate both husbands and wives and should include observations of the couple together as well as separately. The chapter is organized around a series of pragmatic questions faced at each step of the research process. Veroff and Orbuch demonstrate why it is necessary to expand knowledge of both distinctive and more general factors that underpin marital stability and well-being among black couples in order to take into consideration their cultural experiences. They endorse the value of employing a mixed-method approach to the measurement of marital constructs because they found vastly different results between and within the two racial groups depending on which method was used. This chapter offers an extensive assessment of how to deal with ethnic differences in data analysis.

In chapter 7, Copeland-Linder suggests that mainstream research has been slow to examine the historical, social, political, and cultural factors that influence stress and coping among blacks, especially from an international perspective. The chapter provides an overview of the sociocultural context of stress and coping resources among black South Africans and highlights methodological issues and strategies for conducting culturally competent research with blacks in South Africa. Copeland-Linder concludes with several lessons learned when conducting research in an international context and offers a number of suggestions for overcoming challenges in conducting international research with blacks, emphasizing community involvement and ethnographic interviews to understand the political and cultural contexts as well as meaning.

Sellers, Wilson, and Harris (chapter 8) provide specific recommendations for recruiting and retaining low-wage domestic workers (a hard-to-reach population) based on experiences with a research study focused on female immigrants from English-speaking Caribbean countries. They also address the tensions between advocacy and research that may arise when studying hard-to-reach populations. The chapter is organized into three sections. The first offers a brief review of classic and contemporary research on domestic work and immigration. The second section describes the Domestic Workers Project (DWP) that included a survey and a series of in-depth interviews and focus groups with study participants. The last section presents research challenges and approaches for addressing the challenges to successfully conduct research with black immigrant female domestic workers. An emphasis is placed on mixed-methods approaches as valuable for collecting data and understanding the community. With a scarcity of research with hard-to-reach populations, this chapter delineates a process for establishing genuine linkages with community members. The authors suggest that domestic workers are especially vulnerable because of their precarious social status and limited material resources; therefore, there is a vital advocacy function required when conducting research with vulnerable populations. They suggest that advocacy must be part of the research agenda to successfully conduct this type of research.

Part III: Strategies for Obtaining National Data with African Americans, Caribbean Blacks, and Black Churches

In chapter 9, Jackson, Caldwell, Torres, and Sweetman describe both conceptual and methodological issues faced when conducting specific components of the National Survey of American Life (NSAL), which includes national samples of African Americans, Caribbean blacks, and whites. The use of random probes with diverse ethnic groups to determine cultural variation in meaning of specific concepts, the identification of strategies for addressing nonresponse across ethnic groups while emphasizing predictors with cultural significance not previously used in such analyses, and an illustration of how to identify cross-cultural multigenerational black samples that extend beyond U.S. borders are topics discussed in this chapter. The significance of maintaining a firm view of culturally varied life experiences based on race and ethnicity provides the overriding frame for the chapter.

Chapter 10 by Hastings, Kromrei, and Caldwell describes the process used to successfully incorporate cultural traditions and reduce mistrust in the interview training portion of the NSAL. This included adaptations in communication styles, enhancements in race matching of training staff, and appropriate food selections. In a rare opportunity to see the interpersonal dynamics of interviewer training issues that are culturally driven, the authors summarize the transitions between the multiple NSAL interviewer training sessions and provide lessons learned as useful guidelines for future interviewer training for survey research conducted with African American and Caribbean black adults and adolescents. In addition, they offer guidance for improving survey responses through effective interviewer training, especially for adolescent samples. They conclude that when there are potential cultural differences between training staff and interviewers, researchers should include instruction on behaviors and skills needed to gain the cooperation of diverse black interviewers as well as study participants as part of interviewer training.

Chapter 11 by Wolford and Torres addresses the process of conducting longitudinal research with a national sample of black Americans, highlighting a set of unique challenges, including the difficulties of maintaining a representative sample and compensating for the systematic loss of individuals over the course of multiple years. They note that while even the random loss of respondents can create problems by eroding the power of analyses, the most critical problem is the bias that the disproportionate loss of particular subgroups introduces into the analyses. The chapter focuses on the dynamics that are associated with longitudinal nonresponse in the National Panel Survey of Black Americans. They examine the sources of systematic nonresponse in order to compensate for it statistically through the use of weights and to develop better procedures for identifying black respondents most likely to be lost at later waves of data collection. Although they find, based upon their analyses, that home ownership and income are important predictors of nonresponse among blacks just as they are in the general population, educational attainment appears to be more critical for nonresponse among blacks than in the general population. Interestingly, these are all class factors linked to economic equity. Uniquely, however, they also find that respondents' involvement in the community is substantially related to nonresponse. This is a finding with significant cultural implications. Suggestions are made for improving upon nonresponses specifically for conducting longitudinal research in black communities.

The final chapter in part III, by Caldwell, focuses on black churches as pivotal institutions in the lives of African Americans. It describes a number of lessons learned in working with black churches as part of the Black Church Family Project using a community-based participatory research approach (CBPR; Israel et al. 1998, 2005; Minkler and Wallerstein 2003). Caldwell notes that black churches have been embedded in the social, economic, political, health, and educational fabrics of black communities since the establishment of the first black American church in the eighteenth century. The challenges of defining, identifying, and selecting black churches for inclusion in an empirical study are discussed, along with a number of other methodological issues related to conducting a national study of black churches. Caldwell notes that good samples are vital to fully represent denominational differences in church research; therefore the study relied on the NSBA sampling framework to draw a national sample of black churches. Similar to other chapters in this volume, the need for continued contact and special attention to working with church leaders and knowledgeable members is emphasized to gain corporation in the research process and for obtaining richer data.

Part IV: Research Involving Structural Issues Focused on Families, the Mental Health System, and the Media

The first chapter in part IV, by Hunter and Johnson, illustrates how methodological choices serve larger interpretative goals to reveal the nuances of black family life that are evident but often go unexamined. Using a range of studies in child development and family studies, they focus on core areas of family research including family structure and form, family process, and meanings to illustrate varied approaches to studying black families. Throughout, they highlight the ways in which research in the developmental sciences and family studies can be a kind of anthropology and point to the ways that their own work is part of a larger storytelling tradition, infusing the lived experiences of their research participants. They emphasize that capturing a certain angle of vision influences research questions, methodological choices, and interpretative strategies.

In chapter 14, Snowden discusses how we might increase the amount of rigorous research on the mental health of black Americans by examining features of the service delivery system. He suggests that in studying black mental health diverse issues demand that researchers call upon methods associated with a number of disciplines. Investigators must focus on the impact of interventions, paying particular attention to evaluating proposed adaptations to the sociocultural conditions of black life. Empirical studies must consider differential effectiveness, comparing the responses of blacks to standard and adapted forms of the intervention. He delineates the significance of considering resource expenditures as an important part of the equation and suggests directly testing trade-offs between participation in mental health treatments and programs and participation in institutions of public support and social control for blacks. He provides examples of economically based hypotheses and strategies that have been used to test them. He also illustrates how different multivariate statistics can be used to test culturally based assumptions involving African Americans. This chapter makes a strong case for examining community and societal contexts in which mental health problems occur and where solutions are implemented, including the economic circumstances of African Americans, to facilitate mental health research. Overall, Snowden is optimistic that research will improve in quality as a new generation of investigators conduct methodological studies that will advance the state of knowledge, and thereby increase the power of community interventions.

In chapter 15, Ward presents evidence that little is actually known about television's impact on the self- and social conceptions of black youth. Only a handful of studies have examined the influence of media exposure on black youths' conceptions of themselves; even fewer have included black youth in investigations of general media effects. The purpose of this chapter is to summarize the current state of the field and offer lessons learned for future research from a cultural perspective. These include: (1) move away from global assessments of media exposure (e.g., hours of television watched) to consider the specific nature of black youths' media diets; (2) be aware of complexity and heterogeneity of black-oriented media; (3) examine the impact of black portrayals in mainstream media; examine the impact of under- versus misrepresentation; (4) employ a developmental focus, include participants across several age groups, and follow participants over time to explore how the media's influence changes with age. Grounded in the experiences of her work with the media, Ward reminds us how influential the media can be with impressionable black youth.

In the final chapter, Haggins and Squires note that some research on blacks and the media, implicitly or explicitly, assumes that the narrow spectrum of black images in mainstream media may have negative effects on individual blacks' self-esteem. However, to assume that black audiences are always looking toward "mainstream" media representations for pleasure or role models is to overlook the context of media consumption as well as the types of media that are consumed. That is, there may be other aspects of an individual's or group's experiences and knowledge that carry more weight than the preferred or hegemonic meanings of a media text. They note that most quantitative studies have largely ignored alternative media choices made by black audiences. This chapter highlights how qualitative methods, such as ethnographic and cultural-historical research, can lend new insight into which cultural practices, rituals, or ideologies guide black media consumers through what often seems like a minefield of problematic images. In this chapter, Haggins and Squires share their research approach as a way to add to the emerging media scholarship creating different opportunities for understanding black adult audiences and conducting research.

Conclusions

Individually the contributors to this volume are working in diverse areas of focus and on problems of differing levels of complexity, yet they all suggest that researchers must more fully appreciate the lived experiences of black people if we are to advance scientific knowledge about this population. There are a number of common conceptual and methodological threads that bind these chapters together. One overarching framework is the intersectional perspective. Whether a focus on blacks in America, immigrant blacks, or blacks in South Africa, the perspective offered by the intersectional framework suggesting multiple social identities rooted in historical experiences can be applied to research in black communities. Thus, it is critical for researchers to consider how social identities may have implications for defining the cultural context of a study when involving black populations.

Below we list several principles intended to assist researchers in moving forward with such an endeavor.

1. Studies of racial and ethnic minority populations cannot divorce substance and conceptualization from methodological concerns. The intersectionality perspective offers one framework for viewing the connections across multiple social identities for blacks. Racial and ethnic minority populations must be appropriately defined, identified, and sampled if this research is to be successful.

2. Study conceptualizations, analyses, and interpretation of data must be sensitive to the ethnic, cultural, gendered, and class nuances of the historical and contemporary circumstances of racial and ethnic communities, whether done domestically or internationally.

3. Community participation is paramount, and research participants must be viewed as partners and not objects of the research.

4. Quantitative and qualitative, as well as mixed-methods approaches to data collection must be combined with life-course perspectives and longitudinal foci on change in order to give appropriate voice to research participants.

5. New methods in sampling, data collection modes, and more powerful approaches to analyses, especially in survey research, are providing future researchers with better tools to conduct more culturally sensitive and effective research among racial and ethnic minority populations. Researchers must take advantage of these new methodological options in their work.

6. Humility in the face of daunting methodological challenges must be the dominant orientation of all researchers.

We believe that successfully overcoming methodological challenges researchers face in studies of black populations not only furthers the social scientific knowledge base, it also provides the evidence foundation needed for building a more just society. America is becoming an increasingly diverse society. By the middle of this century the majority of Americans will be peoples of color with large numbers of newly arrived immigrants and second-generation children and adults. This profound change in the composition of the country will have consequences for all political, social, and economic institutions. We need sound empirical data to develop effective public policies, educational practices, and service delivery systems attuned to these new realities. Research going forward must be better informed in conceptualization, operationalization, and interpretation and policy recommendations if we are to realize a harmonious and productive society in the near future.

REFERENCES

Alvarez, R. A., E. Vasquez, C. C. Mayorga, D. J. Feaster, and V. B. Mitrani. 2006. Increasing minority research participation through community organization outreach. *Western Journal of Nursing Research* 28:541–60.
Anad, S. S. 1999. Using ethnicity as a classification variable in health research: Perpetuating the myth of biological determinism, serving socio-political agendas, or making valuable contributions to medical sciences? *Ethnicity and Health* 4, no. 4: 241–44.
Arthur, J. A. 2000. *Invisible sojourners: African immigrant diaspora in the United States.* Westport, CT: Praeger.
Brown, T. N., S. L. Sellers, K. T. Brown, and J. S. Jackson. 1999. Race, ethnicity, and culture in the sociology of mental health. In C. S. Aneshensel and J. C. Phelan, eds., *Handbook of the sociology of mental health*, 169–82. New York: Kluwer Academic/Plenum.
Caldwell, C. F., J. S. Jackson, M. B. Tucker, and P. J. Bowman. 1999. Culturally-competent research methods in African American communities: An update. In R. Jones, ed., *Advances in African American psychology: Theory, paradigms, methodology, and reviews*, 101–27. Hampton, VA: Cobb and Henry.
Collins, P. H. 1991. *Black feminist thought: Knowledge, consciousness, and the politics of empowerment.* New York: Routledge.
Crenshaw, K. 1995. Mapping the margins: Intersectionality, identity politics, and violence against women of color. In K. Crenshaw, N. Gotanda, G. Peller, and K. Thomas, eds., *Critical race theory.* New York: Free Press.
Duster, T. 2005. Enhances: Race and reifications in science. *Science* 307, no. 5712: 1050–51.
Finifter, B. M. 1977. The robustness of cross-cultural findings in issues in cross-cultural research. *Annals of the New York Academy of Sciences*, ed. Leonore Loeb Adler, 151–84. New York: New York Academy of Medicine.
Gabard, D. L., and T. L. Cooper. 1998. Race: Constructs and dilemmas. *Administration and Society* 30:339–46.

Harding, S., ed. 2004. *The feminist standpoint theory reader.* New York: Routledge.

Harrison, P. M., and A. J. Beck. 2006. Prisoners in 2005. U.S. Department of Justice, Bureau of Justice Statistics Bulletin, November 2006. Downloaded from the following website: http:// www.ojp.usdoj.gov/bjs/abstract/p05.htm.

Israel, B. A., E. Eng, A. J. Schulz, and E. A. Parker, eds. 2005. *Methods in community-based participatory research for health.* San Francisco: Jossey-Bass.

Israel, B. A., A. J. Schulz, E. A. Parker, and A. B. Becker. 1998. A review of community-based research: Assessing partnership approaches to improve public health. *Annual Review of Public Health* 19:173–202.

Jackson, J. S. 1988. Methodological issues in survey research on older minority adults. In M. P. Lawton and A. R. Herzog, eds., *Research methods in gerontology,* 137–61. Farmingdale, NY: Baywood Press.

Jackson, J. S., ed. 1991. *Life in black America.* Newbury Park, CA: Sage.

Jackson, J. S. 2002. Conceptual and methodological linkages in cross-cultural groups and cross-national aging research. *Journal of Social Issues* 58, no. 4: 825–35.

Jackson, J. S. 2004. Discussion: Genetic explanation for health disparities: What is at stake? In E. Singer and T. C. Antonucci, eds., *Proceedings of the Conference on Genetics and Health Disparities, March 20–21.* Ann Arbor: Institute for Social Research, University of Michigan.

Jackson, J. S., M. B. Tucker, and P. J. Bowman. 1982. Conceptual and methodological problems in survey research on black Americans. In W. T. Liu, ed., *Methodological problems in minority research.* Chicago: Pacific/Asian American Mental Health Research Center.

Johnson-Bailey, J. 1999. The ties that bind and the shackles that separate: Race, gender, class, and color in a research process. *Qualitative Studies in Education* 12, no. 6: 659–70.

Jones, J. 1991. Psychological models of race: What have they been and what should they be. In J. D. Goodchilds, ed., *Psychological perspectives on human diversity in America,* 3–46. Washington, DC: American Psychological Association.

Jones, J. H. 1993. *Bad blood: The Tuskegee syphilis experiment.* Rev. ed. New York: Free Press.

Katz, R. V., S. S. Kegeles, N. R. Kressin, B. L. Green, S. A. James, M. Q. Wang, S. L. Russell, and C. Claudio. 2008. Awareness of the Tuskegee Syphilis Study and the US presidential apology and their influence on minority participation in biomedical research. *American Journal of Public Health* 98, no. 6: 1137–42.

Krieger, N., D. R. Williams, and N. E. Moss. 1997. Measuring social class in US public health research: Concepts, methodologies, and guidelines. *Annual Review of Public Health* 18:341–78.

Labov, W. 1972. *Sociolinguistic patterns.* Philadelphia: University of Pennsylvania Press.

LaVeist, T. 1996. Why we should continue to study race . . . but do a better job: An essay on race, racism, and health. *Ethnicity and Disease* 6:21–29.

Lindsey, L. 1994. *Gender roles: A sociological perspective.* Upper Saddle River, NJ: Prentice-Hall.

Manly, J. 2006. Deconstructing race and ethnicity implications for measurement of health outcomes. *Medical Care* 44, no. 11: S3, S10–S16.

Mays, V. M., S. D. Cochran, and N. W. Barnes. 2007. Race, race-based discrimination, and health outcomes among African Americans. *Annual Review of Psychology* 58:201–25.

Megargee, E. I. 1995. Assessment research in correctional settings: Methodological issues and practical problems. *Psychological Assessment* 7:359–66.

Minkler, M., and N. Wallerstein, eds. 2003. *Community-based participatory research for health*. San Francisco: Jossey-Bass.

Murry, V. M., B. A. Kotchick, S. Wallace, B. Ketchen, K. Eddings, L. Heller, and I. Collier. 2004. Race, culture, and ethnicity: Implications for a community intervention. *Journal of Child and Family Studies* 13:81–99.

Neighbors, H. W. 1989. Needed research on the epidemiology of mental disorder in black Americans. In A. Harrison, J. S. Jackson, C. Munday, and N. Bleiden, eds., *A search for understanding: Michigan research conference on mental health services for black Americans*. Oakland, MI: Oakland University Press.

Neighbors, H. W., and J. S. Jackson. 1996. Mental health in black America: Psychosocial problems and help-seeking behavior. In H. W. Neighbors and J. S. Jackson, eds., *Mental health in black America*. Thousand Oaks, CA: Sage.

Omi, M., and H. Winant. 1994. *Racial formation in the United States: From the 1960s to the 1990s*. New York: Routledge.

Prelow, H. M., J.-Y. Tein, M. W. Roosa, and J. Wood. 2000. Do coping styles differ across socio-cultural groups? The role of measurement equivalence in making this judgment. *American Journal of Community Psychology* 28, no. 2: 225–44.

Sampson, R. J., and W. J. Wilson. 1995. Toward a theory of race, crime, and urban inequality. In J. Hagan and R. D. Peterson, eds., *Crime and inequality*, 37–54. Stanford: Stanford University Press.

Satel, S. 2002. I am a racially profiling doctor. *New York Times*. May 5.

Sellers, S. L., organizer, chair, and presenter. 2002. Gender and mental health: Patterns, problems, and promising new directions. The 8th International Interdisciplinary Congress on Women, Kampala, Uganda, July.

Shields, S. A. 2008. Gender: An intersectionality perspective. *Sex Roles* 59:301–11.

Silver, B. D., P. R. Abramson, and B. A. Anderson. 1986. The presence of others and overreporting of voting in American National Elections. *Public Opinion Quarterly* 50:285–39.

Silver, E. 2000. Race, neighborhood disadvantage, and violence among persons with mental disorders: The importance of contextual measurement. *Law and Human Behavior* 24:449–56.

Smith, A. W. 1993. Survey research on African Americans. In J. H. Stanfield II and R. M. Dennis, eds., *Race and ethnicity in research methods*. Newbury Park, CA: Sage.

Stanfield, J. 1993. Epistemological considerations. In J. H. Stanfield II and R. M. Dennis, eds., *Race and ethnicity in research methods*, 16–35. Newbury Park, CA: Sage.

Sue, S. 1999. Science, ethnicity, and bias: Where have we gone wrong? *American Psychologist* 54:1070–77.

Tanur, J. 1983. Methods for large-scale surveys and experiments. In Samuel Leinhardt, ed., *Sociological methodology, 1983–1984*, 1–71. San Francisco: Jossey-Bass.

U.S. Census Bureau. 2007. Website: http://www.census.gov.

Washington, H. A. 2006. Profitable wonders: Antebellum medical experimentation with slaves and freedmen. In H. A. Washington, eds., *Medical apartheid: The dark history of medical experimentation on black Americans from colonial times to the present,* 52–74. 1st ed. New York: Doubleday.

Williams, D. R., R. Haile, H. M. Gonzalez, H. Neighbors, R. Baser, and J. S. Jackson. 2007. The mental health of Black Caribbean immigrants: Results from the National Survey of American Life. *American Journal of Public Health* 97:52–57.

Williams, D. R., R. Lavizzo-Mourey, and R. C. Warren. 1994. The concept of race and health status in America. *Public Health Reports* 109:26–41.

Williams, D. R., H. Neighbors, and J. S. Jackson. 2003. Racial/ethnic discrimination and health: Findings from community studies. *American Journal of Public Health* 93, no. 2:200–209.

Zuberi, T., and E. Bonilla-Silva. 2008. *White logic, white methods: Racism and methodology.* Lanham, MA: Rowman and Littlefield.

2 | Researching "Black" Educational Experiences and Outcomes: Theoretical and Methodological Considerations

Carla O'Connor, Amanda Lewis, and Jennifer Mueller

In recent years, Black student achievement in the United States has garnered substantial attention. In particular, there has been sustained focus on the persistence of racial gaps in educational outcomes and on why Black students are underperforming in school. In analyzing how and why the educational experiences and outcomes of Blacks differ from those of other racial groups—particularly Whites—the concept of race is regularly invoked. At the same time, race is often undertheorized in education research (Ladson-Billings and Tate 1995; Pollock 2004; Tate 1997). Although some research of the past decade offers more complex conceptualizations of race, we argue that there is still much work to be done in the interest of capturing the meaning and consequences of race for educational experiences and outcomes. The absence of conceptual (and, by implication, methodological) precision impinges on our ability to interpret accurately how and why Black students fare in school as they do and to develop policy that will ameliorate racial gaps in achievement.[1]

To delineate how race has been undertheorized in contemporary education research, we zero in on two dominant traditions in which race has been captured as a social category in research conducted in the past 40 years. The first tradition treats race as culture; the second treats it as a variable. We outline the two traditions and discuss their conceptual limitations. We analyze how one tradition (race as a variable) confounds causes and effects in the estimation of when and how race is "significant" to Black achievement. We then discuss how both traditions not only mask the heterogeneity of the Black experience and its relationship to the differentiated academic performance of Black youth but also underanalyze institutionalized productions of race and racial discrimination. We subsequently discuss how future studies on the Black educational experience might correct for these limitations. Finally, we recommend productive directions for reorienting empirical and analytical foci, a move that will necessitate a shift in research design and methodology.

The Dominant Traditions

Race as Culture

During the past 40 years, education researchers have variously defined and examined the impact of culture on Black student achievement. Initially, researchers conceptualized culture as consisting of norms and beliefs, and they sought to document differences in the norms and beliefs that governed the life of the poor, who were disproportionately Black, as contrasted with the middle class, who were imagined as White (e.g., language practices, parenting approaches and child-parent interactions, educational attitudes and aspirations). They concluded that the differences elucidated deficiencies in lower-class and Black culture and explained why Blacks underperformed in school relative to Whites (e.g., Bloom, Whiteman, and Deutsch 1965; Deutsch 1964a, 1964b).

Critics, however, argued that researchers working in this tradition had not in fact captured culture in their analyses but had only isolated and described selected behaviors of the (Black) poor (Gordon 1965; Valentine 1968). In the process, researchers had imposed their own meanings on the behaviors, positioned Whites as the normative referent, and obfuscated native understandings of what was being communicated by Blacks who engaged in or eschewed particular actions.

To disrupt this White normative referent, a growing community of scholars sought to define Black culture in terms of competencies and practices. They documented the linguistic codes, learning styles, and social orientations that distinguished Blacks. In doing so, they attempted to curtail the invidious comparisons between presumably Black and White practices. These scholars highlighted the productive qualities of these codes, styles, and orientations and faulted schools for institutionalizing norms and practices that failed to build on the competencies that Black children brought to school (e.g., Kochman 1981; Labov 1982; Reissman 1962). Critics responded that this school of thought often fell short of exploring the meanings that undergirded "Black" competencies and practices and also offered oversimplified conceptualizations of culture (research like that in Heath 1982, Irvine 1990, and C. Lee 2007 being notable exceptions). For example, Ogbu (1999) noted that the Ebonics debates that emerged in response to the Oakland School District's effort to use African American Vernacular English as a scaffold for teaching and learning focused almost exclusively on differences in dialects per se.

"Some people agreed . . . that the academic problems [of Blacks] are caused by large differences between Black students' home dialect and school standard English. Others contended that the differences are not large enough to cause problems. The two groups, however, missed the point: It is not only the degree of differences in dialects per se that counts. What also seems to count is the cultural *meanings* of those dialect differences" (148).

Fordham (1999) similarly noted that researchers should not limit analyses to how Ebonics "parallels or deviates from . . . standard dialect" (272) but must examine how "the meaning of the linguistic practices of Black youths operate as markers of Black identity" (274).

In alignment with these claims, contemporary scholars have examined how Blackness is articulated through meaning making rather than through objectified competencies and practices. In accordance with this orientation, Blacks are distinguished from other racial groups in light of how they make sense of publicly available tools or symbols. This conceptual emphasis is consistent with larger trends in sociology and anthropology to characterize culture "by the publicly available symbolic forms through which people experience and express meaning" (Swidler 1986, 273). Through this emphasis on meaning making, researchers have begun mapping, conceptually and empirically, how Black people interpret, act upon, and produce material (e.g., art forms, tools) as well as social texts (e.g., interaction, identity, ideology, strategies for action; Yosso 2005).

Despite exceptions (e.g., Carter 2005; Tyson 2002), this continued progression in researchers' efforts to develop ever more complex renderings of culture in relation to race often stops short of escaping what Michaels (1992) refers to as the "anticipation of culture by race" (677). That is, we presume that "to be Navajo you have to do Navajo things, but you can't really count as doing Navajo things unless you already are Navajo" (677). Although we must substitute *Black* for *Navajo* in this instance, the effect is the same. Such anticipation reifies race as a stable and objective category and links it deterministically to culture.

When race is operationalized in this way, we lose sight of Black heterogeneity and underconceptualize accordant intersectionalities. In addition, we overlook the extent to which Blackness is reflected not only in the meanings students bring with them to school but also in the meanings that are imposed on them by school structures. In the process, we underestimate the emergent and dynamic meanings of race and the impact of racial discrimination.

Race as a Variable

Education research that treats race as a variable also tends to conceptualize race as a stable, objective category and to demonstrate the aforementioned limitations that derive from this conceptualization. For example, in their efforts to explain a range of educational outcomes—
particularly gaps in Black-White achievement—researchers rely on statistical models where race is included as one of many control variables
(e.g., social class, previous achievement, school resources) and is treated
as an individual attribute. These models "test" whether mediating factors
decrease the significance with which race is associated with educational
outcomes.

When interpreting the cause of the racial differences in educational
outcomes, scholars in this tradition often collapse conceptually the statistical relationships they document between race and the moderating variable under study. For instance, if IQ scores predict educational achievement and Blacks have lower scores than Whites, then being Black is seen
as equivalent to being intellectually deficient (e.g., Herrnstein and Murray
1994). Alternatively, if two-parent households and the presence of a father
in the home correlate with more competitive educational outcomes, and
Blacks are shown to grow up in households headed by single women at
disproportionately higher rates than are Whites, the prevalent family
structure of Blacks (even if founded in economic inequities) is reduced to
a cultural dysfunction (e.g., see Bankston and Caldas 1998; A. A. Ferguson
2001; Moynihan 1965). In both of these examples, being Black functions
as a conceptual proxy for something else (i.e., biology or culture). What
was once a statistical correlation is now conceived as a trait embodied in a
coherent "Black" community. So, although "race as biology" has been dis-
proved in biological and anthropological literature, scholars continue to
conceptualize it as a proxy for bad genes or a lack of the "cultural 'right
stuff'" (Darity 2002, 1). The logic of these analyses parallels that found in
the cultural arguments, thus delineating a place of convergence between
the treatment of race as culture and race as a variable. Bonilla-Silva (2001)
calls this approach the "biologization of culture."

Although other scholars in this tradition examine the impact of social and institutional inequities on observed racial differences in achievement, their analyses also treat race as if it were an individual attribute
that is stable across time. For example, researchers have controlled for
social class and educational resources in the interest of exploring
whether their differential distribution across racial groups explains

racial gaps in achievement and diminishes the significance with which race "predicts" educational outcomes. Although researchers have found that these resources account for some of the documented differences in racial achievement gaps, their effect is minimal and does not reduce substantially the statistical significance with which race correlates with educational outcomes (e.g., Coleman 1966; Grissmer et al. 1994; Hallinan 2001; Jencks and Phillips 1998). In addition, changes in the socioeconomic status (SES) of racial groups across time do not predict changes in racial achievement gaps, and the gaps between middle-class Whites and Blacks (even among those attending resource-rich schools) are greater than those between lower-class Whites and Blacks ("Confronting a Widening Racial Gap" 2003; "The Expanding Racial Scoring Gap" 2002; Hallinan 2001).

Looking to explain these findings, researchers argue that studies that control for the influence of social class generally assume that the effects of social class are constant across racial groups (J. Lee 2002) and historical time and are comparable at the top and bottom tails of achievement distributions (Hedges and Nowell 1999). In making these arguments, researchers attribute to social class a sociohistorical dynamism but stop short of attributing the same dynamism to race. Without considering how the meaning and effect of race are differentially articulated across space, time, and reference groups, researchers relegate race to a unified and stable social category that powerfully predicts Blacks' educational outcomes. The conceptual dilemma is that "Black" is not a biological category that can be reduced to an individual trait (Brayboy, Castagno, and Maughan 2007). It is a social group united by a long history of racialized experiences in the United States (Davis 1991; Takaki 1993). Unfortunately, education researchers are often inattentive to this when they interpret findings of statistical significance. Moreover, in these analyses race is often mistakenly situated as a cause for educational outcomes (Zuberi 2001). Although racial discrimination, for example, may be a cause of some specified outcome, race itself merely marks a social location. It is an ascribed characteristic and a political classification system.

We do not mean to suggest that we should not collect or analyze racial data. Nor are we diminishing the importance of quantitative education research. Collecting and analyzing racial data are essential for understanding and tracking racial inequalities and for charting progress on a range of social outcomes such as SES, individual well-being, and educational attainment. However, we must be theoretically precise in our articulations of what is being captured when race is a variable in the analysis. This means, in part, that racial data should not be used as proxies for traits (such as intelligence or motivation) and subsequently interpreted as innate or culturally ingrained. In the absence of theoretical precision, not only do we misinterpret findings of racial "significance," but as in previously discussed studies that treat race as culture, we are also inclined to homogenize the Black community and underestimate the effects of racial discrimination. What follows is a delineation of these limitations across the two traditions.

Conceptual and Methodological Limitations

Masking the Heterogeneity of the Black Experience

When researchers in the race-as-culture tradition report on norms and values, competencies and practices, or subjectivity and meaning making, usually they are reporting on findings that are specific to a particular segment of the Black community that is subject to a host of social phenomena including, but not limited to, race-related dynamics. Although researchers often allude to these other influences in their elaborated descriptions of the research participants (e.g., by referring to the gender or social class of those under study) and the research settings (e.g., by referring to the demographics, organization, and location of the site of the study), these influences are rarely analyzed. For example, although the majority of studies that have situated race as culture have focused on lower-income Blacks in urban spaces, the ways in which social class and place may have shaped these reported expressions of "Black" culture are not examined. In turn, researchers inadvertently cast the Black poor as a homogeneous social category and overlook the ways in which space, time, and social class moderate the experience of being Black and the consequent norms, values, competencies, practices, and subjectivities that derive from that experience.

Space, Time, and Intersecting Identities.   These are problems because, in terms of space, Black life in large urban cities in the Northeast, Midwest, and South is marked more profoundly by both racial and social-class segregation than in the West (Massey and Eggers 1990). Moreover, researchers have documented how the Black experience varies from one school system to the next, in part as a consequence of how the economy differentially frames the demographics and funding of school systems

(Anyon 1997; Kozol 1991). Scholars have also documented how the specifics of neighborhood (Patillo-McCoy 1999) and school (e.g., Bryk, Lee, and Holland 1993; Hemmings 1996) affect Black life.

Racial experiences are also marked by historical time. However, although there are some important exceptions (e.g., Galletta and Cross 2007; MacLeod 1995; O'Connor 2002), education researchers have approached their analyses as if Blacks' race-related constraints and opportunities did not vary from one historical era to another. To provide one example, Ogbu's cultural-ecological model (CEM) denies the dynamism of Black subjugation across time.[2] The model operates as if there were only one story to be told about Black subjugation and as if it were only this tale that framed Black youths' renderings of opportunity and their consequent performance in school. However, sociologists have marked critical shifts in Black people's experience with oppression. They have discerned shifts from "economic racial oppression" to "class subordination" (Wilson 1978), from "overt" racism to "color blind racism" (Bonilla-Silva 2001), and from "traditional" to "laissez-faire" racism (Bobo, Kluegel, and Smith 1997). Operating within the logic of CEM, we would expect that Black adults coming of age in different eras would generate distinct narratives about opportunity and thus differentially affect how Black youths come to interpret their life chances. Failure to attend to how the demands of particular geographic or historical contexts influence the norms, practices, and meaning making of Black youth is not uncommon. As indicated by Spencer, Swanson, and Cunningham (1991), "Studies that explore contextual effects are seldom conducted on minority youth" (368).

Beyond time and space, Blacks are also classed. The impact of social class as a moderating influence may be growing in significance, given the increased income polarization among Blacks. This polarization, which is defined by "proportionate declines in the middle class, and sharp increases in the proportions of both the affluent and the poor," suggests that the experiences of Black "haves" and "have-nots" have become more differentiated (Massey and Eggers 1990, 1166). Researchers continue to document distinctions not only in how poor and affluent Blacks interpret their life chances but in how they define their interests and ideologies (Hochschild 1995). Differentiation also occurs among Blacks who are similarly classed and are operating in the same space and time. For example, O'Connor (1997) documented how Blacks who share the same class standing and operate in the same social spaces vary considerably in their social encounters and worldviews. Horvat and Lewis (2003) examined how SES mediated the ways that Black families were able to access social networks and influence school decisions.[3] In failing to attend to variation in the Black experience, we construct Blackness as a static social category.

In research that treats race as a variable, this static expression of Blackness is made evident when we scrutinize the methods by which respondents are categorized as Black. To begin, survey research categorizes individuals as Black when they or their parents identify them as such. However, this research does not account for how the context of administration and the design of the survey influence the respondents' designations. Depending on how demographic questions are asked, the range of available options, and the context in which the asking occurs, we may well get different responses. For example, in a recent analysis of national data, Harris and Sim (2000) found that multiracial students responded differently to questions about their racial identification depending on the mode of the questioning (self-administered survey or interview) and the location of the questioning (school or home).

In addition, surveys regularly prevent Hispanics from claiming a racial designation. The racial and ethnic options provided on surveys often situate "Hispanic" as a category that parallels "Black not of Hispanic origin" and "White not of Hispanic origin." By defining racial and ethnic choices in this way, we blur the distinction between race and ethnicity and deny respondents the ability to claim an ethnic and a racial affiliation.[4] Even when surveys enable Hispanics to claim a racial designation, the choices—to the chagrin of many Hispanics—are usually dichotomized, for example, between White and Black (Rodriguez 2000). Moreover, researchers rarely use the information, thus avoiding race-related analyses. And although place of birth on the same surveys can signal the ethnic affiliations of Blacks (e.g., African or West Indian), researchers do not often take advantage of such data.[5] With some exceptions (e.g., Butterfield 2006; Farley and Allen 1989; Waters 1994), the ethnic differentiation among Blacks and its relation to their educational outcomes is under-studied.

Such issues are suggested in Portes and MacLeod's (1996) study of the educational progress of children of immigrants to the United States from Cuba, Vietnam, Haiti, and Mexico. This study focuses our attention on the importance of the context of reception in the differential performance of these immigrant groups. The researchers do not, however, analyze how race may have moderated the nature of that reception and how race and ethnicity intersect to explain variation in educational outcomes and experiences. For example, they found that Cuban and Vietnamese immigrants, in contrast to Haitian and Mexican immigrants, were "received sympathetically by the U.S. government and were granted numerous forms of federal assistance" (260). Portes and MacLeod indicate that the Cubans and Vietnamese used the subsidies to "create solidary and dynamic entrepreneurial communities" that, in part, framed their more competitive achievement performance. The authors also note that earlier waves of Cubans received generous governmental assistance that was denied to those who arrived later. Although the authors report that the first wave of Cubans were of higher social-class origins, they fail to point out that the first wave was also disproportionately "White," whereas later waves were primarily "Black" and "Brown" (Pedraza and Rumbaut 1996). The analyses did not explore how race (signaled by phenotype) might be implicated in institutionalized access to resources.[6] Although Portes and MacLeod did not pursue this study in the interest of examining how race and ethnicity influence reception and educational outcomes, their sample calls attention to the ways that the reception and subsequent outcomes of Black Haitians and Black Cubans may have been similar. The study unintentionally illustrates the importance of exploring when, how, and why educational experiences and outcomes vary (or do not vary) among Blacks of different ethnic groups.

The issues of design and analysis discussed earlier raise two important questions: (1) Who is being captured in and who is being excluded by the category "Black"? and (2) How does this categorization impinge on our comparative analyses of Blacks vis-à-vis others? Although these questions can be addressed in part with the use of control variables (e.g., SES, region, nationality), some of the variation is left out because of limitations in data collection.

It is not beyond the scope of a survey to assess how participants make sense of the racial options with which they are provided. We can design surveys with the intent of examining how respondents understand their selected racial options in relation to researcher-selected parameters of interest. We might, for example, use Sellers and colleagues' (Sellers et al. 1998) multidimensional model of racial identity to gauge, among other things, (1) the extent to which being Black is central to the identity of the person under study, (2) whether the person assesses being Black in positive or negative terms, or (3) whether the self-designation as Black is aligned with a specific racial ideology. This model contributes significantly to our understanding of the multidimensionality of Black racial identity. However, like other survey approaches, it also restricts the respondent's ability to impose categories unanticipated by the researcher. Consequently, we are unable to assess dimensions of racial identity that were not targeted a priori. Nor can we make adequate sense of those dimensions that are represented by performance (e.g., style, dress, language) rather than by cognition and would be better captured by observation.[7]

We are also unable to explore how the social construction of these categories (through macro- or microdynamics or historical or contemporary forces) informs a participant's interpretation of or election into one category over another (Cornell 1996; Hall 1990). For example, researchers (e.g., Vickerman 1999) have found that many immigrants of dark phenotype who had not previously imagined themselves as "Black" adopted that identity after their arrival in the United States, given the power with which skin color signals race in the U.S. context.

Our failure to attend to the aforementioned methodological and conceptual issues necessarily influences how we make sense of the statistically robust relationships that are reported in research that features race as a variable. That is, although this research is often focused on identifying correlates for Black educational outcomes, it often prevents us from interpreting how race, operating as a social phenomenon, impinges on these relationships. Thus, when some research finds that income and occupation are less robust predictors of achievement for Blacks than for Whites, we cannot unpack the relationship. Is the relationship a function of the ways in which Blacks across social class groups similarly make sense of and display what it means to "be" Black in the school setting? Is it due to the frames of Blackness that are imposed by schooling agents on Black bodies in ways that diminish the significance of social class? Or is it how social class, as signaled by income and occupation, marks culture and determines opportunity differently and less powerfully than when it is signaled by wealth (a measure in which Blacks across income categories have huge deficits relative to Whites)?

When studies fail to account analytically for Black heterogeneity, we construct oversimplified notions of what it means to be Black and thereby compromise our ability to make sense of the substantive variation in achievement performance that occurs among Blacks in and across time. Despite overarching accounts of Black underperformance in school, Black performance in school varies. For example, the differences between Black and White educational attainment narrowed during the 1970s, but by the mid-1980s the gap began to grow (Nettles and Perna 1997). Similarly, researchers documented the dramatic narrowing of the

Black-White test-score gap during the 1970s, which leveled off during the 1980s and began to reverse itself on some measures, such as reading and science scores (Grissmer et al. 1994). Across the same span of time, Black test-score gains were somewhat larger in the Southeast and smallest in the Northeast (Grissmer et al. 1994). Black students at Catholic and "effective" schools outperformed Blacks in public and unreformed neighborhood schools (Bryk et al. 1993; Wang and Gordon 1994). The performance of Black subgroups also varies. Although Black men now lag behind Black women in the rates at which they earn advanced degrees (Nettles and Perna 1997), this was not always the case. During the mid-1970s, for example, Black men outperformed Black women on this measure (Cross and Slater 2000).

Certainly, our account of research on the variation in Black achievement is not exhaustive. These findings nevertheless signal the need to specify which Blacks are being studied and the conditions under which they are operating. We cannot stop with naming and describing who, when, and where but must analyze and theorize how these specificities are implicated in the cultural formations that we attach to achievement outcomes. In our struggle to establish conceptual links between the heterogeneity in the Black experience and the heterogeneity in Black educational outcomes, we must also contend with intersectionalities.

The Underconceptualization of Intersectionalities.   As noted earlier, Black variation is marked not only by space, time, and ethnicity but also by gender and social class (Carter 2005; O'Connor 2002). Recognizing this, researchers have conducted studies that contrast the experiences of Black men with those of Black women (e.g., Cross and Slater 2000; Grant 1984). In other instances, researchers have focused on Black men and women and have used Whites or members of other ethnic groups of the same gender category as comparative referents (e.g., A. A. Ferguson 2001; Fordham 1996; Holland and Eisenhart 1990). Similarly, researchers have captured the experiences of middle-class, working-class, and poor Blacks (Hemmings 1996; Lareau and Horvat 1999). Still others have sought to examine the intersections of race, class, and gender (Cousins 1999; Horvat and Antonio 1999).

Although some of the works cited offer notable exceptions (e.g., Carter 2005; Lareau and Horvat 1999), much of this work stops short of examining intersectionalities substantively. In some instances, researchers who compare Blacks of different genders or social classes or Whites and Blacks of the same gender and social class simply list the differences in the groups' educational experiences or outcomes. They do not offer a concomitant analysis of how the participants' social class or gender locations interface with racial location to explain the noted differences. When such analyses are attempted, one group position is often privileged over another. For example, Holland and Eisenhart (1990), in their study of Black and White women in college, identify distinctions in how the two groups of women negotiate the culture of femininity in relation to how they achieve in and experience college. The authors note that the culture of femininity and its accordant relationship with women's college achievements and experiences are differently framed for the two groups, in part because of the different peer cultures operating at the two colleges. However, the authors offer no analysis regarding how race shapes these differences. The marginalization of race as an analytical category is especially problematic because the Black women were attending a historically Black college and the White women were attending a predominantly White college.

Feminist scholars warn us against establishing hierarchal relationships between social positions (e.g., King 1988). They compel us to examine how these positions are "inextricably intertwined and circulate together in the representations [or structuring] of subjects and experiences of subjectivity" (A. A. Ferguson 2001, 22). Many researchers have been hesitant to examine class and gender out of concern that the significance of race will be trumped in the process. Some of those who have done so have been criticized for their efforts (e.g., Wilson 1978). If, however, we examine these positions as intertwined rather than as isolated and independent, we evade the risk of displacing the significance of race.

Underanalyzing Institutionalized Productions of Race and Racial Discrimination

Related to these concerns, the framing of race as culture can have the effect of ignoring or minimizing how race is produced institutionally. Although some cultural analyses have attended to racialized meaning making and have made strides in reporting on intersectionalities, such work is generally focused on examining the racialized understandings that Black youths bring with them to school. For example, Fordham (1993) examined how gender and race intersected in the production of Black women's conceptions of womanhood and how these conceptions were implicated in the pursuit of competitive academic outcomes. Alternatively, Lareau and Horvat (1999) showed how the race and social class of the Black parents in their study simultaneously framed how they gauged the racial terrain of their children's schools and how they went about advocating on their children's behalf. Works such as these provide insight into how Blacks produce classed and gendered interpretations of themselves as racial subjects and of their status in social settings. Such works also elucidate how these raced, but not solely raced, interpretations influence how some Blacks think about and behave in school in their efforts to influence their own or their children's educational outcomes. In delineating how Blacks make sense of their status and experience as raced (but not solely raced) subjects and then act accordingly in school, studies such as these often stop short of examining how schools and their agents simultaneously racialize Black subjects and in turn structure racism (Dolby 2001; Lewis 2003a).

A. A. Ferguson's (2001) work substantiates the need for such analyses. She found that although both Black and White boys perform their masculinity by breaking school rules, Black boys more often find themselves in trouble because of how their performances are interpreted. When White boys transgressed, school officials presumed that "boys will be boys," attributed "innocence to their wrongdoing," and believed that "they must be socialized to fully understand the meaning of their acts" (80). In contrast, when Black boys transgressed, their acts were "adultified." That is, "their transgressions [were] made to take on a sinister, intentional, fully conscious tone . . . stripped of any element of naivete" (83). Having framed them as "not children," the interpreters (most of whom were White and constituted authority in the school setting) were necessarily directed toward treatment "that punishes through example and exclusion rather than through persuasion and edification, as is practiced with the young White males in the school" (90). The relationship between these institutionalized productions of race and the higher rates at which Black boys find themselves in trouble is evident. Other researchers have contributed to our growing understanding of how school-based productions of race shape race-related inequities in educational access and opportunity (e.g., Dolby 2001; Lewis 2003a; Pollock 2001, 2004) and ultimately function as institutionalized racism (even if not explicitly labeled as such by the researchers). Researchers who fail to build on this emerging approach to studying race in schools will likely underestimate the effects of racial discrimination.

The risk of underestimating the effects of racial discrimination also emerges in education research that deploys race as a variable. One example comes from national studies of secondary school that "control" for previous achievement (most often operationalized as eighth-grade test scores) in the effort to determine whether race is significant in predicting educational outcomes. Such studies, often drawing on large, longitudinal national data sets (e.g., the National Education Longitudinal Study), may underestimate the effects of institutionalized racism on educational outcomes by including measures of previous achievement as if they were good controls for academic ability rather than measures of previous opportunity. The studies fail to recognize that previous achievement may well serve as a proxy for racial discrimination—systematically poor educational experiences and opportunities in the early years that are captured in eighth-grade test scores.

In an example from the research on track placements, Dauber, Alexander, and Entwistle (1996) discuss how the effects of social background factors (race, SES, etc.) can be masked as "objective academic qualifications" (300). They found that sixth-grade course placement (i.e., advanced, regular, or remedial) was the main predictor of eighth-grade course placement. However, they found that the main predictors of sixth-grade course placement included social background factors—race being one of the most significant. The authors state that "by the eighth grade, social background differences in mathematics are almost entirely hidden by their strong association with sixth-grade placements" (300). This illustrates how using seemingly objective academic outcomes from early in a student's career as controls in analyzing later academic outcomes can mask other effects. Specifically, in the sixth grade, Black students were much less likely than similar White peers to be placed in high-track classes and were more likely than similar White peers to be placed in low-track classes. Those patterns held in the eighth grade, but any analysis that used sixth-grade placement as an objective measure of prior achievement would find almost no race effects—as they were almost entirely captured by the variable "sixth-grade placement."

In another example, Mickelson (2001), using longitudinal data, found that attending a racially isolated Black elementary school had both direct and indirect negative effects on achievement and track placement, even with controls for numerous individual and family indicators. This measure is often not available and thus is not usually included in analyses. But, given persistently high levels of school segregation, it might well be one factor that is typically captured in the variable "race." In fact, ample evidence exists suggesting that institutionalized racism of various kinds shapes access to educational opportunity and resources

(Bonilla-Silva and Lewis 1999; Feagin, Vera, and Imani 1996; R. Ferguson 1998; Johnson, Boyden, and Pittz 2001; Lewis 2003b; Mickelson 2003; Roscigno 1998). But research that includes prior achievement and race in a regression model and concludes that race is not significant has the potential to miss such effects. This kind of analysis implies that race and prior achievement occur or have effects at the same time, when, in fact, race (as a proxy for institutionalized racism) potentially has causal significance in shaping prior achievement.

Our call for more purposeful theorization of how racism is implicated in Black educational experiences and outcomes is consistent with that of education scholars who build on the social science and legal literature in critical race theory. These scholars challenge researchers to examine how racism shapes educational experiences and outcomes, in part by studying (1) how the discourses that emerge in and around schools and students are not neutral but, rather, have "embedded in them values and practices that normalize racism" (Duncan 2002, 131; Rousseau and Tate 2003); (2) how the historical legacy of racism structures group advantage and disadvantage in school (Ladson-Billings and Tate 1995); and (3) how the narratives of people of color are central to analyzing and understanding these phenomena (Solorzano and Yosso 2002; see Dixson and Rousseau 2005, for further discussion).

Orienting Future Research

Our analysis of research on Black educational experiences and outcomes yields several theoretical and methodological considerations for future efforts, including (1) theoretical attention to how race-related resources shape educational outcomes, (2) attention to the way race is a product of educational settings as much as it is something that students bring with them, (3) a focus on how everyday interactions and practices in schools affect educational outcomes, and (4) examination of how students make sense of their racialized social locations in light of their schooling experiences. Such studies will continue to unveil how schools produce race as a social category.

Toward that end, researchers are only just beginning to examine how race can variously shape capital in educational settings (A. A. Ferguson 2001; Horvat and Lewis 2003; Lewis 2003b). As defined by Bourdieu (1977), *capital* consists of the resources that serve to advance one's position or status in a given context.[8] Race shapes (1) economic capital, given how it defines historical access to economic resources, particularly wealth (Oliver and Shapiro 1995), and therefore influences who has access to "good" schools (Kozol 1991; Orfield, Eaton, and The Harvard Project on School Desegregation 1996); (2) cultural capital, given how it affects which cultural resources are rewarded in schools (Carter 2002; Lareau and Horvat 1999); (3) social capital, given how it informs patterns of segregation that affect social networks, which in turn affect educational access and achievement; and (4) symbolic capital, given how skin color influences which bodies are privileged in school. For example, theorizing in terms of symbolic capital reveals how such capital can serve as a resource, affecting our expectations and interpretations. Like what some call "White privilege," race as symbolic capital captures the daily, sometimes subtle forms of discrimination that can affect daily educational experiences.

Despite the potential benefits of such investigations, analyses of how race shapes everyday practices and experiences in schools—including how those practices and experiences affect the production of capital and the institutionalization of racism—are in short supply. Important work has emerged in recent years, such as that by A. A. Ferguson (2001), Horvat, Weininger, and Lareau (2003), Lewis (2003b), and Lareau and Horvat (1999) on elementary schools; Davidson (1996), Dolby (2001), Fergus (2004), Jewett (2006), Kenny (2000), O'Connor (2001), Peterson-Lewis and Bratton (2004), and Pollock (2001, 2004) on middle and high schools; and Feagin et al. (1996) on college settings. However, there is still not enough work examining how Black educational experiences and outcomes are founded in everyday experience with race and racism. Moreover, the works cited here do not reflect in full the kind of multilevel ecological studies that we call for later in this chapter. These works, all of which are ethnographic in orientation, nevertheless indicate that ethnographic research provides one critical starting point for these multilevel studies.

Ethnographic research involves entering a social setting and getting to know the people who move within it. Thus researchers can use ethnography to unearth how various school contexts affect Black students and how Black students experience and understand various school contexts. As Emerson (1983) articulates, ethnography assumes context as a resource for understanding. Ethnography permits the study of relationships as they happen rather than abstracting people from their lives and treating them as if they lived, acted, and believed "in isolation from one another" (Feagin, Orum, and Sjoberg 1991, 8). Thus ethnography has the potential to provide insight into how race shapes interactions in schools. For example, why do disciplinary sanctions differ across race and gender categories? What are the perceptions of these sanctions on the bodies on which they are enacted? Ethnography has the potential also to illuminate what race means for particular Black students in particular contexts and how their understandings of themselves and others develop. Especially in the study of race and race relations, this kind of research is crucial for capturing the workings of complex social processes and for capturing the inconsistencies between what people say and do.

The promise of ethnographic methods rests with their ability to capture the everydayness of racism, a second recommendation for future research. More ecologically grounded studies of how race is implicated in the education of Blacks, including how its impact is realized through institutionalized racism, are warranted. This recommendation is consistent with current efforts to integrate multiple levels of analysis when interpreting educational outcomes (Bryk and Raudenbush 1992; DiPrete and Foristal 1994; Frank 1998). In the interest of explaining racial gaps in achievement, researchers have linked microprocesses (e.g., student subjectivity and actions, student-teacher interactions) with mesoinfluences (e.g., school- and district-level policies, demographics, and organization) and macroinfluences (e.g., the economic forces or systems of racial hierarchy that are specific to the time and space in which the study is being conducted; DiPrete and Foristal 1994; Roscigno 2000; Roscigno, Tomaskovic-Devey, and Crowley 2006). By establishing empirical and analytical links between these levels of interaction and influence, they have generated more precise estimations of how context affects the educational realities of Blacks operating in a specific place and time (Spencer, Dupree, and Hartmann 1997). Such multilevel and historically specific studies are essential to the task of unpacking why Black students, operating in one space and time, have educational experiences and outcomes different from those of Black students operating in other contexts.

When we wed multilevel and historically specific analyses with ethnography, we establish the groundwork for exploring with more conceptual rigor the operation and impact of institutionalized racism on the experiences and outcomes of Blacks in school. As Holt (1995) argues, the analysis of racism requires us to resolve the linkage between the individual actor and the social context. In other words, we must analyze the levels of the problem, such that we establish "continuity between behavioral explanations sited at the individual level of human experience and those at the level of society and social force" (Holt 1995, 7). Consequently, education researchers must explore how contemporary social forces nourish the racial knowledge, structures, and practices that sustain and reward everyday racism (Essed 1991; Tate 1997).

> It is at . . . [the] level [of the everyday] . . . that race is reproduced via the marking of the racial Other and that racist ideas and practices are naturalized, made self-evident, and thus seemingly beyond audible challenge. It is at this level that race is reproduced long after its original historical stimulus—the slave trade and slavery—have faded. It is at this level that seemingly rational and ordinary folk commit irrational and extraordinary acts. (7)

The irrational and extraordinary acts to which Holt directs us should not be reduced to explicitly racist actions. They consist of the many complicated social processes whereby educational opportunities are facilitated or circumscribed. Within this frame, we can explore more subtle forms of racism that are not signaled by overt behavior (Forman 2001). Thus—like A. A. Ferguson (2001), Lewis (2003b), Duncan (2002), or Morris (2006)—we can study how the interpretations and responses of individual school actors shape Black students' experiences in schools in ways that systemically deny them privilege and educational access. In this way, we come to understand how culture can operate as structure (Hays 1994), and we establish an analytical lens for revealing the meso- and macrolevel forces that legitimate and institutionalize that operation.

Black education research also needs to analyze how race intersects with social class and gender. This includes studying not only variation in Black school experiences but also how and why class and gender shape Black students' school experiences differently than they shape other groups' experiences. As discussed previously, it is essential that work of this kind examine race, class, and gender as intertwined rather than as independent social positions (Akom 2003; Carter 2005; Mickelson and Velasco 2006; Tyson 2002). As indicated by McCarthy and Crichlow (1993), one cannot interpret the educational experiences of minority groups "from assumptions about race pure and simple" because different gender and class identities within minority groups often "cut at right angles" to racial politics and identities. In addition, ethnic variation of Blacks has only recently gained attention in education research, although it is an important component of complex racial identities (Bryce-Laporte 1972; Butterfield 2006; Fergus 2004; Goodstein 1990; Portes and Rumbaut 2001; Rong and

Brown 2002; Waters 1999). Ideally, analyses of intersectionalities should be conducted in accord with the kind of multilevel analysis we discussed earlier. In this instance, examining "levels of the problem" is warranted because "the relative significance of race, sex, or class [or ethnicity] in determining the conditions of [people's] lives is neither fixed nor absolute, but rather is dependent on the sociohistorical context and the social phenomenon under consideration" (King 1988, 49).

In addition, research needs to incorporate multiple methodological strategies. For example, challenges abound in the effort to understand fully why we continue to have racial gaps in achievement. Recent research has shown that students often enter kindergarten with different skill sets. Gaps in skills increase in the first years of school (Denton and West 2002). We have yet to develop a complete understanding of how this process unfolds over time and why it is that Black students are being undereducated. This issue, along with other research questions about Black educational experiences, can be more precisely addressed with productive pairings of quantitative and qualitative methodologies (Anyon 2005; Mickelson and Velasco 2006; Tyson, Darity, and Castellino 2005). The pairing of survey research and qualitative interviewing is an especially productive option. Young (1999, 206) argues that qualitative interviews provide the entrée to what Goffman (1974) identified as "schemata of interpretation. These are the meanings that actors formulate about their social encounters and experiences." Consequently, when an understanding of these meanings is coupled with individuals' forced-choice selections (i.e., on a survey), we are provided with a phenomenological framing of the responses.

This pairing of methodologies not only provides possibilities for clarification and elaboration of survey findings but also serves an important corrective function. For example, recent studies on racial issues, both in school and beyond, have found important inconsistencies between survey and qualitative data. Bonilla-Silva and Forman (2000) found gaps between people's responses to abstract survey items about race (e.g., whether they approved of interracial marriage in general) and their expanded responses in in-depth interviews (e.g., how they felt about interracial marriage and whether they would ever marry someone of a different race). In addition, in recent school research, one of the coauthors found inconsistencies between teachers' and parents' reported views and the ways they then interacted with someone of another racial group (Lewis 2003b). These are not mere contradictions but provide more complex information about how race works in and across settings.

Finally, as we have argued throughout, research on Blacks' educational experiences needs to have more theoretically informed interpretations of the constructs it includes (e.g., race, culture, racism; Ladson-Billings and Tate 1995; Pollock 2004). In particular, research in this tradition needs more robust conceptualizations of race. The question of what meaning race has for Black students' educational outcomes is one that must be theorized, not assumed or implied. Our ability to develop more accurate interpretations of how and why Black students fare in school as they do depends on our ability to attend to race with greater conceptual precision. This challenge is relevant to a range of methodological issues, including the productive framing of research questions, the proper specification of statistical models in quantitative analyses, and the appropriate selection of research designs.

Lessons Learned

- The construct of race must be theoretically informed to be useful in research with African Americans so that more meaningful interpretations of findings are possible.
- The intersections of race, class, and gender warrant serious consideration in determining the conditions of people's lives as they collectively reflect the sociohistorical context of the phenomenon to be examined.
- More complex information about how race works in and across settings can be obtained using multimethod research strategies.
- The advantage of greater conceptual and methodological clarity of research on race will have important implications for both educational practice and policy.

Our emphasis on developing more theoretically informed relationships between key constructs and research design and methodology is not simply an academic matter. Education research influences policy decisions, which in turn have an impact on life outcomes. For example, scholarship suggesting that Black students' underperformance in school is a matter of individual or group deficiencies leads to very different policy proposals than does scholarship suggesting that school policies and practices are responsible. Moreover, studies that suggest that Blacks are a monolithic cultural group facing the same issues across space and time flatten the complex topography of Black life, ignoring important variations in educational experiences. In failing to establish more theoretically rigorous relationships between research designs, methodologies, and central concepts such as race, we limit our ability to improve educational opportunity for Blacks and impinge negatively on Black people's already narrowed educational chances.

NOTES

This chapter was originally published as an article in *Educational Researcher* 36, no. 9: 541–52, 2007. It has been reproduced here with permission from the publisher, Sage Publications, Thousand Oaks, CA.

The analyses recorded herein were supported in part by funding from the William T. Grant Foundation.

1. Although this article elucidates the analytic imprecision with which researchers have studied Black educational outcomes, similar arguments can be made about understanding the educational experiences of other racial and ethnic groups.

2. According to the cultural ecological model, Black youths learn about their group's historical and contemporary subjugation through the experiences and narratives of Black adults. In response, they generate theories of "making it" that contradict dominant notions of status attainment and that produce disillusionment about the instrumental value of school. They thus develop distrust for schools and their agents, and an oppositional cultural identity emerges. Situating schooling as a White domain that requires Blacks to "think" and "act" White in exchange for academic success, Black youths are said to limit their efforts in school because they do not want to compromise their racial identity or their affiliation with the Black community.

3. We found limited literature on class differences in the educational experiences and outcomes of Blacks. For some recent examples, see Diamond and Gomez (2004), Harding (2006), Horton-Ikard and Miller (2004), Horvat, Weininger, and Lareau (2003), Lareau (2000, 2003), Rothstein (2004), and Sirin and Rogers-Sirin (2004).

4. For example, in their recent analysis of multiracial identities among adolescents using the Add Health data, Harris and Sim (2000) exclude Hispanics altogether from their study. This is because, as they state, Add Health follows the convention of asking separate questions about race and Hispanic origin. In treating Hispanicity as distinct from race, Add Health deviates from conventional academic uses of race that tend to contrast Hispanics with non-Hispanic Whites, Blacks, and Asians (Farley 1996), as well as understandings of race among Hispanics, many of whom treat Hispanic, White, Black, Asian, and American Indian as comparable identifiers (Hirschman, Kasinitz, and DeWind 1999; OMB [Office of Management and Budget] 1997). The two-question approach lowers the threshold for identifying as Hispanic (Hirschman et al. 1999) and leads to confusing responses. Comparisons cannot be made between Hispanic and non-Hispanic multiracials, because selecting two or more responses to the race question is very

different from selecting a Hispanic origin in one question and a race in another. Moreover, it is not clear what people mean when they select a Hispanic origin and a race. Some are indicating mixed ancestry (e.g., mestiz mother from Mexico and a White father from Ireland), while others are indicating an ancestry and a nationality (e.g., Japanese from Peru, German from Argentina).

5. Nativity is not always an adequate proxy for ethnicity. Some Blacks claim ethnic affiliations that are not signaled by their places of birth; for example, some Blacks who were born in the United States claim West Indian identity (Waters 1999).

6. The question of how race may factor in the U.S. resistance to defining Haitians as political refugees and therefore eligible for federal subsidies also warrants exploration (Lennox 1993).

7. In addition, the forced-choice nature of the survey prevents respondents from providing commentary that would qualify their responses in significant ways and possibly require the researcher to reinterpret findings (Bonilla-Silva and Forman 2000).

8. Bourdieu (1977) discussed four types of capital: economic (money and property), social (connections, social networks), cultural (cultural knowledge, educational credentials), and symbolic (symbols of prestige and legitimacy). Each form of capital can be converted into the others to enhance or maintain positions in the social order. For example, families use economic capital to buy housing in neighborhoods with good schools or to pay for private schooling. These schools can bestow important cultural capital and social connections (social capital), which can then be converted back into economic capital when deployed in gaining access to elite colleges and good employment opportunities.

REFERENCES

Akom, A. A. 2003. Reexamining resistance as oppositional behavior: The Nation of Islam and the creation of a Black achievement ideology. *Sociology of Education* 76, no. 4: 305–25.

Anyon, J. 1997. *Ghetto schooling.* New York: Teachers College Press.

Anyon, J. 2005. *Radical possibilities: Public policy, urban education, and a new social movement.* New York: Routledge.

Bankston, C. L., III, and S. L. Caldas. 1998. Family structure, schoolmates, and racial inequalities in school achievement. *Journal of Marriage and Family* 60:715–23.

Bloom, R., M. Whiteman, and M. Deutsch. 1965. Race and social class as separate factors related to social environment. *American Journal of Sociology* 70, no. 4: 471–76.

Bobo, L., J. R. Kluegel, and R. A. Smith. 1997. Laissez-faire racism: The crystallization of a "Kinder, Gentler" anti-Black ideology. In S. A. Tuch and J. K. Martin, eds., *Racial attitudes in the 1990s: Continuity and change,* 15–44. Westport, CT: Praeger.

Bonilla-Silva, E. 2001. *White supremacy and racism in the post–Civil Rights era.* Boulder: Lynne Rienner.

Bonilla-Silva, E., and T. A. Forman. 2000. "I am not a racist, but . . .": Mapping college students' racial ideology in the United States. *Discourse and Society* 11:50–85.

Bonilla-Silva, E., and A. Lewis. 1999. The new racism: Racial structure in the United States, 1960s–1990s. In P. Wong, ed., *Race, ethnicity, and nationality in the United States,* 55–101. Boulder: Westview.

Bourdieu, P. 1977. *Outline of a theory of practice.* Cambridge, UK: Cambridge University Press.

Brayboy, B. M. J., A. E. Castagno, and E. Maughan. 2007. Equality and justice for all? Examining race in educational scholarship. *Review of Research in Education* 31:159–95.

Bryce-Laporte, R. S. 1972. Black immigrants: The experience of invisibility and inequality. *Journal of Black Studies* 3, no. 1: 29–56.

Bryk, A. S., V. E. Lee, and P. B. Holland. 1993. *Catholic schools and the common good.* Cambridge: Harvard University Press.

Bryk, A. S., and S. Raudenbush. 1992. *Hierarchical linear models.* Newbury Park, CA: Sage.

Butterfield, S. 2006. To be young, gifted, Black, and somewhat foreign: The role of ethnicity in Black student achievement. In E. Horvat and C. O'Connor, eds., *Beyond acting White: Reframing the debate on Black student achievement,* 133–55. Lanham, MD: Rowman and Littlefield.

Carter, P. 2002. Balancing "acts": Issues of identity and cultural resistance in the social and educational behaviors of minority youth. Unpublished manuscript, Harvard University.

Carter, P. 2005. *Keepin' it real.* New York: Oxford University Press.

Coleman, J. S. 1966. *Equality of educational opportunity.* Washington, DC: U.S. Department of Education.

Confronting the widening racial scoring gap on the SAT. 2003. *Journal of Blacks in Higher Education* 41 (Autumn): 84–89. Special report.

Cornell, S. 1996. The variable ties that bind: Content and circumstance in ethnic processes. *Ethnic and Racial Studies* 19, no. 2: 266–89.

Cousins, L. H. 1999. "Playing between classes": America's troubles with class, race, and gender in a Black high school and community. *Anthropology and Education Quarterly* 30, no. 3: 294–316.

Cross, T., and R. B. Slater. 2000. The alarming decline in the academic performance of African-American men. *Journal of Blacks in Higher Education* 27:82–87.

Darity, W. A. 2002. Intergroup disparity: Why culture is irrelevant. Unpublished manuscript, University of North Carolina, Chapel Hill.

Dauber, S., K. Alexander, and D. Entwistle. 1996. Tracking and transitions through the middle grades: Channeling educational trajectories. *Sociology of Education* 69, no. 4: 290–307.

Davidson, A. 1996. *Making and molding identity in schools: Student narratives on race, gender, and academic engagement.* Albany: SUNY Press.

Davis, J. 1991. *Who is Black? One nation's definition.* University Park: Pennsylvania State University Press.

Denton, K., and J. West. 2002. *Children's reading and mathematics achievement in kindergarten and first grade.* NCES 2002125. Washington, DC: National Center for Education Statistics.

Deutsch, M. 1964a. Early social environment: Its influence on school adaptation. In D. Schreiber, ed., *The school dropout,* 89–100. Washington, DC: National Education Association.

Deutsch, M. 1964b. Social and psychological perspectives on the development of the disadvantaged learner. *Journal of Negro Education* 33, no. 3: 232–44.

Diamond, J., and K. Gomez. 2004. African American parents' educational orientations: The importance of social class and parents' perceptions of schools. *Education and Urban Society* 36, no. 4: 383–427.

DiPrete, T. A., and J. Foristal. 1994. Multilevel models: Methods and substance. *American Sociological Review* 200:331–57.

Dixson, A. D., and C. K. Rousseau. 2005. And we are still not saved: Critical race theory in education ten years later. *Race, Ethnicity, and Education* 8, no. 1: 7–27.

Dolby, N. 2001. *Constructing race: Youth, identity, and popular culture in South Africa.* Albany: SUNY Press.

Duncan, G. A. 2002. Beyond love: A critical race ethnography of the schooling of adolescent Black males. *Equity and Excellence in Education* 35, no. 2: 131–43.

Emerson, R. M. 1983. *Contemporary field research: A collection of readings.* Boston: Little, Brown.

Essed, P. 1991. *Understanding everyday racism: An interdisciplinary theory.* Newbury Park, CA: Sage.

The expanding racial scoring gap between Black and White SAT test takers. 2002. *Journal of Blacks in Higher Education* 37 (Autumn): 15–16, 18–20.

Farley, R. 1996. *The new American reality: Who we are, how we got here, where we are going.* New York: Russell Sage Foundation.

Farley, R., and W. R. Allen. 1989. *The color line and the quality of life in America.* New York: Oxford University Press.

Feagin, J. R., A. M. Orum, and G. Sjoberg. 1991. *A case for the case study.* Chapel Hill: University of North Carolina Press.

Feagin, J. R., H. Vera, and N. Imani. 1996. *The agony of education: Black students at White colleges and universities.* New York: Routledge.

Fergus, E. 2004. *Skin color and identity formation: Perceptions of opportunity and academic orientation among Mexican and Puerto Rican youth.* New York: Routledge.

Ferguson, A. A. 2001. *Bad boys: Public schools in the making of Black masculinity.* Ann Arbor: University of Michigan Press.

Ferguson, R. 1998. Teachers' perceptions and expectations and the Black-White test score gap. In C. Jencks and M. Phillips, eds., *The Black-White test score gap,* 273–317. Washington, DC: Brookings Institution Press.

Fordham, S. 1993. "Those loud Black girls": (Black) women, silence, and gender "passing" in the academy. *Anthropology and Education Quarterly* 24, no. 1: 3–32.

Fordham, S. 1996. *Blacked out: Dilemmas of race, identity, and success at Capital High.* Chicago: University of Chicago Press.

Fordham, S. 1999. Dissin' "the standard": Ebonics as guerilla warfare at Capital High. *Anthropology and Education Quarterly* 30, no. 3: 272–93.

Forman, T. A. 2001. Social determinants of White youth's racial attitudes. *Sociological Studies of Children and Youth* 8:173–207.

Frank, K. 1998. Quantitative methods for studying social context in multilevels and through interpersonal relations. *Review of Research in Education* 23:171–216.

Galletta, A., and W. Cross. 2007. Past as present, present as past: Historicizing Black education and interrogating "integration." In A. Fuligni, ed., *Contesting stereotypes and creating identities: Social categories, social identities, and educational participation*, 15–41. New York: Russell Sage.

Goffman, E. 1974. *Frame analysis: An essay on the organization of experience.* New York: Harper and Row.

Goodstein, C. 1990. America's cities: The new immigrants in the schools. *Crisis* 98, no. 5: 28–29.

Gordon, E. 1965.Characteristics of socially disadvantaged children. *Review of Educational Research* 35, no. 3: 377–88.

Grant, L. 1984. Black females' "place" in desegregated classrooms. *Sociology of Education* 57, no. 2: 98–111.

Grissmer, D. W., S. N. Kirby, M. Berends, and S. Williamson. 1994. *Student achievement and the changing American family.* Santa Monica, CA: RAND.

Hall, S. 1990. Cultural identity and diaspora. In J. Rutherford, ed., *Identity: Community, culture, and difference,* 222–37. London: Lawrence and Wishart.

Hallinan, M. 2001. Sociological perspectives on Black-White inequalities in American schooling. *Sociology of Education,* Special issue, 50–70.

Harding, N. 2006. Ethnic and social class similarities and differences in mothers' beliefs about kindergarten preparation. *Race, Ethnicity, and Education* 9, no. 2: 223–37.

Harris, D. R., and J. J. Sim. 2000. *Who is mixed race? Patterns and determinants of adolescent racial identity.* Ann Arbor: University of Michigan Press.

Hays, S. 1994. Structure and agency and the sticky problem of culture. *Sociological Theory* 12:57–72.

Heath, S. B. 1982. *Ways with words: Language, life, and work in communities and classrooms.* Cambridge, UK: Cambridge University Press.

Hedges, L., and A. Nowell. 1999. Black-White gap in achievement test scores. *Sociology of Education* 72:111–35.

Hemmings, A. 1996. Conflicting images? Being Black and a model high school student. *Anthropology and Education Quarterly* 27, no. 1: 20–50.

Herrnstein, R. J., and C. Murray. 1994. *The bell curve: Intelligence and class structure in American life.* New York: Free Press.

Hirschman, C., P. Kasinitz, and J. DeWind. 1999. *The handbook of international migration: The American experience.* New York: Russell Sage Foundation.

Hochschild, J. L. 1995. *Facing up to the American dream: Race, class, and the soul of the nation.* Princeton: Princeton University Press.

Holland, D. C., and M. A. Eisenhart. 1990. *Educated in romance: Women, achievement, and college culture.* Chicago: University of Chicago Press.

Holt, T. C. 1995. Marking: Race, race making, and the writing of history. *American Historical Review* 100, no. 1: 1–20.

Horton-Ikard, R., and J. F. Miller. 2004. "It is not just the poor kids": The use of AAE forms by African-American school-aged children from middle SES communities. *Journal of Communication Disorders* 37, no. 6: 467–87.

Horvat, E. M., and A. L. Antonio. 1999. "Hey, those shoes are out of uniform": Black girls in an elite high school and the importance of habitus. *Anthropology and Education Quarterly* 30, no. 3: 317–42.

Horvat, E. M., and K. Lewis. 2003. Reassessing the "burden of acting White": The importance of Black peer groups in managing academic success. *Sociology of Education* 76:265–80.

Horvat, E. M., E. Weininger, and A. Lareau. 2003. From social ties to social capital: Class differences in the relations between schools and parent networks. *American Educational Research Journal* 40, no. 2: 319–51.

Irvine, J. J. 1990. *Black students and school failure: Policies, practices, and prescriptions.* Westport, CT: Greenwood.

Jencks, C., and M. Phillips. 1998. *The Black-White test score gap.* Washington, DC: Brookings Institution Press.

Jewett, S. 2006. "If you don't identify with your ancestry, you're like a race without a land": Constructing race at a small urban middle school. *Anthropology and Education Quarterly* 37, no. 2: 144–61.

Johnson, T., J. E. Boyden, and W. J. Pittz. 2001. *Racial profiling and punishment in US public schools.* Oakland, CA: Applied Research Center.

Kenny, L. 2000. *Daughters of suburbia: Growing up White, middle class, and female.* New Brunswick: Rutgers University Press.

King, D. 1988. Multiple jeopardy, multiple consciousness: The context of Black feminist ideology. *Signs: Journal of Women in Culture and Society* 14, no. 1: 42–72.

Kochman, T. 1981. *Black and White styles in conflict.* Chicago: University of Chicago Press.

Kozol, J. 1991. *Savage inequalities.* New York: HarperCollins.

Labov, W. 1982. Objectivity and commitment in linguistic science: The case of the Black English trial in Ann Arbor. *Language and Society* 11:165–201.

Ladson-Billings, G., and W. F. Tate IV. 1995. Toward a critical race theory of education. *Teachers College Record* 97, no. 1: 47–68.

Lareau, A. 2000. *Home advantage: Social class and parental intervention in elementary education.* Lanham, MD: Rowman and Littlefield.

Lareau, A. 2003. *Unequal childhoods: Class, race, and family life.* Berkeley: University of California Press.

Lareau, A., and E. M. Horvat. 1999. Moments of social inclusion and exclusion: Race, class, and cultural capital in family-school relationships. *Sociology of Education* 72:37–53.

Lee, C. 2007. *Cultural literacy and learning: Taking bloom in the midst of the whirlwind.* New York: Teachers College Press.

Lee, J. 2002. Racial and ethnic achievement gap trends: Reversing the progress toward equity? *Educational Researcher* 31, no. 1: 3–12.

Lennox, M. 1993. Refugees, racism, and reparations: A critique of the United States' Haitian immigration policy. *Stanford Law Review* 45, no. 3: 687–724.

Lewis, A. E. 2003a. Everyday race-making: Navigating racial boundaries in schools. *American Behavioral Scientist* 47, no. 3: 283–305.

Lewis, A. E. 2003b. *Race in the schoolyard: Reproducing the color line in school.* New Brunswick: Rutgers University Press.

MacLeod, J. 1995. *Ain't no makin' it: Aspirations and attainment in a low-income neighborhood.* Boulder: Westview.

Massey, D. S., and M. L. Eggers. 1990. The ecology of inequality: Minorities and the concentration of poverty, 1970–1980. *American Journal of Sociology* 95:1153–88.

McCarthy, C., and W. Crichlow. 1993. Introduction: Theories of identity, theories of representation, theories of race. In C. McCarthy and W. Crichlow, eds., *Race, identity, and representation in education,* xiii–xxix. New York: Routledge.

Michaels, W. B. 1992. Race into culture: A critical genealogy of cultural identity. *Critical Inquiry* 18:655–85.

Mickelson, R. 2001. Subverting Swann: First- and second-generation segregation in the Charlotte-Mecklenburg schools. *American Educational Research Journal* 38, no. 2: 215–52.

Mickelson, R. 2003. When are racial disparities in education the result of racial discrimination? A social science perspective. *Teachers College Record* 105, no. 6: 1052–86.

Mickelson, R., and A. Velasco. 2006. Bring it on! Diverse responses to "acting White" among academically able Black adolescents. In E. McNamara and C. O'Connor, eds., *Beyond acting White: Reframing the debate on Black student achievement,* 27–56. Lanham, MD: Rowman and Littlefield.

Morris, E. 2006. *An unexpected minority: White kids in an urban school.* New Brunswick: Rutgers University Press.

Moynihan, D. P. 1965. *The Negro family: The case for national action.* Washington, DC: U.S. Department of Labor.

Nettles, M. T., and L. W. Perna. 1997. *The Black education data book.* Fairfax, VA: Frederick D. Patterson Research Institute of the College Fund.

O'Connor, C. 1997. Dispositions toward (collective) struggle and educational resilience in the inner city: A case of six African American high school students. *American Educational Research Journal* 34, no. 4: 593–629.

O'Connor, C. 2001. *Being Black and achieving in school: Exploring the promise of social context, Black heterogeneity, and the multidimensionality of racial identity.* Paper presented at the annual meeting of the American Sociological Association, August, Chicago.

O'Connor, C. 2002. Black women beating the odds from one generation to the next: How the changing dynamics of constraint and opportunity affect the process of educational resilience. *American Educational Research Journal* 39, no. 4: 855–903.

Office of Management and Budget. 1997. *Provisional guidance on the implementation of the 1997 standards for federal data on race and ethnicity.* Washington, DC: Office of Management and Budget.

Ogbu, J. 1999. Beyond language: Ebonics, proper English, and identity in a Black-American speech community. *American Educational Research Journal* 36, no. 2: 147–84.

Oliver, M. L., and T. M. Shapiro. 1995. *Black wealth/White wealth: A new perspective on racial inequality.* New York: Routledge.

Orfield, G., S. Eaton, and The Harvard Project on School Desegregation. 1996. *Dismantling desegregation: The quiet reversal of Brown v. Board of Education.* New York: New Press.

Patillo-McCoy, M. 1999. *Black picket fences: Privilege and peril among the Black middle class.* Chicago: University of Chicago Press.

Pedraza, S., and R. G. Rumbaut. 1996. *Origins and destinies: Immigration, race, and ethnicity in America.* Belmont, CA: Wadsworth.

Peterson-Lewis, S., and L. M. Bratton. 2004. Perceptions of "acting Black" among African American teens: Implications of racial dramaturgy for academic and social achievement. *Urban Review* 36, no. 2: 81–100.

Pollock, M. 2001. How the question we ask most about race in education is the very question we most suppress. *Educational Researcher* 30, no. 9: 2–11.

Pollock, M. 2004. Race wrestling: Struggling strategically with race in educational practice and research. *American Journal of Education* 111, no. 1: 25–43.

Portes, A., and D. MacLeod. 1996. Educational progress of children and immigrants: The roles of class, ethnicity, and school context. *Sociology of Education* 69, no. 4: 255–75.

Portes, A., and R. Rumbaut. 2001. *Legacies: The story of the immigrant second generation.* Berkeley: University of California Press.

Reissman, F. 1962. *The culturally deprived child.* New York: Harper and Row.

Rodriguez, C. E. 2000. *Changing race: Latinos, the census, and the history of ethnicity in the United States.* New York: New York University Press.

Rong, X., and F. Brown. 2002. Socialization, culture, and identities of Black immigrant children: What educators need to know and do. *Education and Urban Society* 34, no. 2: 247–73.

Roscigno, V. J. 1998. Race and the reproduction of educational disadvantage. *Social Forces* 76, no. 3: 1033–61.

Roscigno V. J. 2000. Family/school inequality and African-American/Hispanic achievement. *Social Problems* 47, no. 2: 266–90.

Roscigno, V. J., D. Tomaskovic-Devey, and M. L. Crowley. 2006. Education and the inequalities of place. *Social Forces* 84, no. 4: 2121–45.

Rothstein, R. 2004. Wising up on the Black-White achievement gap. *Education Digest* 70, no. 4: 27–36.

Rousseau, C., and W. Tate. 2003. No time like the present: Reflecting on equity in school mathematics. *Theory into Practice* 42, no. 3: 210–16.

Sellers, R. M., M. A. Smith, J. N. Shelton, S. A. J. Rowley, and T. M. Chavous. 1998. Multidimensional model of racial identity: A reconceptualization of Black racial identity. *Personality and Social Psychology Review* 2, no. 1: 18–39.

Sirin, S. R., and L. Rogers-Sirin. 2004. Exploring school engagement of middle-class African American adolescents. *Youth and Society* 35, no. 3: 323–40.

Solorzano, D. G., and T. Yosso. 2002. Critical race methodology: Counterstorytelling as an analytical framework for education research. *Qualitative Inquiry* 8, no. 1: 23–44.

Spencer, M. B., D. Dupree, and T. Hartmann. 1997. A phenomenological variant of ecological systems theory (PVEST): A self-organization perspective in context. *Development and Psychopathology* 9:817–33.

Spencer, M. B., D. P. Swanson, and M. Cunningham. 1991. Ethnicity, ethnic identity, and competence formation: Adolescent transition and cultural transformation. *Journal of Negro Education* 60, no. 3: 366–87.

Swidler, A. 1986. Culture in action: Symbols and strategies. *American Sociological Review* 51, no. 2: 273–86.

Takaki, R. 1993. *A different mirror: A history of multicultural America.* Boston: Little, Brown.

Tate, W. 1997. Critical race theory and education: History, theory, and implications. *Review of Research in Education* 22:195–247.

Tyson, K. 2002. Weighing in: Elementary-age students and the debate on attitudes toward school among Black students. *Social Forces* 80, no. 4: 1157–89.

Tyson, K., W. Darity, and D. Castellino. 2005. "It's not 'a Black thing'": Understanding the burden of acting White and other dilemmas of high achievement. *American Sociological Review* 70, no. 4: 582–605.

Valentine, C. 1968. *Culture and poverty: Critique and counter-proposals.* Chicago: University of Chicago Press.

Vickerman, M. 1999. *Crosscurrents: West Indian immigrants and race.* New York: Oxford University Press.

Wang, M., and E. Gordon, eds. 1994. *Educational resilience in inner-city America: Challenges and prospects.* Hillsdale, NJ: Lawrence Erlbaum.

Waters, M. C. 1994. Ethnic and racial identities of second-generation Black immigrants in New York City. *International Migration Review* 28, no. 4: 795–820.

Waters, M. C. 1999. *Black identities: West Indian immigrant dreams and American realities.* Cambridge: Harvard University Press.

Wilson, W. J. 1978. *The declining significance of race: Blacks and changing American institutions.* Chicago: University of Chicago Press.

Yosso, T. 2005. Whose culture has capital? A critical race theory discussion of community cultural wealth. *Race, Ethnicity, and Education* 8, no. 1: 69–91.

Young, A. A. 1999. The (non)accumulation of capital: Explicating the relationship of structure and agency in the lives of poor Black men. *Sociological Theory* 17:201–27.

Zuberi, T. 2001. *Thicker than blood: How racial statistics lie.* Minneapolis: University of Minnesota Press.

3 | Crowded Out? The Racial Composition of American Occupations

Darrick Hamilton and William A. Darity Jr.

Over 35 years ago, Barbara Bergmann (1971) hypothesized that labor market discrimination against black males is manifest in a "crowding" effect, which results in lower earnings. White employers' refusal to hire blacks in certain occupations forces them to cluster and creates crowding in less desirable jobs, reinforcing a condition of lower earnings. Bergmann provided empirical evidence of this crowding phenomenon by reporting the disproportionate presence of black male workers in several low-skilled occupations relative to what would be expected based on educational attainment and population share. In this chapter we provide an update and extension of black male occupational crowding using a more extensive list of occupations that is not limited to low-skilled work based on the 2000 decennial census. Data are examined to determine whether the crowding phenomenon is still evident in the post–Civil Rights labor market. In addition, a correlation analysis is performed to test for a relationship between occupational crowding and earnings.

Since 1959, when the empirical data for Bergmann's study was collected, there has been evidence of persistent economic disparity between white and black men. For example, 11% of white males graduated from college in 1959 compared to 4% of black males; rates in 1970 were 15% versus 5% respectively; in 1980, 22% compared to 8%; in 1990, 25% compared to 12%; and in 2000, 31% of white males graduated college compared to 16% of black males. The ratio of college-educated black males to comparably educated whites rose only moderately between 1959 and 2000, from 0.37 in to 0.52.

White male median income was $21,294 in 1960, rising to $29,696 in 2000; for blacks, median income was $11,202 in 1960, rising to $21,659 in 2000. The ratio of black to white median income rose from 0.53 in 1960 to 0.73 in 2000.[1] Disparities in unemployment rates reveal a similar pattern. For whites, males and females, the unemployment rate in 1970 was 4.5%, 6.3% in 1980, 4.8% in 1990 and 3.5% in 2000, and for blacks the rate was 9.4% in 1973, 14.3% in 1980, 11.4% in 1990 and 7.6% in 2000 (U.S. Statistical Abstract 2001, Table 569).

Undoubtedly, some of the ebbs and flows in earnings and employment for both blacks and whites have been related to economic business cycles. Nonetheless, there is sustained evidence of racial disparity in educational attainment, income, and employment.

What Does Economic Theory Tell Us about Persistent Racial Disparities

Standard economic theory has not been very successful in explaining persistent inequality between blacks and whites. There are two broad possibilities for the existence of these persistent disparities. First, there may be something inherent that inhibits the ability of blacks to achieve economic rewards. This inherent inaptitude may take the form of a biological or a cultural deficiency. Although we do not address it here, there is a substantial literature that debates explanations based on inherent versus structural disparities (see Darity and Mason 1998, Darity and Myers 1998, and Hamilton 2001 for summaries of the economic literature).

The second explanation for this persistent disparity is related to the social structures that privilege whites over blacks in one of two ways: social structures may favor one group's ability to accumulate characteristics that lead to desired economic outcomes, or social structures may provide greater economic returns to the accumulated characteristics of one group. Both mechanisms can be termed discrimination—"pre-market discrimination" for disparities in process of acquisition of productivity-linked characteristics and "in-market discrimination" for disparities in returns to characteristics.

Standard economic theory generally does a poor job of explaining persistent disparity due to in-market discrimination. The two most commonly cited approaches are those based on "taste for discrimination" (Becker 1957) and "statistical discrimination" (Aigner and Cain 1977; Arrow 1972; Coate and Loury 1993; Phelps 1972). The "taste" model asserts that bigoted firms are willing to pay a higher labor cost and forgo profits to appease their own preferences for whites by refusing to hire qualified blacks at a cheaper cost. Conventional economics suggests that, over time, the less efficient firms run by bigoted bosses would be casualties to more efficient firms run by less bigoted bosses who prefer profits over prejudice. The process would continue until all of the less efficient firms are driven out of business, and blacks and whites with comparable skills would end up being paid similar wages.

The "statistical discrimination" model asserts that employers use their *perceptions* of the distributional characteristics of blacks as a group to make employment decisions about individuals who are black. The model suggests that, when making a hiring decision, an employer may believe that he or she does not have enough information to adequately predict the potential employee's productivity, so the employer uses his or her perceptions concerning the potential employee's group attributes in the calculus of their employment decision.

However, Darity and Mason (1998, 83) have observed, "If average group differences are perceived but not real, then employers should learn that their beliefs are mistaken. If average group differences are real, then in a world with antidiscrimination laws, employers are likely to find methods of predicting the future performance of potential employees with sufficient accuracy that there is no need to use the additional signal of race or gender. It seems implausible that with all the resources that corporations put into hiring decisions, the remaining differentials are due to an inability to come up with a suitable set of questions or qualifications for potential employees." Provided that groups have similar productivity, persistent group inequality resulting from labor market discrimination is inconsistent with either "taste" or "statistical" theories of discrimination.

There are at least two other theories of in-market discrimination that are less cited than the "taste" and "statistical" theories of discrimination: William Darity's (2001) "functionality of discrimination" hypothesis and Barbara Bergmann's (1971) "occupational crowding" hypothesis. The "functionality" theory argues that discrimination serves a "practical" role in maintaining social hierarchy in favor of the dominant group. The theory expands upon the late Nobel laureate Arthur Lewis's (1985) notion that a dominant group is able to maintain the existing social hierarchy by controlling and structuring access to skills and labor market characteristics in a manner that privileges their own group. As a result, members of the subaltern group will be rendered "non-competitive" in labor market settings.

Darity's functionality hypothesis proposes an additional mechanism of social maintenance for the dominant group. Subaltern group members, who, for whatever reason, are able to overcome barriers and attain competitive labor market skills will face in-market discrimination that will be related in intensity to their acquired skills during the premarket stage. Thus, the more competitive members of a subaltern group become, the more intense the degree of in-market discrimination they will face.[2]

Bergmann's (1971) crowding hypothesis suggests that black workers are denied employment in more desirable occupations and crowded into those that are less desirable. The result is an oversupply of workers in the crowded occupations, which has the effect of further lowering wages in those occupations. She goes on to say that black workers who are able to attain employment in white-dominant sectors receive relatively lower earnings because the opportunity cost of their labor involves the threat of employment in the crowded labor sector that is predominantly reserved for blacks.

> [A] Negro's only alternative to a substandard offer in a "white" occupation is employment in a "Negro" occupation which may be overcrowded, which may not make use of his training or talent, and in which he will earn considerably less. Employers know this, so the wage a Negro may be offered by the rare employer who is willing to hire him in a "white" occupation will probably be lower than that earned by a white man in the same occupation. (1971, 298–99)

Bergmann explains that there may be various reasons why an employer would refuse to hire a black worker. The reasons include distaste for associating with blacks, a belief that blacks are less productive, or a fear of a negative reaction from their customers or current employees if a black worker is hired. In particular, she claims that white employees fear a desegregated labor force would reduce their wages by forcing them to compete with black workers in more desirable occupations. So in turn, although not the complete story, white employers maintain the present arrangements to avoid a loss of morale.

However, similar criticisms levied against the "taste" and "statistical" models of discrimination's inability to explain persistent racial inequality are applicable to Bergmann (1971). The crowding hypothesis does not address the incentive for firms to emerge that are willing to hire equally qualified blacks at a lower-than-white labor cost to earn above-normal profits. Employer fear of retribution from disgruntled white employees could be avoided by hiring all black employees. In other words, there could be a short-run scenario of two sets of firms in certain occupations; one with predominately white workers and the other with predominantly black workers resulting in lower labor costs. Despite this criticism, Bergmann does provide an interesting and inadequately examined framework to understand and measure racially segregated labor forces.

Measuring Occupational Crowding

In order to calculate the under/overrepresentation of nonwhite male workers in a low-skilled occupation, Barbara Bergmann used data from the 1960 U.S. Census of Population. Her measure was calculated by subtracting the number of expected nonwhite employees in an occupation from the number of actual nonwhite employees. In 1960 the nonwhite category was predominantly black employees. Since white male educational attainment far exceeded that of their black counterparts in 1960, Bergmann examined 29 occupations where the majority of workers had less than a high school diploma to control for educational requirements. The expected number of nonwhite employees was computed based on the share of nonwhites without a high school diploma.

In 1960, even among the occupations requiring less than a high school diploma, Bergmann found that there was variation with respect to job desirability. If an occupation was composed of more than 10% (the expected number) of blacks, it was considered one where black men were overrepresented; alternatively, if black men constituted less than 10% of the men employed, the occupation was one where black men were underrepresented.

Out of the 29 occupations, Bergmann found that 8 had more nonwhites than expected, while 18 had fewer than expected. The 18 "deficit" occupations were mainly protective services, farm and precision production, and craft and repair type occupations, while the "surplus" occupations consisted mainly of shipping and receiving clerks, nonprotective service workers including private household workers, operators, farm laborers, and other laborers. The "deficit" occupations offered more lucrative pay than the "surplus" occupations.

Gibson, Darity, and Myers (1998) use a revised measure of black concentration within occupations to calculate occupational crowding for Allegheny County (Pittsburgh), PA, and Wayne County (Detroit), MI. Using the 1990 5% U.S. Census Public Use Micro Data Sample (PUMS), they identified an expected occupational share for blacks given the proportionate share of their population meeting the educational require-ments for that occupation. The educational requirements were based on more stringent criteria than Bergmann's. Only black individuals with ed-ucational attainment between the 25th and 90th percentiles of the edu-cational attainment held by all persons in a particular occupation were treated as eligible for the job.

In addition, they computed crowding indices for both male and fe-males, except for those occupations that they deemed "gender typed."[3] If an occupation consisted of at least 90% persons of one sex, it was con-sidered "gender typed." Subsequently, in those cases, only individuals who were members of the occupation's dominant sex group were used to compute the crowding index for that occupation.

Although Bergmann (1971) analyzed only "blue collar" jobs, Gibson, Darity and Myers (1998) analyzed 59 occupations, including both "white" and "blue collar" occupations. Similar to Bergmann, Gibson et al. found that black males are still largely excluded from higher-paying precision production and craft and repair occupations while being crowded into the lower-paying laborer and service occupations. Al-though Bergmann found proportionate representation for black males in operative occupations, Gibson, Darity, and Myers found them over-crowded in those occupations in the two urban areas they examined. For black females, Gibson, Darity, and Myers found them overcrowded in "pink collar" occupations. Finally, in terms of the managerial and pro-fessional occupations, Gibson et al. found black exclusion from higher-paying occupations, except for those in the public sector in Detroit.

The current study adopts the revised crowding measure designed by Gibson, Darity, and Myers and updates their results by using the 2000 5% PUMS to compute occupational crowding indices for black males for 475 occupations defined by the Census. The use of the 5% sample allows for enough observations to compute crowding measures for a large number of occupations at a very detailed level. This current analysis ex-amines only males, largely to avoid any confounding that may be due to differential labor-market treatment based on gender and differential la-bor-supply decisions associated with gender. Unlike Gibson, Darity, and Myers (1998), we analyze crowding across all occupations and the entire United States. The disadvantage is the loss of implicit regional controls, but the advantage is the addition of enough observations to compute crowding scores across a far greater range of occupations.

In addition, having 475 observations on crowding allows us to test a proposition put forth in Bergmann's (1971) original paper. We can examine whether black males are systematically crowded into occupations that have lower pay by regressing their computed occupational crowding scores against the average earnings of those occupations. If we find, after controlling for occupational educational requirements, that black male occupational crowding scores are statistically correlated with the average earnings of their occupations, we view that as statistically significant empirical support for Bergmann's claims.

Results

We have provided on the Web a table that presents all 475 occupations defined by their three-digit census coding along with the number of black respondents in the occupations, the 25th and 90th percentile educational requirement cutoffs for inclusion in the occupational crowding measure, the computed occupational crowding indices, and, finally, the occupation's average earnings for 2000. Recall that our crowding index computes the ratio of the share of blacks within an occupation relative to their share in the total population that meets the educational requirements for that particular occupation. We follow Bergmann (1971) and Gibson, Darity, and Myers (1998) and define occupations with less than 10% of the expected number of black employees as underrepresented (crowded out), and those with 10% less than expected as overrepresented (crowded).

Table 3.1 provides a summary of the crowding results. The first panel of the table displays the results for all occupations, while subsequent panels present results for occupations disaggregated by occupational groupings based on census classifications. The tables display the number of occupations in which black males are underrepresented (crowded out), proportionally represented (not crowded), and overrepresented (crowded), along with the shares and mean occupational earnings for those categories. The last column of the table presents bivariate linear regression coefficients of occupational wages measured in $10,000 increments regressed on occupational crowding in order to statistically test for a relationship between occupational wages and occupational crowding. In addition, figures 3.1 to 3.8 visually summarize these relationships and their regression results.

Beginning with the first panel of all 475 occupations in 2000, table 3.1 indicates that occupations in the United States tend to be racially segregated. Only 14% of the 475 occupations in 2000 demonstrate no crowd-

TABLE 3.1. The Relationship between 2000 Occupational Crowding and Wages

Occupations	Total	Crowded Out[a]	Not Crowded	Crowded	Regression Coefficient[b]
All Occupations					
Number of occupations	475	216	67	192	−0.10*
Share within occupation		0.45	0.14	0.40	(0.01)
Mean occupational wages	36,370	41,414	36,471	30,661	
Managment, Professional, and Related Occupations					
Number of occupations	167	92	23	52	−0.10*
Share within occupation		0.55	0.14	0.31	(0.02)
Mean occupational wages	49,574	53,809	51,014	41,145	
Service Occupations					
Number of occupations	59	14	8	37	−0.11
Share within occupation		0.24	0.14	0.63	(0.08)
Mean occupational wages	24,361	26,601	29,578	22,386	
Sales and Office Occupations					
Number of occupations	68	20	3	45	−0.22*
Share within occupation		0.29	0.04	0.66	(0.04)
Mean occupational wages	34,110	45,392	26,620	29,595	
Farming, Fishing, and Forestry Occupations					
Number of occupations	7	5	2	0	0.01
Share within occupation		0.71	0.29	0.00	(0.16)
Mean occupational wages	20,749	22,020	17,570	NA	
Construction, Extraction, and Maintenance Occupations					
Number of occupations	67	45	12	10	−0.06
Share within occupation		0.67	0.18	0.15	(0.05)
Mean occupational wages	28,770	29,910	27,552	25,100	
Production, Transportation, and Material Moving Occupations					
Number of occupations	103	40	19	44	−0.17*
Share within occupation		0.39	0.18	0.43	(0.04)
Mean occupational wages	29,344	31,446	30,947	26,722	
Military-Specific Occupations					
Number of occupations	4	0	0	4	−0.03
Share within occupation		0.00	0.00	1.00	(0.03)
Mean occupational wages	36,144	NA	NA	36,144	

Note: NA = not applicable. [a]The respective column headings "Crowded Out," "Not Crowded," and "Crowded" indicate occupations where the proportions of blacks is either 10 percent less than, proportional to, or 10 percent greater than the expected number of blacks that would be employed based on the number of blacks that meet the educational requirements for that occupation.

[b]Bivariate regression coefficients of the average occupational wages measured in $10,000 increments regressed on occupational crowding measures, the ratio of black employees in an occupation relative to the expected proportion black with the prerequisite educational requirements of the occupation. Regression coefficient standard errors are presented in parentheses.

*Indicates 90 percent level of statistical significance   **Indicates 95 percent level of statistical significance   ***Indicates 99 percent level of significance

Fig. 3.1. The relationship between occupational crowding and wages

Fig. 3.2. The relationship between occupational crowding and wages:
Management, professional and related occupations

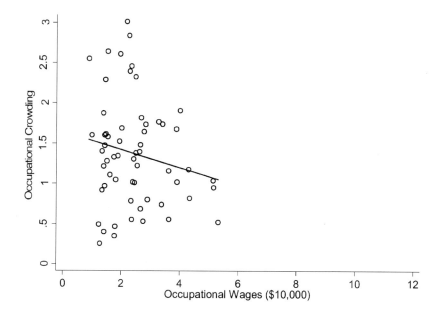

Fig. 3.3. The relationship between occupational crowding and wages:
Service occupations

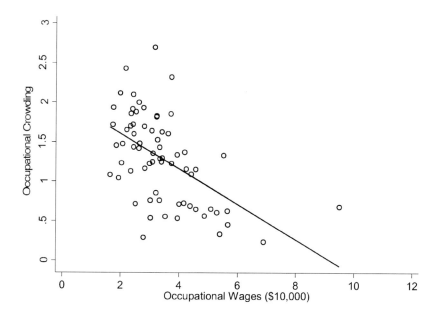

Fig. 3.4. The relationship between occupational crowding and wages:
Sales and office occupations

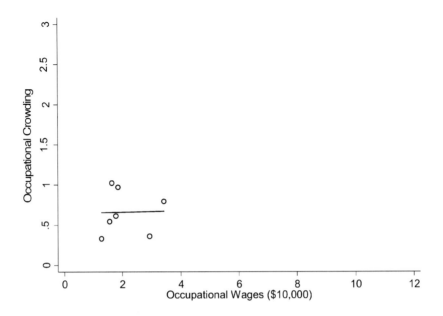

Fig. 3.5. The relationship between occupational crowding and wages: Farming, fishing, and forestry occupations

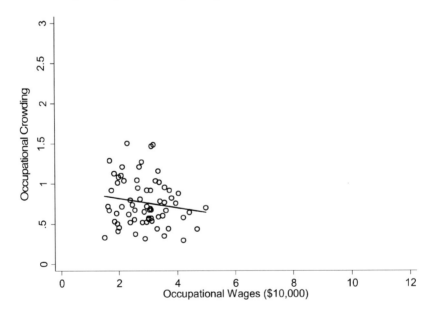

Fig. 3.6. The relationship between occupational crowding and wages: Construction, extraction, and maintenance occupations

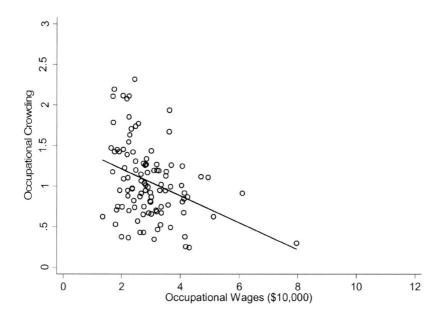

Fig. 3.7. The relationship between occupational crowding and wages: Production, transportation, and material moving occupations

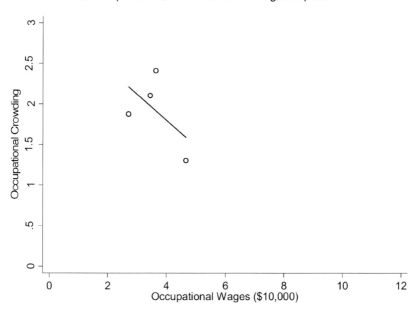

Fig. 3.8. The relationship between occupational crowding and wages: Military-specific occupations

ing; hence 86% of occupations are characterized by either over- or underrepresentation of blacks. Moreover, the 192 occupations in which blacks are crowded offer average occupational wages ($30,661) that are 74% of the wages in the 216 occupations ($41,414) in which they are crowded-out. These descriptive results are consistent with the negative trend between occupational wages and crowding displayed in figure 3.1 and the statistically significant regression coefficient of –0.10 in the last column of the first panel of table 3.1. The regression coefficient estimates that for every $10,000 increase in occupational wages, there is an associated 0.10 point decrease in occupational crowding. This suggest that occupations where blacks are crowded-out offer wages that are at least $10,000 higher than those occupations where they have proportional representation. Alternatively, occupations where blacks are crowded offer wages that are at least $10,000 less than occupations with a proportionate representation of black males.[4]

Thus the first panel of the table provides evidence that, even after accounting for educational attainment, black males are, indeed, crowded into lower-earning occupations. The pattern of crowding observed by Bergmann in 1960 and Gibson, Darity, and Myers in Wayne and Allegheny Counties in 1990 is also present across a national sample in 2000.

Next, we turn to the occupational crowding results disaggregated by major occupational groupings. Managerial and professional related occupations offered the highest wages ($49,574) in 2000. There are 167 managerial and professional related occupations, of which 92 (55%) are characterized by underrepresentation and 52 (31%) are characterized by overrepresentation of black males. Moreover, within managerial and professional jobs, blacks are crowded into occupations that have about 76% lower wages than the occupations from which they are crowded-out ($41,145 vs. $53,809). Gibson, Darity, and Myers (1998) also found blacks to be underrepresented in this occupational category.

The regression coefficient within this cluster of occupations indicates an inverse and highly significant (p value = 0.02) relationship between occupational crowding and earnings. The regression coefficient indicates that a $10,000 increase in the wage of a managerial and professional-related occupation is associated with a 10% reduction in the proportion of black workers in that occupation. This relationship also is exhibited by the downward trend in the regression line in figure 3.2.

The next panel in table 3.1 and figure 3.3 display results for service occupations. Service occupations have average wages that are considerably lower than other occupational categories. The average service sector wage is $24,361, which is only slightly higher than the $20,749 average for farming, fishing, and forestry occupations. Only 14 of the 59 occupations in this category feature black male underrepresentation, while 37 (63%) are overcrowded with black workers.

The clustering of black males in service occupations with their associated low wages is consistent with the Bergmann hypothesis. The regression coefficient and downward trend in figure 3.3 for service occupations indicates an inverse relationship between crowding and occupational wages; however, the relationship is not statistically significant.[5] Nonetheless, the highly crowded and low-wage-yielding service sector is, undoubtedly, a major contributor to the statistically significant finding in support of the crowding theory across all occupations.

For the sales and office category, there is a strong pattern of racially segregated occupations. Only 3 out of 68 (4%) of these occupations have a proportional representation of black workers. There are 45 sales and office occupations that are crowded with black workers, and these jobs offer wages that are 65% lower than the 20 sales and office occupations where black males are crowded-out. This pattern of occupational crowding is further supported by the steep downward trend in figure 3.4, and the large and statistically significant regression coefficient, which indicates that a $10,000 increase in the occupational wage of sales and office jobs is associated with a strikingly large 22% reduction in the proportion of black workers in those jobs.

There are only seven farming, forestry, and fishing occupations; none are overrepresented with black workers. There are five occupations in which black males are largely crowded-out; nonetheless, these occupations offer relatively low wages and hence do not exhibit an inverse relationship between occupational crowding and wages. The flat linear trend in figure 3.5 and the small regression coefficient in table 3.1 indicate that there is no relationship between occupational wages and crowding in this category. It is likely that the spatial mismatch resulting from the concentration of blacks in metropolitan areas and the concentration of farming, forestry, and fishing occupations in rural areas is the explanation for this contradiction of the Bergmann hypothesis.

Next, the categories of construction, extraction, and maintenance, and production, transportation, and material-moving occupations are discussed together. These occupations typically have lower educational requirements and occupational wages than management, professional and related occupations, and sales and office occupations. Given that black males tend to have lower educational attainment than white males, a relatively large number of black males are competing for jobs in these two occupational categories. About 67% of construction, extraction, and maintenance occupations are characterized by black male crowding-out, whereas about 39% of the production, transportation, and material-moving occupations are crowded-out. However, within both of these occupational sectors, these crowded-out occupations have relatively higher wages than other occupations in their respective groupings.

With regard to the regression results, the estimated coefficient for construction, extraction, and maintenance occupations is relatively small and statistically insignificant, while the coefficient for production, transportation, and material-moving occupations is statistically significant. Indeed, a $10,000 increase in occupational wages is associated with a 17% reduction in the crowding of black workers. The stronger relationship between occupational wages and crowding in production, transportation, and material-moving relative to construction is further exhibited by the relative steeper trend line in figure 3.7 compared to figure 3.6.[6]

The final category in table 3.1, military-specific occupations, is made up of only four types of jobs. Figure 3.8 illustrates a steep downward sloping regression trend line. However, contrary to Bergmann's theory that blacks are crowded into low-wage occupations, military occupations offer relatively high wages yet feature concentrations of black men that range from 30 to 140% higher than their expected proportions.[7]

Although not included here, this analysis was performed for females as well. The pattern of black male crowding was not evident for black females when compared solely with white females. However, when compared to white males and females combined, black female crowding was negatively associated with occupational earnings. In addition, female crowding in general is negatively associated with occupational earnings.

According to Mary King's (1993) "access" model, jobs are distributed based on a queuing system that puts white men at the top followed by black men and white women with black women on the bottom. If the "access" model is correct, the relevant comparison is not black women to white women, but rather all groups in comparison to white men. Furthermore, if black females suffer from both racial and gender discrimination, even a comparison among all females will not allow us to separate out the gender and racial components of discrimination.[8]

Lessons Learned

1. The crowding theory initiated by Bergmann provides a useful framework to analyze disparities in labor market outcomes.
2. However, the framework is limited in that it does not address "pre-market" disparities. For example, appendix table 3.2 indicates that blacks are close to proportionately represented among physicians and surgeons. However, the Association of American Medical Colleges states that blacks, based on their population share, are highly underrepresented in these professions. These seemingly contradictory claims are reconciled by the fact that crowding measures only take into account educationally qualified black males.
3. Blacks may be systematically denied access to skill acquirement so as to render them "non-competing" in the labor market settings in the similar manner that blacks with the prerequisite educational attainment may be denied access (crowded-out) of the higher-paying, more-desirable jobs.
4. A challenge to scholars is to develop new or additional theories that account for "pre-market" and "in-market" transactions simultaneously in order to better explain why both education and employment outcomes are so unevenly racially distributed.

Conclusions

This essay finds considerable evidence in support of the theory and findings of Bergmann (1971) and Gibson, Darity, and Myers (1998) that blacks are systematically crowded into lower-earning occupations. This essay improves upon the scope of the other two studies, since it is not limited by occupation or geographical area. The results indicate a general pattern of exclusion in the most desired management, professional, and related sector, even for blacks who have the prerequisite educational attainment for these jobs. This relationship also is evident in sales and office occupations, which, like management, professional, and related occupations, require high levels of education and yield high wages.

In contrast to management, professional, and related occupations, service occupations offer some of the lowest wages; most of these low-wage service occupations contain a disproportionately high concentration of blacks. Construction, extraction, and maintenance, and production, transportation, and material-moving are two other occupation sectors that require less education and offer low wages. Given that most of the construction, extraction, and maintenance occupations had low concentrations of blacks (67%), it appears as though low-skilled blacks have relatively greater access to the production, transportation, and material-moving sector.

Finally, there are two examples of occupational categories that, on the surface, seem counter to the crowding theory. Farm, forestry, and fishing are low-pay occupations that are not well represented by blacks, and military occupations pay reasonably well and are overrepresented by blacks. Exclusion from the farm, forestry, and fishing sector appears to be the result of spatial mismatch, and, at least in modern history, the military seems to have fewer restrictions for blacks than other occupations with similar pay, which may be a compelling factor for crowding in that sector.

The next steps in the research on crowding and the racial composition of American occupations are to develop theories of persistent inequality that account for "pre-market" and "in-market" transactions simultaneously and to examine these theories empirically with enough observations to compute crowding scores for a range of occupations and across race and gender groups.

NOTES

This chapter is largely based on Darrick Hamilton's article "The Racial Composition of American Jobs" in the National Urban League's edited volume *2006 State of Black America.*

1. Both the education and income statistics are obtained from the U.S. Census Bureau (http://www.census.gov/). The median income statistics are measured in year 2000 constant dollars.

2. See Darity (2001) and Hamilton and Darity (2001) for some empirical evidence in support of this hypothesis and Sharpe (2001) for mixed empirical evidence.

3. They also include an appendix with crowding indices for males and females computed separately.

4. We caution the reader that these bivariate regression coefficients do not necessarily indicate a causal relationship.

5. Perhaps the lack of observations and variations of occupational wages in service jobs is the culprit for not detecting statistical significance.

6. Similar to service occupations, perhaps the lack of observations and varia-

tions of occupational wages explains the inability to detect statistical significance in construction, extraction, and maintenance jobs.

7. Moskos and Butler (1996) contend that in the post–World War II period the army has been fairer in hiring and advancement opportunities than other sectors of the economy.

8. However, Holzer (1996) finds a different ordering based on employer-reported preferences for workers; where the sequence of preferred race is white males, white females, black females, and finally black males.

REFERENCES

Aigner, D., and G. Cain. 1977. Statistical theories of discrimination in labor markets. *Industrial and Labor Relations Review* 30:175–87.

Arrow, K. J. 1972. Models of job discrimination. In A. H. Pascal, ed., *Racial discrimination in economic life,* 83–102. Lexington, MA: D. C. Heath.

Becker, G. S. 1957. *The economics of discrimination.* Chicago: University of Chicago Press.

Bergmann, B. R. 1971. The effect on white incomes of discrimination in employment. *Journal of Political Economy* 29, no. 2: 294–313.

Coate, S., and G. C. Loury. 1993. Will affirmative-action policies eliminate negative stereotypes? *American Economic Review* 83, no. 5: 1220–40.

Darity, W., Jr. 2001. The functionality of market-based discrimination. *International Journal of Social Economics* 28, no. 10: 980–86.

Darity, W., Jr., and P. Mason. 1998. Evidence on discrimination in employment: codes of color, codes of gender. *Journal of Economic Perspectives* 12, no. 2: 1–29.

Darity, W., Jr., and S. Myers Jr. 1998. *Persistent disparity: Race and economic inequality in the United States since 1945.* Northampton, MA: Elgar.

Gibson, K., D. William Jr., and S. Myers Jr. 1998. Revisiting occupational crowding in the United States: A preliminary study. *Feminist Economist* 4, no. 3: 73–95.

Hamilton, D. 2000. Issues concerning discrimination and measurements of discrimination in U.S. labor markets. *African American Research Perspectives* 6, no. 3: 116–20.

Hamilton, D. 2006. The racial composition of American jobs. In G. Curry, ed., *The 2006 state of black America,* 4–5. New York: National Urban League.

Hamilton, D., and W. Darity Jr. 2001. A test of the functionality of discrimination: An analysis of the relationship between socioeconomic status and ethnic/racial earnings discrimination. Unpublished manuscript.

Holzer, H. 1996. *What employers want: Job prospects for less-educated workers.* New York: Russell Sage Foundation.

King, M. 1993. Black women's breakthrough into clerical work: An occupational tipping model. *Journal of Economic Issues* 27, no. 4: 1097–1127.

Lewis, W. A. 1985. *Racial conflict and economic development.* Cambridge: Harvard University Press.

Moskos, C., and J. Butler. 1996. *All that we can be: Black leadership and racial integration the Army Way.* New York: Basic Books.

Phelps, E. S. 1972. The statistical theory of racism and sexism. *American Economic Review* 62:659–61.

Sharpe, R. 2001. Does educational attainment reduce labor market discrimination? Paper presented at the Association for Public Policy Analysis and Management Annual Research Conference, Washington, DC, November.

4 | Aging, Physical Health, and Work and Family Role Changes among African American Women: Strategies for Conducting Life-Course Research with African American Women

Letha A. Chadiha and Jewell F. Brazelton

The status of African American women's physical health, work, and family life has improved over that of prior generations of African American women (Leigh and Lindquist 1998). But the quality of their physical health, work, and family life has yet to achieve parity with White women's (Grayson et al. 2001). A gender and life-course perspective recognizes linkages among gender, race, ethnicity, social class, and aging in the human experience, therefore providing an explanatory framework for the inequality in health, work, and family roles for African American women. Specifically, this perspective helps explain how the multiple realities that accompany aging differ in African American women's lives from those of women in other racial and ethnic groups, including the differential access to resources that shape the quality of African American women's physical health and work and family role statuses. This chapter focuses on the status and quality of African American women's physical health, work, marriage, and caregiving roles within an aging context. We begin with an overview of the gender and life-course perspective described in Hatch's (2001) work followed by a brief demographic profile of the Black population and African American women. We discuss evidence bearing on the physical health status of African American women, highlighting heart disease and breast cancer as examples of health concerns influenced by gender and life-course issues. Correspondingly, we discuss evidence bearing on the work, marriage, and caregiving roles of African American women as further support for considering the gender and life-course perspective in conducting research with aging African American women. We conclude with a summary of lessons learned and recommendations for life-course research with African American women.

Overview: The Life-Course Perspective

Prior literature supports using a life-course perspective to address aging and health topics (Jackson 1996). We adopt the gender and life-course perspective in Hatch's (2001) work that emphasizes the role that gender plays along with race, ethnicity, social class, and aging in shaping people's life opportunities. Focusing on gender as a key concept is important, as Hatch notes: "Gender is a fundamental stratifier of people's lives," one that "interlocks with other hierarchies of inequality, including race, ethnicity, social class, sexual orientation, and age, which together help to determine individuals' social locations" (24). Four assumptions of a life-course perspective from Hatch's work inform this discussion. First, prior life experiences influence the present and future life circumstances of individuals. Second, individual life histories do not occur in isolation from social histories. Rather, individual and social histories are shaped by and intertwined with external events occurring within the larger context of society, such as legislative and social changes. Third, individuals occupying similar social positions in society will share common experiences that often contrast with the experiences of individuals occupying different social positions. Gender, race, ethnicity, and social class are contributing factors to these different experiences. Fourth, individuals moving through the life course will enter and exit different and multiple social roles, a process called *role transitions* that may include getting married, becoming a parent, or becoming a caregiver of an aging relative. These four assumptions undergird our discussion on African American women's physical health and work and family roles. Recognizing that critics view a life-course perspective as being too vague and broad, Hatch (2000) notes that the strength of the gender and life-course perspective "lies in the explicit recognition of multiple, interlocking dimensions of human experiences," with gender, race, social class, and aging being at the center of these experiences (36).

Demographic Profile: U.S. Black and Female Population

The total Black population in Census 2000 was 36.4 million, approximately 13% of the total (281.4 million) U.S. population (McKinnon 2003). Women represent more than half (143.4 million) of the U.S. population; the majority are White women of non-Hispanic origin and the remainder are Black or African American women of non-Hispanic origin (13%), Hispanic or Latina women (12%), American Indian and Alaskan Native women (1%), and Native Hawaiian and other Pacific Islander (1%) (Office of Women's Health [OWH] 2000). As with minority women generally, the health concerns, marriage, work, and family roles of African American women over the life-course converge and diverge from those of White women (OWH 2000). The topics of convergence and divergence among women are the core elements in the discussions that follow, focusing on physical health and aging, as well as marriage, work, and family as we highlight the significance of considering research with African American women from the gender and life-course perspective.

Physical Health and Aging: The Case of Heart Disease and Breast Cancer

Heart Disease

The concept of heart disease refers to common heart ailments and coronary heart disease (OWH 2000). The incidence of coronary heart disease continues to rise in the U.S. population, with African American women at greater risk of dying from heart disease than other minority women or White women (Bolton and Wilson 2005; Jha et al. 2003; Ephraim et al. 2001; OWH 2000). An assessment of African American women's chronic physical health status over the life course directs researchers' attention to the high rate of mortality from heart disease—the number one leading cause of death among African American women in the United States (Jha et al. 2003; OWH 2000).

What might account for these racial and ethnic disparities in the rate of heart disease and mortality from it among African American women? Researchers have established common risk factors for women's heart disease including hypertension, diabetes, high blood cholesterol, being overweight, engaging in a low amount of physical activity, smoking cigarettes, drinking alcohol, and using illicit drugs (Bolton and Wilson 2005; OWH 2000). African American women are at high risk for heart disease and associated mortality, in part owing to a higher vulnerability to hypertension, diabetes, obesity, and low physical activity (Ephraim et al. 2001; Leigh and Lindquist 1998; OWH 2000). A disproportionate number of African American women are represented in low social and economic positions (OWH 2000), and as Hatch (2001) notes, "Those with greater socioeconomic resources tend to have better health, fewer disabilities, and lower risks for mortality" (24).

Studies also document race as an influential factor in the health and health care of African Americans (Bolton and Wilson 2005; Hummer 1996; Williams, Lavizzo-Mourey, and Warren 1994). African Americans are less likely to receive critical medical services and procedures, even when services are being delivered to patients covered by government insurance, and critical demographic variables (e.g., age, sex, Medicaid status, income, education, residence) are controlled (Ayanian et al. 1993; Schneider, Zaslavsky, and Epstein 2002). In addition, researchers contend that hypertension, a key risk factor for African American women's high rate of heart disease and associated mortality, is more severe among African Americans because of greater and more persistent exposure to chronic life stressors like racism than Whites (Krieger 1990; Leigh and Lindquist 1998; Macera, Armstead, and Anderson 2001; Williams 1999). Studies report African American and Hispanic women diagnosed with heart disease are less likely than White women to receive aspirin as a form of preventive treatment (Correa-de-Araujo et al. 2006; Jha et al. 2003). The consequences of racial disparities in health care quality for African American women are reflected in these conclusions of Schneider and colleagues (2002): "To the extent that [African Americans] fail to receive quality care, they may be at risk for complications that could otherwise have been ameliorated or prevented altogether" (1288).

Genetic or biological factors have not been dismissed in discussions on risk factors for high rates of heart disease and associated mortality among African American women (see Bolton and Wilson 2005), but researchers caution that such explanations await more conclusive scientific evidence (Bolton and Wilson 2005; Hummer 1996; Landrine and Klonoff 1992; Williams et al. 1994). Furthermore, Hummer argues, "Missing from [genetic or biological] interpretations is an understanding of the social significance of race in U.S. society and, especially, how health and mortality outcomes may be affected by many social and biological factors related to race that are both difficult to statistically control and genetically determined" (108).

In sum, the high rates of heart disease and associated mortality rates among African American women are critical topics in discussions on minority women's health and well-being over the life course. In addressing the prevailing high rates of heart disease and associated mortality rates among African American women through prevention and intervention, current evidence suggests that researchers should consider the health disparities arising from the interplay of biological factors, common risk factors, equality in health care services, and issues of socioeconomic status and racism.

Breast Cancer

Breast cancer is the most frequent occurring malignancy among U.S. women (Dignam 2000). Although the incidence rate (i.e., the number of new annual cases per 100,000 persons) of breast cancer is greater among White women than African American women, more African American women die annually from breast cancer (OWH 2000; Chu, Tarone, and Brawley 1999; Dignam 2000). Overall, breast cancer mortality rates decreased in the last decade for White women but not for African American women (Chu et al. 1999; Dignam 2000). African American women aged 75 years and over have the lowest breast cancer survival rate (OWH 2000). Moreover, African American women, as a group, are more likely to be diagnosed with breast cancer prior to 40 years of age, whereas White women are more likely to be diagnosed after 40 years of age (OWH 2000). At time of diagnosis, more African American women present with a more advanced stage of breast cancer than White women (see Campbell 2002), even when African American and White women have similar mammography use (Chu et al. 1999).

Risk factors for cancer and cancer mortality among African American women include a younger age at menarche, less likelihood to breastfeed, high levels of obesity, low levels of physical activity, psychosocial/cultural factors (e.g., illness beliefs and dietary practices), and lack of access to clinical trials (Bernstein, Teal, Joslyn, and Wilson 2003; Campbell 2002; Forshee, Storey, and Ritenbaugh 2003; Guidry, Matthews-Juarez, and Copeland 2003). Although White women have these risk factors, they are more intense among African American women (Campbell 2002). Other cancer risk factors, such as an extended history of estrogen replacement therapy and high intake of alcohol, associated with increased cancer risk among White women, appear less likely to be risk factors for African American women (Bernstein et al. 2003; Campbell 2002).

Researchers acknowledge that African American women's high rate of breast cancer mortality and their more advanced-stage breast cancers at diagnosis cannot be fully explained in terms of genes or biology (Chu et al. 1999; Dignam 2000). Furthermore, practicing preventive health behaviors in cancer control, such as early detection of breast cancer through mammography screening, appears to benefit White women more than African American ones (Jones, Patterson, and Calvocoressi 2003). African American women with breast cancer also face a pattern of higher rates of morbidity as they age. Older African American women, in particular, are less likely to report having a mammogram compared to younger African American women (Leigh and Lindquist 1998), and older African American women face greater disease morbidity, including hypertension, heart disease, stroke (a complication of hypertension), end-stage renal disease, and dementia (Leigh and Lindquist 1998). Nor have researchers abandoned the role that racial, social, and economic inequalities may play in higher breast cancer mortality rates of African American women (see Campbell 2002). Dignam (2000) has concluded that linking these inequalities to treatment access and health care utilization in breast cancer research is difficult to establish because of inadequate data sources.

In sum, African American women face greater risk than White women of being diagnosed with breast cancer at an earlier age and dying from breast cancer. Within-race variations in breast cancer survival rates for different age cohorts of African American women, such as those under 40 years of age versus over 74 years of age, support the importance of using a gender and life-course perspective in investigating survival patterns. Scientific evidence is accumulating about racial and ethnic variations in breast cancer risk factors and survival rates; however, it is largely inconclusive because few studies have included adequate samples of African American women in cancer clinical trials (Bernstein et al. 2003).

We conclude this section with Rodin and Ickovics' description of health as "a complex and multidetermined issue, influenced by a wide variety of factors," both internal and external to people (1990, 1018). This definition coupled with the gender and life-course perspective helps clarify divergences in heart disease and breast cancer patterns among African American and White women. Current scientific evidence points to a set of standard risk factors for African American women's high rate of heart disease and associated mortality as well as the high rate of breast cancer mortality that likely evolve from the interplay of gender, race, social class, individual health practices, and inequality in access to health care.

Work, Marriage, and Caregiving Roles

The gender and life-course perspective recognizes the importance of understanding shifts or transitions in people's lives resulting from role changes. Work and family role transitions, such as getting a job, becoming a spouse, and becoming a caregiver of an elderly relative, are common role occurrences in human societies.

Work Role

Many African American women spend much of their adult life in the labor market. According to U.S. Census (2001) data, younger African American women, 16 years of age and over, were more likely to be working in the labor force than non-Hispanic White women in year 2000. Specifically, 64% of African American women 16 years and over were working compared to 61% of non-Hispanic White women in this age group. The high labor market participation of African American women in younger years of life may not translate into greater economic advantage over the life course, as the risk of women living in poverty generally is likely to increase across the life span (Rank and Hirschl 1999a, b).

The gender and life-course perspective suggests that the economic disadvantage of older African American women is a cumulative and lifelong process shaped by the intersection of gender, race, social class, and aging (Hatch 2001). For instance, Ozawa (1995) reports African American and Hispanic women received most of their retirement income from public assistance; whereas White women received most of their retirement income from private pensions, annuities, and assets. In addition, African American and Hispanic women spent most of their working years in low-wage, low-skill jobs; whereas White women spent most of their working years in higher-wage, high-skill jobs. In contrast to both White and Hispanic women, African American women spent significantly more years in the labor market but reaped lower lifetime total earnings (Ozawa 1995).

According to the gender and life-course perspective, individuals holding similar social positions in society will share common experiences that contrast with those holding different social positions or statuses. We focus on African American women's work experience; but older African American and Hispanic women, as women of color and minority status, share similar labor market inequality and income disadvantage (see Angel, Jimenez, and Angel 2007). Furthermore, older African American and Hispanic women's similar labor market experiences in the younger years of adult life help explain the convergence in income and asset disadvantage in late life. African American women nonetheless diverge the most from White women in work histories by spending more time in the labor market and receiving less earnings for labor market participation (Ozawa 1995), and this fact suggests how gender and race may interact differently than gender and ethnicity in women's work experiences.

Marriage and Caregiving Roles

Marriage continues to be an important life transition for U.S. women, as indicated by studies examining the link between women's economic status and marital status. Although evidence is inconclusive, research indicates that marriage may have consequences over the life course for women's economic well-being. Married families fare better economically than single families with a female head of household (U.S. Census Bureau 1999). Economic disadvantage is most extreme for unmarried older women, with a disproportionate number of unmarried older African American women bearing a higher burden of economic disadvantage by living in poverty (Ozawa 1995). More recent evidence pinpoints linkages between race, ethnicity, marital status, and aging women's economic security. A study documented that marital disruptions, especially widowhood, resulted in significant income and asset losses for aging non-Hispanic White, Hispanic, and African American women (Angel et al. 2007). When demographic measures were controlled, income and asset losses were greater for aging Hispanic and African American women than for aging White women. This study's investigators explained minority women's greater economic losses in terms of their greater lifelong economic disadvantage (Angel et al. 2007). Unraveling the economic benefits to aging women of marriage is a complex task, as suggested in a study examining aging women's income security and personal employment (Willson and Hardy 2002). This study documented that marriage provided notable income security for aging women. Still, their personal employment not only contributed to better income security but also reduced economic insecurity in the transition to old age (Willson and Hardy 2002). Of significance to this discussion is the finding that marriage provided more security for aging White women, whereas personal employment was indispensable to aging Black women's financial security.

In addition to the economic consequences that marriage may have for aging women's financial security, marriage may also impact the physical health of aging women and the availability of partners in the role of caregiving. Being married is associated with good physical health (Young and Kahana 1995) and, especially for relatively younger women, being married may mean that they have someone to share the role of parenting young children (Tucker and Mitchell-Kernan 1995).

Notwithstanding support for the notion that marriage may serve to protect aging women from economic disadvantage, unprecedented numbers of young African Americans are postponing marriage beyond their twenties as compared to 30 years ago (Tucker and Mitchell-Kernan 1995). Furthermore, more African American women than White women or African American men are delaying marriage or never marrying at all (National Marriage Project 2001; Tucker and Mitchell-Kernan 1995), therefore suggesting a nexus of gender and race. The commitment to marriage or a romantic relationship, although it varies by gender and age within the Black population, appears to be lower among African American women. Men and younger respondents in a national survey of Black Americans were more likely than women and older respondents to be married, involved in a romantic relationship, or desire a romantic relationship (Tucker, Taylor, and Mitchell-Kernan 1993). With more African Americans postponing marriage today than three decades ago, this might mean that the timing of contemporary marriage represents an out-of-conventional-sequence or off-time life event for many African American women.

In U.S. society, an inverse relationship exists between age and the probability of women entering marriage. The prospects of older African American women marrying are greatly reduced, owing to the relatively low number of older African American males (Manton et al. 1987). Although more African Americans than ever are marrying outside their racial group, cultural and societal norms of U.S. society strongly dictate within-race marriages (Tucker and Mitchell-Kernan 1995). Older African American women, particularly those entering adulthood prior to the Civil Rights Movement, grew up and were socialized in a context where laws and cultural norms did not sanction mixed-race marriage. Therefore, older African American women are less likely than younger generations of women, who grew up and were socialized in a more liberal context, to cross racial boundaries in marriage, a circumstance providing support for life-course theory as it relates to the interfacing of individual histories, social histories, and social events.

In addition to work and marriage roles, providing care and aiding other people is a key family role for African American women. As caregiving is highly gendered, and women are socialized into the role of caregiver at an early age (Walker, Pratt, and Eddy 1995), African American women are more likely than African American men to assume responsibility in caring for children, grandchildren, and elders over the life course. Proportionately more African American women than White, Hispanic, or Asian women provide care to an older adult; furthermore, African American women are more likely to provide care to an extended family member, such as an aunt or uncle, than White, Hispanic, or Asian women are (National Alliance for Caregiving and AARP 2004).

African American women report more rewards than challenges in the role of caregiving, as indicated by reports of relatively low levels of psychological stress (see review, Chadiha et al. 2004). Still, consistent evidence indicates that African American women and also Hispanic women caring for elderly relatives rate their overall health as worse compared to White women (Pinquart and Sörensen 2005). This raises concerns about the negative consequences of caregiving on aging African American women's health, particularly those involved in multiple caregiving roles such as rearing grandchildren in the absence of biological parents (Casper and Bryson 1998; Whitley, Kelley, and Sipe 2001). Women's multiple roles have been documented as a risk factor for poor physical and mental health (Belle 1990; McBride 1990), and research has established a link between women's work role, caregiving role, and well-being over the life course (Moen, Robison, and Dempster-McClain 1995; Moen, Robison, and Fields 1994). Participation in multiple caregiving roles by women is likely to increase over the life course (Robison, Moen, and Dempster-McClain 1995), particularly for aging African American women who may care for not only grandchildren but also a spouse or adult child with a health disability (see Magana 2004).

Support for concerns about negative caregiving consequences for aging African American women is found in Burton's (1996) work on the timing of African American women's childbearing, family norms, and transitioning to parent and grandparent roles. Burton found that when younger African American women had children at a time in their lives that conformed to conventional norms of becoming a parent, the birth of a child resulted in mutual assistance in the caregiving role for mothers and grandmothers. In contrast, grandmothers were unprepared for the role of grandparent and, consequently, faced greater challenges in the caregiving role when the timing of younger women's childbearing fell out of synch with conventional family norms of becoming a parent. These findings underscore the significance of using a gender and life-course perspective for understanding the linkage between individual role transitions, family role transitions, and aging African American women's caregiving role.

Conclusions

We began this chapter by acknowledging improvements in African American women's physical health and work and family life. We further acknowledged a gap between the health, work, and family life of African American and White women, as evidenced by a high prevalence of heart disease and a high mortality rate associated with both heart disease and breast cancer. Despite improvements in African American women's longevity, it may not equate with better quality physical health. Neither does the prevalence of heart disease and breast cancer equate with old age, given that relatively young African American women are highly vulnerable to a high rate of heart disease and associated mortality as well as a high rate of breast cancer mortality. Viewed through the lens of gender and the life-course perspective, African American women's greater vulnerability to these chronic diseases and associated mortality during the younger years may impact their health and functioning in late life, thus contributing to poorer health, greater morbidity, and disability, as well as poorer functioning in old age (Leigh and Lindquist 1998).

Lessons Learned

- Multiple risk factors, such as institutional racism in the health-care delivery system, poor health behaviors, and the lack of preventive health methods and economic advantages, shape the status of African American women's physical health, work, and family roles. Future research in this area could benefit from employing the gender and life-course perspective that emphasizes the intersection of gender, race, ethnicity, social class, and aging, as this perspective would facilitate the understanding of how these different factors operate together.

- Older African American women may be at greater risk of poor physical health and high mortality from breast cancer because they may not practice preventive health behaviors, such as mammography screening. Drawing on gender and life-course perspectives that posit that past experiences may bear upon present circumstances, older African American women's failure to seek mammography screening may be deeply rooted in past experiences of real and perceived discrimination within the U.S. health system. Future research, both intervention and prevention, may be more successful when taking into account not only the attitudes and beliefs African American women may hold about preventive health behaviors but also how such attitudes and beliefs may be linked to those held about sexism and racism.
- Variability exists across age-specific groups and birth cohorts in breast cancer mortality among African American women. To capture this variability and gain better understanding of high breast cancer mortality rates among African American women, longitudinal research using the gender and life-course perspective is needed that considers the incidence of breast cancer in age-specific groups and birth cohorts. Longitudinal studies using this perspective also may facilitate understanding African American women's caregiving roles, particularly how these are shaped or altered by the role transitions of women themselves and those of other family members.
- Research on aging, physical health, and work and family roles over the life course involving African American women could benefit from more qualitative research that aims to provide a more in-depth understanding of the concerns of these women.
- African American women are a diverse group. The gender and life-course perspective emphasizes the importance of examining multiple experiences and realities. Therefore, future research should seek to understand the issues of physical health, work, and family roles while addressing the heterogeneity (e.g., including middle- and upper-class women, women of different age groups and nationalities) within African American women.

The gender and life-course perspective underscores the role of gender, aging, race, ethnicity, and social class as interlocking inequalities in shaping the work, marriage, and family caregiving roles of African American women. Most important, this perspective facilitates understanding how the inequalities of health, work, and family roles translate into disadvantages for these women in old age. We draw upon the gender and life-course perspective and supporting empirical evidence to recommend strategies for conducting life-course research with African American women based on lessons learned in doing this type of research with African American women.

REFERENCES

Angel, J. L., M. A. Jimenez, and R. Angel. 2007. The economic consequences of widowhood for older minority women. *Gerontologist* 47:224–34.

Ayanian, J. Z., I. S. Udvarhelyi, C. A. Gatsonis, C. L. Pashos, and A. M. Epstein. 1993. Racial differences in the use of revascularization procedures after coronary angiography. *Journal of American Medical Association* 269:2642–46.

Belle, D. 1990. Poverty and women's mental health. *American Psychologist* 45:385–89.

Bernstein, L., C. R. Teal, S. Joslyn, and J. Wilson. 2003. Ethnicity-related variation in breast cancer risk factors. *Cancer* 97 (1 Supplement): 222–29.

Bolton, M. M., and B. A. Wilson. 2005. The influence of race on heart failure in African-American women. *Medsurg Nursing* 14:8–15.

Burton, L. M. 1996. Age norms, the timing of family roles transitions, and intergenerational caregiving among aging African-American women. *Gerontologist* 36:199–208.

Campbell, J. B. 2002. Breast cancer-race, ethnicity, and survival: A literature review. *Breast Cancer Research and Treatment* 74:187–92.

Casper, L., and K. Bryson. 1998. *Co-resident grandparents and their grandchildren: Grandparent maintained families.* Population Division, Working Paper No. 26, U.S. Bureau of the Census. March. Washington, DC: U.S. Government Printing Office.

Chadiha, L. A., P. Adams, D. E. Biegel, W. Auslander, and L. Gutierrez. 2004. Empowering African American women informal caregivers: A literature synthesis and review. *Social Work* 49:97–108.

Chu, K. C., R. E. Tarone, and O. W. Brawley. 1999. Breast cancer trends of Black women compared with White women. *Archives of Family Medicine* 8:521–28.

Correa-de-Araujo, R., B. Stevens, E. Moy, D. Nilasena, F. Chesley, and K. McDermott. 2006. Gender differences across racial and ethnic groups in the quality of care for acute myocardial infarction and heart failure associated with comorbidities. *Women Health Issues* 16:44–55.

Dignam, J. J. 2000. Differences in breast cancer prognosis among African-American and Caucasian women. *CA—A Cancer Journal for Clinicians* 50:50–64.

Ephraim, P., D. Misra, R. Nguyen, and A. Vahratian. 2001. Chronic conditions. In D. Misra, ed., *The Women's Health Data Book,* 64–103. Menlo Park, CA: Jacobs Institute of Women's Health and The Henry J. Kaiser Family Foundation.

Forshee, R. A., M. L. Storey, and C. Ritenbaugh. 2003. Breast cancer risk and lifestyle differences among premenopausal and postmenopausal African-American women and White Women. *Cancer* 97 (1 Supplement): 280–88.

Grayson, H., C. Minkovitz, D. Misra, and D. Strobino. 2001. Impact of social and economic factors on women's health. In D. Misra, ed., *The women's health data book*, 2–3. Menlo Park, CA: Jacobs Institute of Women's Health and the Henry J. Kaiser Family Foundation.

Guidry, J. L., P. Matthews-Juarez, and V. Copeland. 2003. Barriers to breast cancer control for African-American women. *Cancer* 97 (1 Supplement): 318–23.

Hatch, L. R. 2000. Beyond gender differences: Adaptation to aging in life course perspective. Amityville, NY: Baywood.

Hummer, R. A. 1996. Black-white differences in health and mortality: A review and conceptual model. *Sociological Quarterly* 37:105–25.

Jackson, J. S. 1996. A life-course perspective on physical and psychological health. In R. J. Resnick and R. H. Rozensky, eds., *Health psychology through the life span*, 39–57. Washington, DC: American Psychological Association.

Jha, A. K., P. D. Varosy, A. M. Kanaya, D. B. Hunninghake, M. A. Hlatky, D. D. Waters, C. D. Furberg, and M. G. Shlipak. 2003. Differences in medical care and disease outcomes among Black and White women with heart disease. *Circulation* 108: 1089–94.

Jones, B. A., E. A. Patterson, and L. Calvocoressi. 2003. Mammography screening in African American women. *Cancer* 97 (1 Supplement): 258–72.

Krieger, N. 1990. Racial and gender discrimination: Risk factors for high blood pressure. *Social Science and Medicine* 30:1273–81.

Landrine, H., and E. A. Klonoff. 1992. Culture diversity and health psychology. In A. Baum, T. A. Revenson, and J. E. Singer, eds., *Handbook of health psychology*, 851–91. Mahwah, NJ: Lawrence Erlbaum.

Leigh, W. A., and M. A. Lindquist, eds. 1998. *Women of Color Health Data Book*. Bethesda, MD: Office of Research on Women's Health.

Macera, C., C. A. Armstead, and N. B. Anderson. 2001. Sociocultural influences on health. In A. Baum, T. A. Revenson, and J. E. Singer, eds., *Handbook of health psychology*, 427–40. Mahwah, NJ: Lawrence Erlbaum.

Magana, S. 2004. African American families who care for adults with developmental disabilities or mental illness: A call for research. *African American Research Perspectives* 10:129–39.

Manton, K., C. Patrick, and K. Johnson. 1987. Health differentials between Blacks and Whites: Recent trends in mortality and morbidity. *Milbank Quarterly* 65:129–99.

McBride, A. B. 1990. Mental health effects of women's multiple roles. *American Psychologist* 45:381–84.

McKinnon, J. 2003. The black population in the United States: March 2002. *Current Population Reports*. Series P20-541. Washington, DC: U.S. Census Bureau.

Moen, P., J. Robison, and D. Dempster-McClain. 1995. Caregiving and women's well-being: A life course approach. *Journal of Health and Social Behavior* 36:259–73.

Moen, P., J. Robison, and V. Fields. 1994. Women's work and caregiving roles: A life course approach. *Journals of Gerontology* 49B:S176–S186.

National Alliance for Caregiving and AARP. 2004. *Caregiving in the U.S.* National Alliance and AARP.

National Marriage Project. 2001. *The state of our unions, 2001.* Rutgers, NY: National Marriage Project.

Office of Women's Health (OWH). 2000. The health of minority women. http://www.4women.gov/owh/pub/minority/. Accessed June 10, 2007.

Ozawa, M. 1995. The economic status of vulnerable older women. *Social Work* 30:323–31.

Pinquart, M., and S. Sörensen. 2003. Associations of stressors and uplifts of caregiving with caregiver burden and depressive mood: A meta-analysis. *Journals of Gerontology* 58B:P112–P128.

Rank, M. R., and T. A. Hirschl. 1999a. Estimating the proportion of Americans ever experiencing poverty during their elderly years. *Journals of Gerontology* 54B:S184–S193.

Rank, M. R., and T. A. Hirschl. 1999b. The likelihood of poverty across the American adult life span. *Social Work* 44:201–16.

Robison, J., P. Moen, and D. Dempster-McClain. 1995. Women's caregiving: Changing profiles and pathways. *Journals of Gerontology* 50B:S365–S373.

Rodin, J., and J. R. Ickovics. 1990. Women's health. *American Psychologist* 45:1018–34.

Schneider, E. C., A. M. Zaslavsky, and A. M. Epstein. 2002. Racial disparities in the quality of care for enrollees in Medicare managed care. *Journal of American Medical Association* 287:1288–94.

Tucker, M. B., and C. Mitchell-Kernan, eds. 1995. *The decline in marriage among African Americans.* New York: Russell Sage Foundation.

Tucker, M. B., R. J. Taylor, and C. Mitchell-Kernan. 1993. Marriage and romantic involvement among aged African Americans. *Journals of Gerontology* 48B:S123–S132.

U.S. Census Bureau. 1999. *The Black population in the United States.* Washington, DC: U.S. Department of Commerce.

U.S. Census Bureau. 2001. *Census Bureau Facts for Features.* CB01-FF.02. February. http://www.census.gov/Press-Release/www/2001/cb01ff02.html.

Walker, A. J., C. C. Pratt, and L. Eddy. 1995. Informal caregiving to aging family members: A critical review. *Family Relations* 44:402–11.

Whitley, D. M., S. J. Kelley, and T. A. Sipe. 2001. Grandmothers raising grandchildren: Are they at increased risk of health problems? *Health and Social Work* 26:105–14.

Williams, D. 1992. Racism and health: A research agenda. *Ethnicity and Disease* 6:1–6.

Williams, D. 1999. Race, socioeconomic status, and health. The added effects of racism and discrimination. *Annals of the New York Academy of Sciences* 896:173–88.

Williams, D., R. Lavizzo-Mourey, and R. Warren. 1994. The concept of race and health status in America. *Public Health Reports* 109:26–42.

Willson, A. E., and M. A. Hardy. 2002. Racial disparities in income security for a cohort of aging American women. *Social Forces* 80:1283–1306.

Young, R., and E. Kahana. 1995. The context of caregiving and well-being outcomes among African and Caucasian Americans. *Gerontologist* 35:225–32.

PART II | Research with U.S. and International
Populations involving Children,
Couples, and Women

5 | Research with High-Risk African American Infants and Children: Insights from a Longitudinal Study

Dolores G. Norton, Jacquelyn Vincson, and Melissa Wilhelm

This chapter examines research issues of specific relevance in studying African American infants and children born to young mothers residing in impoverished urban neighborhoods. It draws on experiences gained in conducting a longitudinal study following a small sample of African American infants from birth through age 19, *Children at Risk: The Infant and Child Development Research Project* (ICDRP) (Norton 1993, 1996).

In keeping with the goals of this volume, we focus upon issues in four areas of particular importance in carrying out valid and reliable research with young, low-income African American children and their families. These areas are: (1) research conceptualization and design; (2) sample criteria and recruitment; (3) data collection methods and appropriate assessment measures; and (4) maintenance of the sample: fostering retention and limiting attrition. Each area is discussed in terms of the questions and challenges involved, the advantages and limitations of specific decisions made, and the lessons learned. At the end of each area, recommendations based upon pertinent literature and research and the experiences of the ICDRP are summarized.

The ICDRP Research Concerns and Goals

Researchers have consistently cited the population of African American children growing up in impoverished social and physical urban environments as being at high risk for early academic and social failure (Dupree et al. 1997; McLoyd 1990, 1998; Reynolds 1999; Snow et al. 1991). In a multicultural country where education remains one of the most viable paths to choice and opportunity, the development of these children continues to be of concern to policymakers and researchers (Dupree et al. 1997; Garcia Coll et al. 1996; McCarthy 2000; McLoyd 1998; Reynolds 1999; Spencer 1999). Studies indicate that early school achievement and literacy have their roots in individual parent-child communication, patterns of interaction, daily routines, and child-rearing practices, beginning very early in a child's life (Bronfenbrenner 1986, 2005; Huttenlocher et al. 1998; Snow 1993). In addition, the relationship between children and their primary caregivers is nested within the reality of their specific racial/ethnic, sociocultural, and socioeconomic location in society (Dupree et al. 1997; Garcia Coll et al. 1996; Huttenlocher, et al. 1998; Snow 1991). However, there has been and still is a need for more systematic information about the early preschool experiences and relationships of vulnerable African American children growing up in urban poverty and how these experiences relate to the children's developmental outcomes (Dupree et al. 1997; McLoyd 1998).

The major goal of the ICDRP is to contribute to knowledge of those factors in the child's early life that are related to positive life outcomes for African American children, despite the presence of numerous risk factors in their lives. The overall research question asks how specific factors and processes in the children's early environment are related to their social and cognitive development.

Research Conceptualization and Design

A major challenge in conceptualizing research with this group of children is to create a design that considers the children's specific racial/ethnic, social, and economic realities and their relationship within those realities, and that leads to a better understanding of individual developmental outcomes. To meet these challenges for the ICDRP, we decided to employ a within-group, longitudinal, naturalistic, modified ethnographic research design.

We selected a within-group study design, holding race and socioeconomic status constant, in order to relate experiences of the children who succeed in school despite the presence of risk factors to those from the same population who do not succeed. A within-group study could contribute to unpacking the "black box" of findings in many large studies that report high positive correlations between race and socioeconomic status and academic outcomes when comparing children across groups (Snow et al. 1995). These high correlations often result in race and socioeconomic status being the primary explanatory variables for academic achievement. Many researchers contend that such broad variables do little to help us understand the processes of individual child and family variables on outcomes within groups, and they stress that a more precise examination of specific individual factors within groups and their relationship to outcomes would be more informative (Burton et al. 1996; Garcia Coll and Magnuson 2000; Luster and McAdoo 1994; McLoyd 1998; Norton 1996; Ogbu and Simons 1998; Rogoff 2003; Snow 1993; Snow et al. 1995; Spencer 1999; Spencer and Cunningham 1999).

These researchers advocate within-group study because they believe that within-group individual comparisons of those who face the same environmental and contextual conditions are more informative. One studies phenomena from within the system (Lett 1996). This emic perspective involves using internal observations from within the group to study what is meaningful to the group and its behavior in contrast to the etic approach where observers use information external to the group to assess its behavior.

A longitudinal study design was chosen because it allowed the examination of experiences and related outcomes of the same children at various ages. The benefits resulting from the ability to relate early features of children's experiences to their outcomes over time would outweigh the expense and complexity of a longitudinal study. By studying the same children at frequent, systematic intervals, hypotheses suggested by earlier researchers based on cross-sectional studies could be tested.

Another advantage of longitudinal research is the opportunity to uncover "truth" or at least more objective fact over time. For example, in the hospitals where we recruited our sample, seven mothers originally reported being married. However, as we got to know them through systematic videotaping in the homes every six weeks in the first year, we found that four of the seven were not married and had never been.

The ICDRP questions required that the research design permit the observation of naturalistic, interactive behavior, in order to capture the children's and parents' behavior as it occurs in their normal everyday environments. We used semiethnographic methods to capture natural behavior as closely as possible, as well as the contextual information vital to understanding African American children embedded in their family culture and environment. Casper (1996) stated that the ethnographer: (1) makes systematic, consistent observations over time (as does the ICDRP with its frequent, periodic videotaping, discussed later under the section on data collection); (2) uses multiple sources of data (in the ICDRP, videotapes, hospital records, standardized test scores, behavior checklists from mothers and teachers, and personal interviews); (3) collects artifacts of the lives of those studied (e.g., report cards in the ICDRP); and (4) interviews others (teachers, parents, other caretakers in the ICDRP).

Ethnography's primary interest in the context and culture in which be-havior and growth take place makes it a potentially useful method for studying African American children and their families living in high-risk neighborhoods (Burton et al. 1996; Rogoff 2003).

It is important to emphasize that an adequate amount of time must be set aside to conceptualize an overall research design that can yield appro-priate data to answer the major research questions and to evaluate the ad-vantages and limitations of the various elements of the design. Time must also be allotted to determine the practical feasibility of the design being considered. For example, longitudinal studies cannot be planned without doing homework on potential funding sources, such as foundations, cor-porations, private philanthropists, and local, state, and federal sources in-terested in research on this population. At the time the ICDRP was de-signed in 1982, it was almost impossible to obtain federal funding for a within-group study because of the prevailing prominence of compari-son-group research. Fortunately, by addressing this problem during the design stage, we were able to locate two foundations who believed that within-group individual comparisons of those who faced the same envi-ronmental and contextual conditions could also be informative.

During the design phase, researchers should seek consultation with the appropriate institutional review boards (IRBs). This is especially critical when the study centers on very young, low-income, minority children and their families. For example, one IRB member questioned whether the amount of money[1] being offered by the ICDRP to the moth-ers was "coercive" (i.e., pressuring them to participate because of their great financial need). To address this concern, we gathered data from community gatekeepers, other researchers, and similar families, to sup-port our strong belief that the families should be paid for their partici-pation in the study. Backed by these data, we were able to convince the IRB that the families should be paid since no service was being offered, the research would demand a great deal of their time, and their partici-pation was as vital as that of our research assistants and videotapers who were being compensated.

Suggestions for Designing a Study of African American Children in Impoverished, High-Risk Neighborhoods

1. Continuously link the developing design to the major study questions.
2. Evaluate losses and benefits of each study design decision.

3. Allocate adequate time to design the research and to obtain necessary and appropriate input.
4. Determine the practical feasibility of the research design.

Sample Criteria and Recruitment Methods

To operationalize the concept of "high risk," we considered both environmental and familial aspects of the children's lives. In reviewing the demographics of high-risk children, we found that neighborhood factors such as per capita income, overcrowding, transience, the condition of housing units, education, unemployment, health, and neonatal mortality were often associated with stress and high risk (Chicago Area Geographic Information Service 1982). We calculated indices for these factors for individual neighborhoods (indices of neighborhood income level included median value of rental units, median value of single family homes, median family income, etc.), using the latest census figures for the neighborhoods, and compared these with the city indices on the same factors (Norton 1983). This method permitted us to identify those neighborhoods that placed children at high risk, that is, those above the city indices on factors such as neonatal mortality and housing density and below city indices on factors such as employment, per capita income, and education. Children from families living in neighborhoods with seven to eight negative indices were considered at high risk.

The family high-risk criteria included: (1) mothers who did not live with their parents or any older relative, since children of mothers living with older extended-family members have been found to be less at risk than those living alone or with boyfriends or siblings (Egeland and Brunnquell 1979; Furstenberg 1976); (2) maternal age of 18–22 years old, since hospital computer records indicated that most mothers under 18 in the census tracts being sampled lived at home with their mothers; (3) mothers whose education did not go beyond high school at the time of the child's birth; and (4) mothers who did not work at all or who worked less than half-time (Caldwell and Bradley 1978).

With these two aspects of the sampling criteria defined we proceeded to look for children as they were being born, since we wanted to observe parent-child interactions as early as possible during the time when the groundwork was laid for their future interaction. We could find few other studies on this population beginning at birth with the same goals. For example, in a recent study with a major goal similar to that of the

ICDRP, the researchers obtained their large sample of children at age three through an ongoing early childhood program (Reynolds 1999).

Mothers from the selected neighborhoods who gave birth in two major metropolitan hospitals and who met the environmental criteria for participation in the study, as well as the family criteria of high risk, were asked to participate. We decided that a maximum sample of 35 to 40 mothers was all we could enroll and study adequately, due to the frequency and length of the videotaped sessions, as well as the other extensive methods and sources of data collection. Conferences with the hospitals' IRBs and study of the hospitals' computer printouts for the previous year (of the number of young African Americans giving birth from the selected neighborhoods, as well as with whom they lived) indicated that we could probably obtain enough mothers and babies over a three- to four-month period.

Sample Recruitment

In recruiting young African American mothers and their children to research, it is imperative that the methods and expectations be fully and clearly explained, and respondents' questions be actively encouraged. The mothers must understand what is being asked of them, especially in a longitudinal study, for example, how long the study will go on, how we will collect information, how often, who will come, where, how the information will be used, and the limitations of its use. We found that it was also a good practice to routinely read aloud with the potential participant any written study explanations, informed consent forms, or any other materials or forms. This practice gave potential participants time to ask questions and assured that all received the same information despite differential reading skills.

In recruiting participants, we learned that it is necessary to explain not only the goals of the study but also what led the researchers to a particular participant. For example, although she stated that she understood what the study was about, one potential ICDRP mother wanted to know why she was selected and how we found her. When we explained how the procedure of finding newborns whose mothers lived in specific neighborhoods led us to her, she was visibly relieved. Her child's father believed we had received her name through the local department of public welfare because the mother had drugs in her system when her first baby was born. The mother thought the public welfare "system" may have given us her name in order to monitor how she was caring for the second child. We recommend that a description of how participants are located be added to the recruitment discussion with potential participants.

To ensure that the initial recruiters, who were trained social workers, had enough time to begin to build rapport, demonstrate respect, encourage questions, and answer them fully, the principal investigator (PI) arranged to pay for a monthly percentage of one social worker's time at each of the hospitals. In return, the social workers were given time to monitor the hospitals' births during the four months we drew the sample, identify any mothers giving birth who lived in the mapped high-risk U.S. Census areas, establish that they also met the family criteria, present the description of the study, and ask them to participate in the research. In a series of meetings with these social workers (who were master's level graduate social workers with experience working in their hospitals' obstetrics department with young African American mothers giving birth), the study goals, its methods, and the neighborhood maps were discussed. We emphasized that all contacts and interaction with the mothers be conducted in an atmosphere of respect. Despite good intentions, research indicates that some institutions serving poor and ethnic minority communities do not always provide such a climate of interaction (Garcia Coll and Magnuson 2000; McLoyd 1998).

To ensure uniformity in presenting the study, the social workers helped revise the written scripts requesting participation in the study and explaining and obtaining signatures on the informed consent form. If the mother agreed to participate, she signed informed consent forms for the hospital, the university IRB and the ICDRP, and she retained a copy. If the mother did not wish to participate, the PI interviewed her in the hospital. This visit was not to try to convince her to participate but rather to document her reasons for not wishing to participate in order to give us a better understanding of who did not participate and for what reasons.

Suggestions for Sampling High-Risk Children

1. Operationalize the major concepts in an objective and nonpejorative way.
2. Specify locations or institutions where potential participants with such characteristics are likely to be found.
3. Investigate and explore with those locations/institutions the feasibility of finding appropriate participants.

4. Develop practical procedures for making initial contact with potential participants.
5. Establish an atmosphere of respect and rapport; explain study goals and participants' specific involvement, present the process of how participants were found, and encourage questions from potential participants.
6. Fully describe participants' specific involvement.

Data Collection Methods and Appropriate Assessment Measures

Data Collection. As indicated earlier, we chose videotaping as the major method to capture the naturalistic interaction between the children and their families over the years. The mother and child were videotaped for thirty minutes in the hospital at birth, including in the taping whoever might be visiting at the time; at home every six weeks during the first year; every three months in the second year, and every six months thereafter until the child reached age 20. The camera focused continuously on the child being studied, or the target child, for four hours the first two years permitting accurate real-time observation of the children's activities, alone time, sleeping time, and interactions with others.

We attempted to gather information on the child's whole day by alternating between videotaping four hours in the morning on one visit and four hours in the afternoon on the next visit. As a result of this videotaping protocol, the tapes gave us a fairly comprehensive and relatively permanent method with which to record the children's interaction and growth as required by the research design. In addition, the videotapes can be used to generate reliable data, since they can be coded independently by various researchers, and interrater reliability estimates can be obtained.

Given our quest for naturalistic data, we were very much aware that anyone in the home would have some effect on the "natural" behavior of the family, and a camera would certainly heighten that effect. The challenge was to diminish our intrusion as much as possible. No extra lighting was used, and the camera was handheld and as small as could be obtained in 1982.[2] The same videotaper filmed each family over the years, for as long a period as possible to foster familiarity and ease. The four-hour videotaping was also intended to preserve naturalistic interaction as much as possible, since it is difficult to "pretend" for such a long period of time, especially when babies or young children are involved. It should be noted that the videotapers had to be women since many mothers' boyfriends or husbands did not want male videotapers in the homes for such frequent and long periods of time.

As mentioned, the research design called for the camera to focus continuously on the target child. However, by focusing on the child, the camera could miss whatever else was occurring in the child's environment. For example, one baby was crying on camera while the mother off camera attempted to unzip the back of her dress to nurse the crying child. Another six-week-old infant cried on camera for 28 minutes while the mother, off camera, played cards. In analyzing the tapes later, we would have no idea of where the mother was or what she was doing when the baby cried. To address this challenge, we required the videotaper to keep running written notes on the behavior and persons off camera. Although the use of a tripod focused on the children as infants allowed the videotaper to keep on-site running notes, the field-note method of writing immediately after the visit was used when the children became more active.

The notes included who was present, relationship to the child, and the activities in which they were engaged. The videotapers were asked to describe what they observed behaviorally, rather than give their subjective opinion. The running record also attempted to match the activity recorded off camera with the time on the camera recording the child (Norton 1983, Appendix E).

In keeping with the semiethnographic design, we collected data on the children's lives from multiple sources using multiple methods. These methods included interviewing parents and teachers, collecting yearly report cards, obtaining medical information from the hospital records on the child and mother (with informed consent from the mother), and administering social and cognitive measures to the mother and to the child. Additional contextual data came from unsolicited information provided by the mother, other family members, or visitors.

Measurement Issues. As a longitudinal study concerned with individual developmental outcomes of children over the years, the ICDRP clearly needed measures of the children's development, beginning with very early baseline measures. We were faced with the thorny challenge of finding valid measures to use with impoverished African American children. The history of testing racially, culturally, and ethnically diverse children has generated deep concern for many years, and the literature continues to describe the harm and injustice that some interpretations of test results can bring to African American children (Bender et al. 1995; Garcia

Coll and Magnuson 2000; Hilliard 1983, 1987; Jackson et al. 1982; Luster and McAdoo 1994; McLoyd 1990; McLoyd and Randolph 1990; Samuda et al. 1998; Spencer and Dornbusch 1998).

Since one of the ICDRP's major interests was early school achievement, we needed social and cognitive assessments that could be administered at an early age. One of the measures frequently mentioned in the literature at that time was the McCarthy Scales of Children's Abilities (MSCA). The MSCA was designed to measure the cognitive and motor skills of children from 2½ to 8½ years old (Kaufman and Kaufman 1973; McCarthy 1972). Its goal was to use tasks that were "intrinsically interesting to young children" but also "fair to boys and girls of various ethnic, socioeconomic, and regional backgrounds" (McCarthy 1972, 196). The MSCA consists of 18 short subtests weighted and combined to yield five scales evaluating the child's verbal, perceptual, quantitative, memory, and motor abilities. The first three scales are combined to yield a General Cognitive Index (GCI) similar to an IQ score (Trueman, Lynch, and Branthwaite 1984).

We decided to use the MSCA for several reasons: (1) it was standardized on both black and white children, matched geographically, by socioeconomic status, age, sex, and father's occupation; (2) its scales correlated with other assessment instruments; (3) we were not using the results for prediction or labeling; (4) the tasks seemed to engage the small children we were studying in a pilot session; and (5) it was sensitive to the diverse needs of preschool and minority group children (McCarthy 1972). The improved MSCA, now called the Kaufman Assessment Battery for Children (K-ABC) has been recently cited as one of the most useful attempts to take culture into account in the assessment of children (Samuda et al. 1998).

The children were evaluated on the McCarthy at ages three and six by a trained evaluator with experience in testing children from the same population as the ICDRP sample. The testing was done at the ICDRP office to ensure relatively uniform conditions for each child. Transportation was provided, as was child care for other children, if the mother had to bring them along. The children were made as comfortable as possible before they were tested, with treats and visits to their mother who would be interviewed in another room across the hall. Everyone was patient until the child was willing to remain in the testing room without visiting the mother and had established some rapport with the evaluator.

We also needed some assessment of the mothers' social and cognitive ability to add to our understanding of the individual differences among the children. The mothers were given the Wechsler Adult Intelligence Scale (WAIS) when the children were approximately six years old. Although we did not consider the WAIS a measure of the mother's competence, we reasoned it might be a useful variable to contribute to our understanding of the overall context of the child's development. Mothers were paid for all testing and interviewing, both for themselves and the target child; when the children became 16, they themselves were paid and had to sign their own informed consent documents.

In summary, we recommend videotaping as an effective means of recording naturalistic family interaction despite its obvious intrusiveness. The intrusion can be somewhat muted with the use of a familiar videotaper with whom the family has rapport, long periods of videotaping up to four hours, use of a digital camera, and no extra lighting. The camera should be focused on the child being studied at all times to capture the real-time organization of their day and life. In order to obtain a comprehensive picture, the videotaper should keep a running record (or field notes) of the off-camera presence and behavior of others with the child.

In selecting the most appropriate assessment measures, the researcher needs to do a thorough search of the literature from psychology, education, and child development with special emphasis on development of African American children. Professional consultation with assessment experts can also be helpful. The search should be guided by a continuous focus on the study purpose and questions.

Suggestions for Data Collection and Appropriate Assessment

1. Videotape for naturalistic observation if possible.
2. Keep a running record of off-camera activities.
3. Use multiple sources of data.
4. Employ multiple methods of data collection.
5. Thoroughly investigate validity of assessment measures.
6. Relate all measures to study goals, design, and questions.

Maintenance of the Sample: Limiting Attrition and Fostering Retention

Attrition is one of the major threats to any longitudinal study. Losing participants before the end of the study compromises data collection, interpretation of findings, and generalizability. The questions the researcher must ask in relation to attrition must not only focus on what the research itself requires but also on the participants' needs. These questions include: What do participants need to remain in the study? How can we best support their needs and satisfy the study needs to maintain contact with the participants?

Sullivan and his colleagues (1996) recommend that strategies to prevent attrition should be built into the original research design. We made one of our most serious mistakes in not including plans to minimize attrition in the original ICDRP research plan but also learned some of the most valuable lessons. Some of the strategies we used, based on those lessons learned, are listed below as recommendations.

1. Involve all of the research staff in ongoing contact with the participants.

We learned that positive ongoing contact between all research staff and participants is one of the strongest influences on retention. The videotaper with her systematic, frequent home visits was a key person in identifying participants' needs in relation to the study and developing strategies to meet them. The videotaper was not able to be the "fly on the wall" as proposed in our original research plan; many of the mothers needed to talk. We found that the videotaper's relaxed responses and easy, friendly, sharing relationship with the mother were actually far less intrusive than adhering to the "still face" approach. The mothers seemed to be more comfortable when the videotaper responded as a friendly, interested person. We also found that mothers who perceived responses as friendly tended to call the videotaper between tapings, and they usually alerted her to any new moves and addresses.

Other research staff should also call study participants between data collections (Sullivan et al. 1996; Wright, Allen, and Devine 1995). For all members of the research team, the operant words for reasonably successful retention seemed to be respect, sensitivity, and caring. Ribisl and his colleagues (1996) found that the quality of naturally occurring relationships can push participants away or bring them closer. We recommend that every staff contact with participants be viewed as an opportunity to foster retention and to respond to their concerns related to the research.

2. Use financial compensation.

Although financial compensation for participating in the study was built into the original plan, we had not considered it originally as a primary retention strategy; however, we found it did aid retention. For example, in the interest of accountability, our outside funding sources and the university required all cash disbursements from the research to the participants to be delivered in the form of a check. Few mothers had bank accounts, and several told us that their local currency exchange charged exorbitant fees to cash their checks. We worked with the university comptroller's office to set up accounting procedures to establish a petty cash fund to be used to pay the mothers. This flexibility regarding cash payments contributed to retention by sending a message of respect and understanding for the participants' financial world.

3. Log every contact. Make contact regular and consistent.

Every contact with study participants must be documented, along with contacts with other relatives, schools, and teachers in a central log no matter how minor the contact seems. Phone numbers and addresses should be checked and logged with the date at every encounter. The ICDRP staff found that updating our information on next of kin, other relatives, and boyfriends was sometimes more important than having a participant's telephone number, since the mothers were often unable to pay telephone bills, and phones were disconnected.

4. Conduct Internet searches.

When participants cannot be located, Internet searches should be conducted using the names of relatives or friends. In the ICDRP, we learned the importance of having in our files the names of grandmothers, next of kin based on hospital records, friends, and other log contacts. We called each of these contacts to see if they had information on the participant's whereabouts. It should be noted that the permission for such calls should be included in the informed consent.

5. Use school records.

The children's schools should be considered as an important source of information. Once the children entered school, ICDRP staff systematically obtained Release of Information consent forms from the mothers for the children's schools to obtain information from standardized test scores administered through the schools, report card information, health information, and attendance information.[3] We used these forms not only to obtain information from the current school but to locate new schools when the children moved. When a mother moved and we were not able to locate her, we contacted the research division of the city public schools. We described the ICDRP and asked that our letter be forwarded to the parent if the child were still enrolled in the public school system. The parent could then contact us if they wished. The director of the research division usually agreed to this if we had a signed and dated informed consent form from the mother from the previous school.

Fostering Retention and Limiting Attrition

1. Maintain consistent, continuous contact.
   - Involve all research staff in retention efforts.
   - Recognize that every contact can foster retention.
   - Develop strategies for ongoing contact between data collection times.
   - Maintain atmosphere of respect and rapport.
2. Use financial compensation.
   - Develop flexible payment methods.
3. Log every contact.
4. Conduct Internet searches.
5. Use school records.

Conclusions

This chapter discussed four areas of research that offer particular challenges to the longitudinal study of high-risk African American infants and children growing up in impoverished urban neighborhoods. Drawing from the rich experiences gained in conducting the ICDRP, this chapter aims to contribute to the continuing development of effective early parenting, child-care, preschool, and elementary school curricula for this population of African American children.

NOTES

1. Over the years payments to mothers and later the adolescents have ranged from $20.00 to $50.00 per interview, videotaping, or testing.

2. We later used a digital camera.

3. This also should be considered for preschool programs in which the participants are enrolled.

REFERENCES

Bender, S. L., L. E. Ponton, M. R. Crittenden, and C. O. Word. 1995. Response to commentary. For underprivileged children, standardized intelligence testing can do more harm than good. *Developmental and Behavioral Pediatrics* 16:428–30.

Bronfenbrenner, U. 1986. Ecology of the family as a context for human development: Research perspectives. *Developmental Psychology* 22, no. 6: 723–42.

Bronfenbrenner, U., ed. 2005. *Making human beings human: Bioecological perspectives on human development.* Thousand Oaks, CA: Sage.

Burton, L. M., D. A. Obeidallah, and K. Allison. 1996. Ethnographic insights on social context and adolescent development among inner-city African-American teens. In R. Jessor, A. Colby, and R. Schweder, eds., *Ethnography and human development: Context and meaning in social inquiry,* 395–418. Chicago: University of Chicago Press.

Caldwell, B. M., and R. H. Bradley. 1978. *Manual for the home observation for measurement of the environment.* Little Rock: University of Arkansas.

Casper, V. 1996. Making the familiar unfamiliar and the unfamiliar familiar. *Zero to Three* 16:14–20.

Chicago Area Geographic Information Service. 1982. *Quality of Life.* Public service report series number two. Chicago: Department of Geography, University of Illinois at Chicago.

Dupree, D. P., M. B. Spencer, and S. Bell. 1997. The ecology of African American child development: Normative and non-normative outcomes. In G. Johnson-Powell and Y. Yamamoto, eds., *Transcultural child psychiatry: A portrait of America's children,* 237–68. New York: John Wiley and Sons.

Egeland, B., and D. Brunnquell. 1979. An at-risk approach to the study of child abuse: Some preliminary findings. *Journal of the American Academy of Child Psychiatry* 8:219–35.

Furnstenburg, F. F. 1976. The social consequences of teenage parenthood. *Family Planning Perspective* 8:148–64.

Garcia Coll, C. T., G. Lamberty, R. Jenkins, H. Pipes McAdoo, K. Cronic, B. H. Wasik, and H. V. Garcia. 1996. An integrative model for the study of developmental competencies in minority children. *Child Development* 67:1891–1941.

Garcia Coll, C. T., and K. Magnuson. 2000. Cultural differences as sources of developmental vulnerabilities and resources. In J. P. Schonkoff and S. J. Meisels, eds., *Handbook of early childhood intervention,* 94–114. Cambridge: Cambridge University Press.

Hilliard, A. G. 1983. *Testing African American students.* Special issue of the Negro Educational Review, 1987. San Francisco: Julian Richardson Associates.

Hilliard, A. G. 1987. The learning potential assessment device and instrumental enrichment as a paradigm shift. *Negro Educational Review* 38:200–208.

Huttenlocher, J., S. Levine, and J. Vevea. 1998. Environmental input and cognitive growth: A study using time period comparisons. *Child Development* 69:1012–29.

Jackson, J. S., M. B. Tucker, and P. J. Bowman. 1982. Conceptual and methodological problems in survey research on Black Americans. In W. T. Liu, ed., *Methodological issues in minority research.* Occasional Paper No. 7. Oakland, CA: Pacific/Asian American Mental Health Research Center.

Kaufman, A. S., and N. L. Kaufman. 1973. Black-white differences at ages 2½–8½ on the McCarthy Scales of Children's Abilities. *Journal of School Psychology* 11:196–206.

Lett, J. 1996. Emic/etic distinctions. In D. Levinson and M. Ember, eds., *Encyclopedia of Cultural Anthropology,* 382–83. New York: Henry Holt.

Luster, T., and H. P. McAdoo. 1994. Factors related to the achievement and adjustment of young African American children. *Child Development* 65:1080–94.

McCarthy, D. 1972. *McCarthy's scales of children's abilities.* Cleveland: Psychological Corporation.

McCarthy, S. J. 2000. School connections: A review of the literature. *Journal of Educational Research* 93:145–53.

McLoyd, V. C. 1990. Minority children: Introduction to the special issue. *Child Development* 61:263–66.

McLoyd, V. C. 1998. Socioeconomic disadvantage and child development. *American Psychologist* 53:185–204.

Norton, D. G. 1983. Year end report to funder. Unpublished manuscript. University of Chicago, Illinois, School of Social Service Administration.

Norton, D. G. 1993. Diversity, early socialization, and temporal development: The dual perspective revisited. *Social Work* 38:82–90.

Norton, D. G. 1996. Early linguistic interaction and school achievement: An ethnographical, ecological perspective. *Zero to Three* 16:8–14.

Ogbu, J. U., and H. D. Simons. 1998. Voluntary and involuntary minorities: A cultural-ecological theory of school performance with some implications for education. *Anthropology and Education Quarterly* 29:155–88.

Reynolds, A. J. 1999. Educational success in high-risk settings: Contributions of the Chicago longitudinal study. *Journal of School Psychology* 37:345–54.

Ribisl, K. M., M. A. Walton, C. T. Mowbray, D. A. Luke, W. S. Davidson, and J. Bootsmiller. 1996. Minimizing participant attrition in panel studies through the use of effective retention and tracking strategies: Review and Recommendations. *Education and Program Planning* 19:1–25.

Rogoff, B. 2003. The cultural nature of human development. New York: Oxford University Press.

Samunda, R. J., R. Feuerstein, A. S. Kauffman, J. E. Lewis, and R. J. Sterberg. 1998. *Advances in cultural assessment.* Thousand Oaks, CA: Sage.

Snow, C. E. 1991. The theoretical basis for relationship between language and literacy in development. *Journal of Research in Childhood Education* 6:5–10.

Snow, C. E. 1993. Families as social context for literacy development. In C. Daiute, ed., *The development of literacy through social interaction,* 11–24. San Francisco: Jossey-Bass.

Snow, C. E., P. O. Tabors, P. A. Nicholson, and B. F. Kurland. 1995. SHELL: Oral language and early literacy skills in kindergarten and first grade-children. *Journal of Research in Childhood Education* 10:37–48.

Spencer, M. B. 1999. Social and cultural influences on school adjustment: The application of an identity-focuses cultural ecological perspective. *Educational Psychologist* 34:43–57.

Spencer, M. B., and M. Cunningham. 1999. Patterns of resilience and vulnerability: Examining diversity within African American youth. In G. K. Brookins and M. B. Spencer, eds., *Neighborhood poverty: Context and consequences for children,* 132–44. New York: Russell Sage Foundation Press.

Spencer, M. B., and S. M. Dornbusch. 1998. Challenges in studying minority youth. In H. D. Porton, ed., *Adolescent behavior and society,* 316–30. 5th ed. Cambridge: Harvard University Press.

Sullivan, C. M., M. H. Rumptz, R. Campbell, K. K. Eby, and W. S. Davidson. 1996. Retaining participants in longitudinal community research: A comprehensive protocol. *Journal of Applied Behavioral Science* 32:262–76.

Trueman, M., A. Lynch, and A. Branthwaite. 1984. A factor analytic study of the McCarthy Scales of Children's Abilities. *British Journal of Educational Psychology* 54:331–35.

Wright, J. D., T. L. Allen, and J. A. Devine. 1995. Tracking non-traditional populations in longitudinal studies. *Evaluation and Program Planning* 18:267–77.

6 | Studying Marital Relationships

Joseph Veroff and Terri L. Orbuch

In this chapter we will review our experiences in conducting a large-scale project of the progressive development of marriage during the early years. The original study began with a representative sample of newly married African American couples ($N = 199$) and white couples ($N = 174$) who had filed for marriage licenses in the spring of 1986 in Wayne County, Michigan. The couples were recontacted in their second, third, fourth, seventh, fourteenth, and sixteenth years of marriage. The aims of the project have been to delineate both the processes that generally underlie positive development of marital relationships in the early years and the processes that are specific to such development in African American couples in comparison to white couples. Many different factors have been under scrutiny, such as network support and closeness, self-concept and interpersonal factors, parenting, and patterns of economic and work life. The research is unique in its capacity to provide a white/African American cultural analysis within a longitudinal investigation of marriage. For that reason, we will highlight for this volume features of conducting this project that made it useful for this kind of cultural analysis.

While most of our presentations will focus on the methodological issues at stake when doing research on marriage with African Americans, some of our discussion will by necessity deal with issues that come up when doing research on marriage in general. Consider an important case in point. From the beginning we were interested in studying couples and not individual spouses. We had been convinced by many marriage theorists, especially Bernard (1972), that "his marriage" and "her marriage" are different experiences, and to get a full picture of an ongoing marriage, both members of a couple need to be observed. We therefore reasoned that any methods we used to examine marital processes over time should incorporate both husbands and wives and include observations of the couple together as well as separately. We needed to compare the reports of both husband and wife, as well as be sensitive to the couple level in all of our analyses over time. These methodological issues come up whether a researcher is dealing with a majority white sample or an African American sample. Thus, we will be integrating some of these general issues in with our discussion of methodological concerns specifically relevant in the study of African American marriages.

Our presentation is organized around a series of pragmatic questions we faced at each step in obtaining the sample, interviewing, coding, data analysis, and reporting the results. In this way we hope we can cover the concerns that any researcher might have in developing a study of marriage or other family relationships within the African American community.

Obtaining the Sample

What basic sample should we approach for an investigation of marriage? This study was not the first systematic study of marriage. There have been many, but most of the past studies were based on ad hoc samples and often on couples seeking marital counseling. We wanted the study to be representative in some way. Further, we wanted couples right at the start of their marriages, so that we could examine the development of marital processes in the early years. We selected Wayne County in Michigan, both for its convenience to the Institute for Social Research in Ann Arbor where the research was headquartered and for its capacity to generate a reasonably large sample of African American newly married couples. We obtained our sample by contacting all couples who applied for marriage licenses within that county in 1986 during a three-month period. Any other sample design (e.g., a sample of weddings occurring in given churches or at given courts where marriages were performed) would have given us a population of newlyweds that was more limited in its range. As it turned out, even in Wayne County we had to oversample African American licenses in order to get a large enough group of African Americans for the study.

Since ethnic identity is not indicated on a Michigan marriage license, we obtained permission from the county clerk to provide forms for couples to fill out when they filed in person for their license. These forms not only called for their names and "race" (with "black," "white," and "other" as alternatives) but also asked for telephone numbers and addresses. The couples were told that this form was part of a project being conducted at the University of Michigan and that they were not obligated to fill it out. The form also contained a few other questions, such as whether they were planning a church wedding, to justify its being a "study," but in fact it was largely a means of establishing the ethnic identities of the spouses. When a couple refused to fill out the form, the clerk accepting the marriage license application noted the race of the couple. All of these fine points of gathering the sample were discussed with the county clerk and the staff in meetings before the actual sampling occurred. Rapport with these staff members was essential to the success in sampling on this project.

Should we limit the sample in any way? There are distinct advantages and disadvantages to limiting any population considered for research on marriages or families. We decided to limit our population to first marriages only, since these were not further complicated by previous experiences in marriage, and this information was available on the Michigan marriage license; to couples where the woman was under 35, since childbearing was a realistic alternative for the couple and we were interested in the potential effects of having children on marriage; and to marriages where both members of the couple were white or African American, since interracial marriages have their own special dynamics. If we had not excluded these sample characteristics, we would have had a smaller usable sample for large-scale analysis, and too small a number of these excluded groups to perform any clear analysis of them either as subsamples or as control variables.

It is interesting to point out that we were tempted to also limit the sample to only couples who had no children at the time of marriage, but in our pretest questionnaire we found that a very high percentage of the couples (50% of the African American couples and 20% of the white couples) had children going into the marriage. We reasoned that if we limited the sample to childless couples we would be missing an important experience in a good number of marriages that occur at this time in American society.

What size sample did we want to draw? While one has to limit the size of a sample in any research due to pragmatic issues of time and money available for interviewing and coding, we also calculated that around 400 couples would be needed for reasonable power in any statistical analyses using multiple regressions of couples' data as the unit of analysis and ethnicity as a predictor variable. This sample size would permit us to have approximately half the number of couples within each ethnic group, which would also give us enough power to analyze data within ethnic groups. Further, since previous studies had found that African American couples divorce at a higher rate than white couples (Cherlin 1998) and that those who are lost to attrition tend to be from minority backgrounds (Karney and Bradbury 1995), we should start with a larger number of African American couples than white couples. By oversampling African American couples, we reasoned that any sample attrition over time would still give us enough couples for analyses of marital stability over time with the African American couples.

To obtain the sample sizes we desired we ran a pretest at the county clerk's office for a week prior to actual sampling to see how many African Americans would register for licenses within the week's time. It was that information which pressed us into a strategy of using the entire sample of African American couples registering for marriage licenses over a three-month period, while drawing only a random third of the white couples.

Recruiting Couples to Participate

What special techniques should we use to get couples to participate? It is one thing to start with an interesting population from which to draw a sample that could be representative of that population, but it is another thing to get that sample to participate in the study so that it remains representative. In our case, each couple selected was sent an invitation to participate by mail, addressed to where the couple designated they would be living once married. In the initial contact, couples were offered $25 for participating in one individual spouse interview and one couple interview, each of which lasted one hour.

For efficiency, the interviewer who handled the spouse interviews was usually different from the interviewer who handled the couple interviews. Standard survey research procedures were used to induce cooperation in all cases. The response rate was 65% with 22% refusals and 13% not located. The African American and white rates were almost identical. We were pleased with these rates, given the fact that both members of the couple had to agree to participate. We felt comfortable about considering this a relatively representative sample of the original population. It should be noted that in no case did we feel that our honesty in the initial signed consent form—saying that personal issues may come up in the interviews—presented any obstacle to getting couples to participate. Once a couple agreed to participate in the first year, it was easy to maintain participation over the years if we were able to locate a workable address.

Each year we sent out a newsletter and anniversary card to the participants giving them some innocuous feedback (e.g., percentages fitting certain demographic categories, moved during the year). This yearly mailing kept our participants invested in the project, and it alerted us to any changes of address, either directly from the couple when they returned a prestamped postcard that asked for any changes in their address or marital status, or from having the newsletter returned stamped "no longer at this address." We then were able to submit these "old" addresses to the National Change of Address database (NCOA). This is a database that maintains all of the "Moved" records for the U.S. Postal Service. The database can be matched to the sample files to catch those respondents who have moved and notified the USPS of their move. When possible and necessary, we sent interviewers out to the old address to ask about the move with neighbors, store owners, or Federal Express workers.

An important piece of information in the first interview, the names and addresses of people who knew a couple's whereabouts, was also helpful in relocating participants with changed addresses. Because some of these contact persons were uneasy about telling us where the respondents were located or moved to, we wrote personal letters to respondents that were then passed on to them by these contact persons. Sometimes we provided monetary incentives to contact persons for assisting us in relocating the respondents. We also designed a project website where respondents could update their address and/or contact information. Last, we went to the three-county-area divorce records office where we were able to locate any couples who divorced since 1986. In most cases, these divorce records also included the last known address of each spouse (but in all cases the last known address of the person who filed the divorce claim). Depending on the year of divorce (and whether the couple had children together), one ex-spouse also might give us address information on the other ex-spouse.

Data Collection

Could we use telephone interviews since they are much cheaper? We generally opted for the face-to-face interview largely because we had complicated sets of questions, lists that required visual control, and procedures that generally required both partners there for some of the interview. However, for two of the panels (Years 2 and 4), we resorted to phone interviews just to get some updated information and some quick responses about the couples' general and marital well-being. In one of these panels we interviewed the African American couples face-to-face as part of a methodological investigation of differences between face-to-face and telephone interviews on the distribution of responses among blacks, given that face-to-face interviewing identifies race matching but telephone interviewing does not. In fact, there was little race matching in the telephone interviewing. In this methodological investigation, we found that there were no significant differences between the two groups in response distribution.

What methods of data collection are called for? We knew from the start that we were committed to a mixed-methods approach, which permits researchers to be sensitive to an especially wide array of constructs and to track the reliability and validity of these constructs with considerably more confidence than they would have had using a single method. We are aware that modern survey research has drifted more and more to a singular, closed-ended approach of asking relatively direct questions of their respondents for a number of reasons. Closed-ended questions are simpler to administer, code, and analyze than open-ended questions or behavioral observations. Even within closed-ended questions, however, a variety of methods can and should be used to assess the same construct.

In doing research on marriage it behooves us to get into methods more difficult than direct survey questions. For example, the topic of conflict is paramount in the study of marriage, and while we can ask couples about how much they fight and how they cope with conflict, we thought we really needed to observe live conflicts between the spouses and see how these conflicts get resolved. We also felt that the meaning couples make of their relationship in their own words was important to understand and analyze. It was for these reasons that in addition to the standard survey research methods, we introduced two techniques that were important to our study. Before describing these techniques, it is important to note that these were expensive additions, especially in the data analysis stage, and so a researcher has to make sure the addition of such measures will have a rich return before undertaking them.

One of these additional techniques was to set up a task that required the couple to interact verbally, which we could then code from an audiotape. We were interested in how they resolve conflicts. The task required them to come to a consensus on a rank ordering they made individually of the importance of a number of rules for marriage. From that, Crohan (1992) was able to code constructive and destructive approaches to resolving differences. Observing couples in conflict settings has become the mainstay of many marital research programs, particularly the work coming out of Gottman's laboratory (see Gottman 1994) in which physiological assessment measures are used to track emotional reactions to conflict-resolving episodes. Conger and his colleagues also assess complex family interactions by videotaping families with adolescents (see Conger et al. 1990). We ruled out the physiological assessments and the videotaping because they were not only expensive but unmanageable in surveys conducted in respondents' homes.

The second complex technique was to have the couple tell the story of their relationship from the time they first met until the present and their thoughts about the future, with the stories audiotaped. Similar narrative approaches can be found in the research on couples by Buehlman, Gottman, and Katz (1992) and Surra, Batchelder, and Hughes (1995). This narrative technique permits the couple to tell their story in their own words. These stories were audiotaped. It is important to underscore that this was the couple's story since each spouse was present and encouraged to participate. As a jointly constructed narrative, data must be analyzed at the couple level. Regrettably, we did not have the time or money to get each spouse's own story. It would have been an exciting venture to compare spouses' stories with each other and with the couple's joint story. With the limits of funding and respondents' patience, we opted to gather the couple story, justifying that this information comes closest to what couples experience in their social lives together.

In order to have some comparability across couples, we gave them a story board to follow the development of their narrative with such cues as "When we became a couple," "The wedding," and "Right after we were married." Interviewers were given special training for the prompts they were permitted to use if the story began to lag, in order to standardize interviewer probes. In training, interviewers recorded their interviews with several couples and were given feedback from the researchers. From the tapes we constructed many different types of codes. Some codes dealt with the feelings expressed (e.g., Were they jointly experienced?); some dealt with the themes brought up about their courtships, weddings, honeymoons, present lives, and future lives as they see them; some dealt with the styles they used in conveying these themes (e.g., how dramatic they were in telling the story); and some dealt with how the couple interacted while telling their story (e.g., Did they collaborate or disagree about aspects of the story?). We should note that since we had a sample of African American couples, we insisted on having African Americans help develop the codes and also participate in the actual coding of the stories of the African American couples.

Some illustrations of the coding schemes we devised are described in the box. The narrative method should not be undertaken lightly. Setting up reliable codes for the stories is a difficult undertaking. So is the actual coding. For us, the narrative coding (establishing the systems and then coding and checking the coding of 311 couples' narratives) took nearly three years of labor-intensive work. Granted, we had many different codes; if the narrative coding had been more limited in its goals, it wouldn't have taken as long. A saving grace, however, was that generally in a longitudinal study the same codes can be used for data collected at a later point.

Parenthetically we should note that the coding difficulties in a narrative approach are akin to what might emerge in any extremely open-ended question procedure, but with a narrative the coding is much more extensive and covers a great deal more potential territory. It may be more economical and feasible to use a number of pointed open-ended questions rather than a completely open narrative. We profitably used some of these types of questions throughout our survey. For example, we asked, "Looking back on it now, what would you say were the main reasons you decided to get married?" (coded primarily for how much being in love characterized the answer) and, for parents, "In what ways has having a child (children) affected things between you and your husband (wife)?" (coded for positive vs. negative perceived effects).

Couples Narrative Coding Scheme Strategies

Feelings Coding Scheme
- Within the *feelings* coding scheme we coded each mention of a feeling (e.g., being sad, happy, loving, liking; feeling a need for something), who had the feeling, to whom or what it was directed, whether it was positive or negative, and whether it accentuated the individual or the communal aspects of feelings.

Thematic Coding Scheme
- Within the *thematic* coding scheme each subphase of the story (courtship, wedding, honeymoon, present, future) was coded separately for a series of themes (e.g., issues raised, tensions mentioned). Our thematic coding was informed by the past work of other people. For example, Gergen and Gergen (1987) had done some exciting work on narratives of relationship development that hinged on whether the development was a gradual positive unfolding or a lot of ups and downs, which we used when coding the courtship stories. Many people have ar-

gued that the wedding represents the social commitment a couple makes to the world about their relationship, so we coded the wedding story for any evidence of the awareness of this kind of commitment.

Stylistic Coding Scheme
- Some couples are merely descriptive; others tell a story in the more dramatic sense of the word. Within the *stylistic* coding scheme we focused primarily on dramatic styles, but we also coded for how coherently a story was told.

Interaction Coding Scheme
- Finally, in the *interaction* coding scheme we coded each change in voice for whether it indicated collaboration, conflict, or confirmation with what the spouse had just said. (See Veroff, Sutherland, Chadiha, and Ortega 1993a for more details regarding each of the coding schemes.)

The narrative may have touched on these two questions, but we wanted to be sure to have definitive responses. We could have had a series of such questions instead of the open-ended narrative, but we decided to go with the narrative, even though it was a major investment, because it lets couples get involved in a storytelling mode from which images and meanings of marriage and/or parenting may emerge that might not have come through in a direct open-ended question on the same topic.

There are, of course, those couples from whom getting a free-flowing narrative was difficult. Nevertheless, our skilled interviewers were able to obtain enough information to give us usable material. For many of the variables we constructed based on the narrative data, the length of the narrative was controlled in the analysis. Altogether, we feel it was worth the effort (see Holmberg, Orbuch, and Veroff 2004 for complete details on our narrative method). For example, Veroff et al. (1993b) showed that a measure of the salience of religion for a couple derived from the narrative produced more meaningful results than a parallel measure derived from standard direct questions about religion.

The closed-ended questions we used covered standard issues, but some required considerable ingenuity and pretesting. The most challenging of these were couples' reports of marital conflict, how they set marital ideals for each other, and how much they loved their spouses.

For getting at marital conflict, we had each spouse "think about the last time they disagreed or argued about something in the past month or so." We asked them what the argument was about, and then we asked them to read from a booklet "different things that sometimes happen when a couple disagrees." The booklet listed 16 types of behaviors that might have occurred first on the part of the wife and then on the part of the husband. Such behaviors included "backing down right from the start," "calmly discussing the situation," "yelled or shouted," "insulting and calling names," and "trying to compromise." These items became indispensable for forming destructive and constructive conflict style scales. Interestingly, the destructive conflict style was predictive of marital stability for the white couples, while for African American couples it was the constructive conflict style scale (Veroff, Douvan, and Hatchett 1995).

Getting at love in a closed-ended scale is a formidable undertaking. We took a multidimensional approach and asked each spouse to estimate how often they had experienced a series of nine positive feelings toward his or her spouse. These included feeling especially caring toward your spouse, enjoying relaxed times just being with your spouse, and feeling your sexual life was joyful and exciting. A factor analysis of these and the other items (Oggins, Veroff, and Leber 1993) revealed that four items hung together to help form a scale that we called affective affirmation, a fancy way of saying they felt loved. That scale proved to be one of our most powerful scales in predicting marital well-being and marital stability as much for African American couples as for white couples. The items on this scale are listed in the box.

Affective Affirmation Scale Questions Used

Now let's talk about the special pleasures and good feelings that come from being married. For each one of the feelings on this list (hand respondent list that includes more items than the ones used for the affective affirmation scale), mark an "x" in the box telling how often during the past month or so you have had such feelings—often, sometimes, rarely, or never.

During the past month how often did you:

Feel that your (wife/husband) felt especially caring toward you?

Feel that your (wife/husband) made your life especially interesting and exciting?

Feel that your (wife/husband) made you feel good about having your own ideas and ways of doing things?

Feel that your (wife/husband) made you feel good about the kind of person you were?

Scoring Index
Sum of z-scores for above four items where often = 4, sometimes = 3, rarely = 2, and never = 1 for each item

(Modeled after Veroff, Douvan, and Hatchett 1995)

To obtain how they set ideals for each other, we had them fill out a 12-item adjective checklist (e.g., bossy, impatient, considerate, cooperative) four times—first to describe themselves, then their own ideals for themselves, then how they perceive their spouse to be, and finally how they would like their spouse to be. This procedure permitted us to get at a number of important aspects of self-other perceptions, but more importantly it provided indirect measures of ideals set for marital partners and how well they think their spouse is meeting those ideals (see Ruvolo and Veroff 1997).

Data Analysis

When researchers focus on married couples they face the dilemma of whether to analyze wives separately from husbands, and white couples separately from African American couples. How do you deal with gender differences in data analysis of couples? For statistical analyses, there are a variety of choices that take into account that the researcher is dealing with couples and thus the observation drawn from a wife is not completely independent from the parallel observation drawn from her spouse. For example, when tests for gender differences were called for we used paired *t*-tests or pairwise analyses of variance or covariance in which the significant effects of gender can be gauged. When we used regression analyses, as we did for much of our work, we used individual levels of assessment from both spouses as separate predictors for either a couple level of analysis (e.g., couple stability) or an individual level (e.g., wife's marital happiness or husband's commitment to the marriage).

We did not enter the husband's report and the wife's report into the same regression model given the issue of the interdependence of these reports. Instead, when doing regressions at the individual level, a comparison between the strength of beta weights for a given variable in predicting, for example, marital happiness for husbands compared to the strength of that variable in predicting marital happiness for the wives can be tested by standard normal curve differences analyses. Are the parallel betas significantly different from one another? Alternatively, we discussed the relative importance of a predictor variable (e.g., conflict) for wives' marital well-being and the importance of that same variable for husbands' well-being (without comparisons).

We should point out that there are extensions of the pairwise correlational approaches for dyadic data (Griffin and Gonzales 1995) that help sort out effects due to individual spouses from the effects due to the interdependence of both spouses. In this way, more complex pairing of husband and wife variables can be considered, adding novel directions for treating gender effects in couples' data.

How do you deal with ethnic differences in data analysis? Similar questions arise when researchers are explicitly pursuing ethnic differences, such as the white versus African American comparisons possible in our marriage data. We used two different styles of data analyses. When the sample sizes permitted it, we ran separate analyses within each ethnic group. This procedure gave us the most direct results. For example, we ran almost all of the multiple regression analyses for the book *Marital Instability* (Veroff et al. 1995) within whites separately from African Americans. In this way we could detect variables that were predictive of marital instability for each of the groups. We then relied on the beta comparisons across the two analyses for testing the significance of differences between the resulting betas to get at variables that were significantly different between whites and African Americans. The latter was an indirect way of getting at instances where there was a significant statistical interaction with ethnicity.

For illustration, we found that among African American couples the following variables significantly predicted marital stability after four years of marriage: husband having low general anxiety; high collaboration by the wife in a joint task in the first year; the couple experiencing together the death of someone close to them; the wife and husband having a role-sharing orientation in the third year; and the wife not having an affair. With regard to these particular variables we ended up with two that seemed to be distinctively predictive for African Americans (whether the husband had low anxiety and whether the wife had a collaborative style), two that were significant for African Americans but not significantly more predictive than they were for whites (experiencing death of a close one and having a role-sharing orientation), and one that was significantly predictive for both groups of couples (whether the wife had an affair). In the same way we can list what variables were distinctively predictive in the white couples but not in the African American couples. Two of these variables were wives' feelings of equity in the marriage and husbands' assumptions of assumed similarity between themselves and their wives in how good their sex lives were. Both of these variables were predictive of marital stability in whites but not in African Americans, and the differences in the betas were significantly different as well.

In the above illustrations we can see the results clearly for each ethnic group but have only an indirect approach to the statistical interaction. Combining both African American and white couples into one overall analysis and permitting tests for statistical interaction with ethnicity allows us to have more direct tests. We used such an approach in some of the more complex analyses especially geared for longitudinal observations.

How do you best take advantage of longitudinal data, especially for ethnic differences? Over the years certain analytic strategies have become especially useful for exploiting the longitudinal nature of data. We wanted to take advantage of these strategies in our study. It was in the context of these analyses that we highlight the tests of the direct statistical interaction effects with ethnicity.

The first analysis strategy is called Survival Analysis or Cox Proportional Hazard Regression, which was used to examine the timing of divorce across the years of our study (Orbuch et al. 2002). It is often used to capture those factors that are predictive of the timing of an event that can occur to a person or people over a period of observations (early or late in the observations or not at all); this analysis is often used in epidemiology to predict death or the occurrence of a disease. The technique is preferable to regression analyses for which certain time-varying covariates (i.e., income, employment status, frequency of conflict) create problems for assessment of a single variable. In addition, this methodology allows us to use data for all couples in our sample (even if they have missing data on certain time points), up to when they drop out due to divorce.

Like regression, survival analysis produces estimates of coefficients and their standard errors, but the interpretation is slightly different. In our context, the coefficient measures the effect of the predictor variable on the hazard of divorce. By *hazard* we mean the probability of divorce among those who are still married, which can loosely be interpreted as the risk of divorce. In a survival analysis of the risk of divorce we introduced ethnicity both by itself as a predictor variable and as a variable in interaction with other variables (Orbuch et al. 2002). Not only were African Americans found to display the greater hazard for divorce, as many other data sets have shown, but we uncovered two interactions with ethnicity that were enlightening. One was with husband's education. Our results indicated a significant interaction between ethnicity and husband's education, which when plotted showed that the risk of divorce does not go down for African American husbands with increased education as it does for African American wives and white husbands and wives. There had been some hints of this phenomenon when Veroff et al. (1995) found that African American men whose fathers were more educated were more likely to be in unstable marriages than African American husbands whose fathers were less educated. These results prompted us to suggest that African American men in our society, unlike the other groups, may still experience considerable obstacles in the world of work that may undermine the advantages that they might have expected when they became more educated. What is more, with education they may experience special advantages in the marriage market and have many more alternatives to their present partner/spouse.

The second analysis strategy is growth curve analysis (see Bryk and Raudenbusch 1992). In these analyses one can, among other things, see how a given variable may change over time, and how those changes may be different in one group compared to another. Thus we could look for ethnicity × year interactions in understanding changes over time. We did such analyses and found some interesting effects. For example, we found that the decrease in marital well-being that is apparent over the early years of marriage for most couples is steeper for African American compared to white couples. Another example, a much more complicated one, comes out of our coding the narrative stories for whether the husband or wife is said to be the primary initiator of the courtship.

Our results suggest that among the white couples there is a steady report of the husband as the primary initiator by those couples who speak at all about who initiated the courtship. However, among the African American couples there is a much higher report of the husband as the initiator during the first telling of the courtship story in year 1, but such reports drop off in subsequent years to about the same level as white couples. For whatever reason, as marriages proceed, African American couples lose the image of the husband as an active suitor in the marriage. That phenomenon does not occur among white couples, who focus less on the husband's role in courtship altogether, even in the first year of marriage.

Interpreting Ethnic Differences

This last result, while interesting, stretches our imagination for interpretation. First, it may suggest that African American wives promote the image of male initiation of the courtship to solidify and normalize the relationship. Relatedly, we also are reminded of a book by Majors and Billson (1992) called *Cool Pose*. In this book, they advance the notion that there are strong norms in the African American community for many males to adopt a "cool pose"—or a detached pose—to display their masculinity, given the challenges of racial oppression that they face. They further suggest that this persona is particularly prevalent in heterosexual pairings among African Americans. We could say that to live up to the "male cool" persona within the African American community, men in good marital bonding should have been the one in charge of the initiation and maintenance of the relationship. When first married, African American couples might be especially prone to speak of male initiation of their courtship, more so than the white couples, but as the marriage progresses this "male cool" perspective withers as the everyday dynamics of the marital connections take over.

There is something unsatisfying about this interpretation, even if it might be relatively accurate. It depends on a psychological persona presumed to be rampant in the African American community when in fact there is little direct evidence that it is any more rampant there than in the dominant white society. We would prefer interpretations bolstered with more empirical data. To get such data would require another big study to corroborate the greater usage of the "male cool" perspective among contemporary young African American couples.

At this point we should note the major advantage of studying different ethnic groups in working on studies of marriages and families. Only with at least two groups can we sort out results from a study into those that are common to both groups and those that are distinctive to one group or other. If results are common to both groups, as was our finding that there was a decrease in marital well-being over the first seven years of marriage whether or not couples divorced, we are in a good place to describe relatively general phenomena without taking into account the particular cultural context in which the phenomena occurred.

Evidently marriages in the early years, whether African American or white, become less gratifying after the initial honeymoon period is over and the couples encounter the inevitable obstacles and conflicts that come in working out a life together and raising a family. Also common to both groups is the importance of feeling affirmed as a person in the marriage and avoiding frequent conflicts for producing stability. Furthermore, within the analyses of the narratives there were far more ways in which the contents of the narratives across the two groups were the same than different. It is always important to keep in mind these common findings. Much more time is generally devoted to explaining distinctive results, which leaves the impression that the marriages of African American and white couples are vastly different. Nothing can be farther from the truth.

The distinctive results often attract the major attention from researchers. There are two major kinds of distinctive results. One is mean or frequency differences, like the results showing that white husbands are less likely than their African American counterparts to participate in household tasks (Orbuch and Eyster 1997) or a number of interesting differences between African American and white couples in the narratives they told (see Veroff et al. 1993; Chadiha, Veroff, and Leber 1998). Sometimes results like these disappear when additional demographic or other controls are introduced; sometimes they do not. One extremely critical difference in our findings is that African Americans divorce or separate more frequently, even when controls for education, income, and having premarital children were introduced into the analysis. Other explanations of this difference need to be explored (see Veroff et al. 1995; Orbuch et al. 2002).

The other set of results and, for our money, the more interesting kind of distinctive results are those based on significantly different relationships between variables. For example, our finding that men's anxiety was significantly predictive of marital instability among African American couples but not among white couples was a distinctive result. So was the finding regarding wives' concerns with equity in the marital relationship being significantly predictive of marital instability in white couples but not in African American couples.

How do we interpret distinctive results like these? One common way is to rely on potentially differential meanings of words used in the assessment procedures. We might turn to the items used in the anxiety scale or the equity scale to see whether in one group or another it has a different meaning. We felt that this was not the case. The anxiety scale, for example, asks how frequent the person feels "nervous, fidgety, or tense," "troubled by headaches, or pains in the head," "that you were going to have a nervous breakdown." The equity scale asks the person to consider how much he/she and his/her spouse put into their marriage and who gets more out of the marriage—the person, the spouse, or both about equal—and then asks the person to evaluate how he or she thinks his or her spouse would answer the same question. We had no obvious reason to think these items would mean something different for white couples compared to African American couples. Our tacit evaluation may be wrong, and perhaps only a study that probes for the meaning of these items would clearly exonerate these measures from any special bias.

Another way to interpret distinctive differences is to suggest ways that we may be measuring a common process that occurs but the process shows up in different forms in the marriage. Orbuch, Veroff, and Hunter (1999), in an article called "Black couples, white couples: The early years of marriage," suggest that an accommodating wife makes for stable marriages in general. However, the meaning of accommodation is seen differently in the two ethnic groups. For the white couples there was greater marital stability when an accommodating wife was seen as cooperative; for the African American couples it was when the accommodating wife was seen as collaborative on the joint narrative task. Therefore, it was not that the processes (accommodating wife) were different but the measures used to get at the processes were distinctive for each group.

Finally, there will be distinctive differences that do indicate different processes within each group. We feel the distinctive results showing that African American men's anxiety predicts couple instability among African American couples, and that white wives' concerns about equity predict marital instability among white couples require a search for distinctive processes for each group. Our interpretation of the African American couples' results was that African American husbands have a special handicap when they are anxious, since they often may encounter racism in the employment world, plus a variety of other threats like the potential for police harassment as well as other perceived suspiciousness in the outside world, phenomena rarely experienced by white males.

This anxiety exacerbates African American men's capacity to withstand such obstacles, and in turn creates marital tensions. This interpretation suggests that had we had a measure of perceived racial discrimination in our data set, we may have been able to work out a causal model to understand marital instability found in our African American sample. Such a measure of discrimination was found useful in Murry et al.'s study (2001) of how stress and racial discrimination are jointly linked to the quality of marital partnerships.

Our interpretation about the distinctiveness of the white couples' results was that the feminist movement, which is largely a white movement, has hammered home the need for equity in marital relationships and, for this reason, has created a standard for evaluating a good marriage for white women that does not exist within the African American context. Thus, women's feeling that the marriage is not equitable has more severe consequences for marital stability among white couples. Further research is needed to ascertain whether African American women have different standards of equity, or whether they are more tolerant of inequities they experience in marriage, possibly because of the lack of eligible African American males in the marriage market.

Conclusions

There were several lessons learned in conducting this research over a number of years. Those presented in this chapter are summarized below. We stress that having both an African American sample and a white sample to compare in a study of marriages and families opens up special perspectives about the interpretation of the results that would not be available had the researcher examined marriages of only one or the other group. The value of a multiethnic community is that there is some general similarity in the overall cultural contexts for the entire community, but there are clear differences in normative structures within each group that govern the meaning of marriage as well as the meaning of the measures used to assess marital relations. If researchers avoid the perspectives that the reactions and experiences of couples in the majority group are what is normative for all, and that the reactions and experiences of African Americans are only important in contrast to the majority (see Collins 1990), we can get closer to understanding processes that are general to any group as well as those processes that are specifically characteristic of one or the other. In so doing we become closer to a contextual understanding of marriages and families.

This research endorses the value of employing a mixed-method approach to the measurement of marital constructs. We found vastly different results between and within the two ethnic groups depending on which method was used. Our interpretations of results speculated about what certain measures meant for one group as opposed to another. What does equity mean for African American wives as opposed to white wives? What does anxiety mean for white males as opposed to African American males? Methodological research directly investigating such questions, along with many others, are much needed, especially as we open the door to methods that stray from the standard question-answer format of the usual survey. Last, we have suggested that a measure of perceived racial discrimination used in marital studies may go a long way in helping researchers unpack some of the differential findings comparing the two ethnic groups.

Lessons Learned

- A high percentage of couples had children going into the marriage; therefore, limiting the sample to childless couples would have missed an important experience in many marriages that occurs in American society at this time.
- Oversampling African American couples was necessary to maintain power for a longitudinal study of African American and White couples.
- Using the National Change of Address Database with the U.S. Postal Service helps with tracking respondents who move and notify the U.S. Postal Service.
- Innovative data collection techniques introduced in this study (e.g., a verbal interaction around conflict resolution and a narrative story of their relationship) added value to the study in understanding ethnic similarities and differences in marital relationships.
- Approaches to data analyses have implications for understanding couple data from both an ethnic and a gender perspective.
- Interpreting results within a cultural context can be challenging, and careful attention must be given to both distinctive results and common findings.

REFERENCES

Bernard, J. 1972. *The future of marriage.* New York: Bantam.

Bryk, A., and S. W. Raudenbusch. 1992. *Hierarchical linear models for social and behavioral research: Applications and data analysis.* Newbury Park, CA: Sage.

Buehlman, K. T., J. M. Gottman, and L. F. Katz. 1992. How a couple views their past predicts their future: Predicting divorce from an oral history interview. *Journal of Family Psychology* 5:295–318.

Chadiha, L., J. Veroff, and D. Leber. 1998. Newlywed's narrative themes: Meaning in the first year of marriage for African American and white couples. *Journal of Comparative Family Studies* 29:115–30.

Cherlin, A. J. 1998. Marriage and marital dissolution among black Americans. *Journal of Comparative Family Studies* 29:147–58.

Collins, P. H. 1990. *Black feminist thought: Knowledge, consciousness, and the politics of empowerment.* Boston: Unwin Hyman.

Conger, R. D., G. H. Elder, F. O. Lorenz, K. J. Conger, R. L. Simons, L. B. Whitbeck, S. Huck, and J. N. Melby. 1990. Linking economic hardship to marital quality and instability. *Journal of Marriage and the Family* 52:643–56.

Crohan, S. E. 1992. Marital happiness and spacial consensus on beliefs about marital conflicts: A longitudinal investigation. *Journal of Social and Personal Relationships* 9:89–192.

Gergen, K. J., and M. N. Gergen. 1987. Narratives of relationships. In R. Burnett, P. McGhee, and D. Clarke, eds., *Accounting for relationships,* 269–88. New York: Methuen.

Gottman, J. M. 1994. *What predicts divorce? The relationship between marital processes and marital outcomes.* Hillsdale, NJ: Erlbaum.

Griffin, D., and R. Gonzales. 1995 Correlation models for dyad-level models: I. Models for the exchangeable case. *Psychological Bulletin* 118:430–39.

Hatchett, S., J. Veroff, and E. Douvan. 1995. Marital instability among Black and White couples in early marriage. In B. Tucker and C. Mitchell-Kernan, eds., *The decline of marriage among African Americans.* New York: Russell Sage.

Holmberg, D., T. L. Orbuch, and J. Veroff. 2004. *Thrice told tales: Married couples tell their stories.* Hillsdale, NJ: Erlbaum.

Karney, B. R., and T. N. Bradbury. 1995. The longitudinal course of marital quality and stability: A review of theory, methods, and research. *Psychological Bulletin* 118, no. 1: 3–34.

Majors, R., and J. M. Billson. 1992. *Cool pose: The dilemmas of black manhood in America.* New York: Simon and Schuster.

Murry, V. B., P. A. Brown, G. H. Body, C. E. Cutrona, and R. L. Simons. 2001. Racial discrimination as a moderator of the links among stress, maternal psychological functioning, and family relationships. *Journal of Marriage and Family* 63:915–26.

Oggins, J., J. Veroff, and D. Leber. 1993. Perceptions of marital interaction among black and white newlyweds. *Journal of Personality and Social Psychology* 65, no. 3: 494–511.

Orbuch, T. L., and S. Eyster. 1997. Division of household labor among black couples and white couples. *Social Forces* 76, no. 1: 301–22.

Orbuch, T. L., J. Veroff, H. Hassan, and J. Horrocks. 2002. Who will divorce: A 14-year longitudinal study of married black couples and white couples. *Journal of Social and Personal Relationships* 19, no. 2: 179–202.

Orbuch, T. L., J. Veroff, and D. Holmberg. 1993. Becoming a married couple: The emergence of meaning in the first years of marriage. *Journal of Marriage and the Family* 55:815–26.

Orbuch, T. L., J. Veroff, and A. G. Hunter. 1999. Black couples, white couples: The early years of marriage. In E. M. Hetherington, ed., *Coping with divorce, single parenting, and remarriage,* 29–46. Mahwah, NJ: Lawrence Erlbaum.

Ruvolo, A. P., and J. Veroff. 1997. For better or for worse: Real-ideal discrepancies and the marital well-being of newlyweds. *Journal of Social and Personal Relationships* 14:223–42.

Surra, C. A., M. L. Batchelder, and D. K. Hughes. 1995. Accounts and the demystification of courtship. In M. A. Fitzpatrick and A. L. Vangelisti, eds., *Explaining family interactions,* 112–41. Thousand Oaks, CA: Sage.

Veroff, J. 1999. Commitment in the early years of marriage. In J. M. Adams and W. H. Jones, eds., *Handbook of interpersonal commitment and relationship stability,* 149–62. New York: Kluwer Academic/Plenum.

Veroff, J., L. Chadiha, D. Leber, and L. Sutherland. 1993. Affects and interactions in newlyweds' narratives: Black and white couples compared. *Journal of Narrative and Life History* 3, no. 4: 361–90.

Veroff, J., E. Douvan, and S. J. Hatchett. 1995. *Marital instability: A social and behavioral study of the early years.* Westport, CT: Greenwood.

Veroff, J., L. Sutherland, L. Chadiha, and R. Ortega. 1993a. Newlyweds tell their stories: A narrative method for assessing marital experiences. *Journal of Social and Personal Relationships* 10, no. 3: 437–57.

Veroff, J., L. Sutherland, L. A. Chadiha, and R. M. Ortega. 1993b. Predicting marital quality with narrative assessments of marital experience. *Journal of Marriage and the Family* 55:326–37.

7 | Conducting Stress Research in Black Communities Abroad: Suggestions and Methodological Strategies for South African Studies

Nikeea Copeland-Linder

Research on life stress can make a valuable contribution to the field of mental health in South Africa. Blacks[1] in South Africa have borne a disproportionate share of hardship due to the history of racially oppressive policies in that country. Apartheid has been brought to an official end. However, the residual effects of apartheid are clearly reflected in the current social conditions and stressful circumstances that threaten the well-being of Black South Africans. Yet, very little is known about Black South Africans' experiences of stress and their resources for coping and thriving under difficult conditions.

The relationship between exposure to stress and subsequent mental health problems (e.g., see Kessler 1997 for review) and/or physical health problems (e.g., Fang and Myers 2001) is well documented in mainstream research. The complexity of the relationship between stress and health has been acknowledged by incorporating the role of coping behaviors and resources into stress paradigms. However, mainstream research has been slow to examine the historical, social, and cultural factors that influence stress and coping in specific communities. Research conducted among Blacks in South Africa needs to be informed by the historical, social, and cultural factors unique to this population. The purpose of the present chapter is twofold: (1) to provide a brief overview of the sociocultural context of stress and coping resources among Black South Africans that helps illuminate important factors to address in this population; and (2) to use examples from a study of stress among Black South African women to highlight methodological issues and strategies for conducting culturally appropriate research in South Africa.

The chapter begins with arguing that it is essential for researchers to have a good sense of the social, cultural, and political context in which they are conducting research. Next, a number of stressors and coping resources that may be particularly salient for Black South Africans are discussed, and a brief overview of a study that examined stressors and coping resources is provided. The chapter concludes with lessons learned and recommendations for future stress research with an international focus.

Incorporating Sociocultural Perspectives into Life Stress Research

The "stress process" conceptual model (Pearlin 2010) is a useful framework for understanding life stress phenomena. This paradigm examines interrelationships among three conceptual domains: (1) sources of stress, (2) moderators and/or mediators of stress, and (3) outcomes or manifestations of stress (Pearlin 2010). Specific sources of stress or *stressors* appear in two general forms: life events (discrete changes in life circumstances; acute stressors) and long-term conditions (chronic stressors) that threaten well-being. The extent to which one is affected by stress varies depending on the type and number of stressors and the personal and environmental resources that are available for coping.

Some scholars have underscored the importance of incorporating sociocultural understanding to all areas of life stress frameworks (e.g., Dressler 1991; Gonzales and Kim 1997; Slavin et al. 1991). Sociocultural perspectives are based on the premise that individual, social, and cultural analyses are inseparable (Rogoff, Radziszewska, and Masiello 1995). Dressler (1991) asserted that stress research should be informed by historical as well as social factors. According to Dressler, "The life stress process is seen as historically conditioned and socially produced. What is stressful, what resources persons use to resist what is stressful are seen as the result of specific social processes occurring within a specific historical period" (xiii). A sociocultural perspective on stress phenomena can contribute to a more refined understanding of not only the sources of stress and coping resources but also the research strategies used to examine these issues.

The Sociocultural Context of Stress among Blacks in South Africa: Linking History To Present Conditions

In 1948 the Afrikaner-based National Party came into power in South Africa. This marked the official beginning of apartheid, although some scholars refer to this period as an exacerbation of race-based processes that had been going on for many years (Reader's Digest Association South Africa 1994). Apartheid restricted every area of life for Blacks. The 30 million Blacks were forced to live on 13% of the country's land, while the remaining 87% was reserved for the country's 5 million Whites. The Group Areas Act prevented Blacks from living in or entering areas designated for Whites. Blacks were forcibly removed from land they had inhabited for many years. Some Blacks were relocated to remote areas, while others were relocated to "townships" (Black residential areas on the periphery of cities reserved for Whites). The government designed townships as residential areas for Blacks who were needed for a variety of low-paying jobs in White cities but not allowed to live in those cities (Barbarin and Richter 2001).

Apartheid greatly limited the educational attainment of Blacks. Under the Bantu Education Act, a separate system of education was set up that was designed to prepare Blacks for labor and low-paying service-oriented jobs (Reader's Digest Association of South Africa 1994). The per capita expenditure on education for Blacks was one-seventh of that spent on Whites (Dlamina and Julia 1993). Education for White children was enforced by compulsory education laws and provided free of cost, while education for Black children was optional, and it was not free (Dlamini and Julia 1993). In addition, the lack of schools and qualified teachers made getting an education particularly difficult for Blacks. Education did not become compulsory and free for all South Africans until 1995 (South African Institute of Race Relations 1996). The lack of educational opportunities for Blacks served to perpetuate inequality and stifle economic advancement.

The effects of past race-based policies are reflected in present-day conditions in South Africa. The creation of "reserves" and "homelands" during apartheid impoverished millions of Blacks by excluding them from the industrial economy (Wilson and Ramphele 1989). In postapartheid South Africa, many Blacks continue to face economic hardship (Leibbrandt, Woolard, Finn, and Agent 2010). Approximately 60% of the country's 32 million Blacks live below the poverty line, while only 2% of the country's 5.2 million Whites live in poverty (South African Institute of Race Relations 1996; Keller 2005).

In the past, the government deliberately limited the number of housing units in townships in order to discourage the growth of the Black population in those areas (Barbarin and Richter 2001). Today, the housing shortage is a major problem in South Africa that has resulted in many Blacks living in overcrowded and inadequate housing units (Shepherd 1994). For example, many Blacks live in corrugated iron shacks with no electricity or running water. In 2001, approximately 82% of African households were without water taps inside dwellings compared to 13% of Whites (Statistics South Africa 2004).

Black South Africans have suffered from past and present exploitation in the labor market. Many Blacks, having been denied access to education, are limited to jobs with little opportunity for advancement or decent wages. Many Black women work as domestics, and for many years there was no legal minimum wage for domestic workers in South Africa (Hickson and Strouss 1993). In 2002 a schedule of minimum wages for domestics went into effect (Blaauw and Bothma 2010). However, currently these minimum wages do not provide a decent standard of living for workers (Bureau of Democracy, Human Rights, and Labor 2007).

The migrant labor system on which apartheid was built and maintained was also responsible for separating family members. Because Blacks were only allowed to live near towns as temporary workers, their family members who were not employed in these areas were not allowed to reside with the working family member. Today, the migrant labor system continues to be an integral part of the labor force in South Africa. Women are particularly vulnerable to the effects of the migrant labor system because they are often financially dependent on men who may be absent from the home for long periods of time.

Cultural Coping Resources among Black South Africans

A focus on factors that serve a protective function and contribute to resilience in the face of difficulties has dominated the field of stress research in recent years. Coping resources may function to: (1) eliminate or modify the conditions leading to problems, (2) alter the meaning of the events or situations, making them less stressful in nature, or (3) manage the level of emotional response to stressors (Pearlin and Schooler 1978). Religiosity and spirituality, traditional health care services, and cooperative economic clubs or *stokvels* are resources that play an integral role in the lives of many Blacks in South Africa.

Religiosity and Spirituality

Religion is a significant social force in South Africa. In a large-scale study conducted among Black mothers in the Johannesburg-Soweto metro-

politan area, 73% of the mothers indicated that religion is very important in their household, and 62% reported that prayer is an integral part
of their lives (Barbarin and Richter 2001). Many Africans attribute life
events, mental illness, physical ailments, and good fortune to the works
of ancestors, God, or spirit possession (Behr and Allwood 1995; Swartz
1998; Thomas 1999).

There is considerable complexity and diversity of religious and spiritual beliefs within the Black population in South Africa. Although approximately three-quarters of all Black South Africans report a Christian
affiliation (Prozesky 1995), the mixture of Christianity and adherence to
indigenous religious practices and traditional African beliefs vary
greatly. Prozesky (1995) writes that while there has been a major Chris-
tianizing of Black South Africans, "so too has there been a major African-
izing of Christianity by Black people in this country." Many African
Christians maintain their traditional beliefs such as communicating
with ancestors, honoring ancestors in ceremonies, and regarding them as
guardians. According to Kiernan (1995), some people may "operate a
dual religious system, compartmentalized in order to avoid contradiction. Depending on their needs and the occasion they can appeal separately to God or the ancestors, but it is in times of personal mental and
physical crises that they bring their ancestors into the foreground" (79).

Other Black South African Christians do not compartmentalize their
beliefs because they do not see them in contradiction. Instead, according
to Kiernan (1995), they may see their traditional and Christian beliefs as
"complimentary aspects of a single integrated religious system" in which
the ancestors "may be regarded as lesser agents of the divinity" and "God
may be cast in the role of super-ancestor" (79). There are also Blacks who
are not Christian and adhere only to traditional beliefs; likewise, some
Christian Blacks eschew traditional African religious or spiritual beliefs.

Traditional Health-Care Resources

In South Africa, traditional healers (THs) are widely consulted by both
urban and rural Blacks across social class (Behr and Allwood 1995; Seedat et al. 2009). Traditional healers fall into three broad categories: traditional doctors, diviners, and faith healers. Traditional doctors use herbs
and other medicines to treat mental, physical, and social problems. Diviners act as mediums for communication with ancestors. Faith healers
integrate religious rituals and traditional practices in their approach to
problem solving (Senekal and Stevens 1996). Traditional healers are

likened to medical doctors, psychologists, or counselors (Behr and All-wood 1995; Senekal and Stevens 1996). They may deal with physical ailments as well as family quarrels, marital difficulties, and other stressors. Although Western medicine is widely practiced in South Africa, traditional healers are sought out because they explain the cause and the meaning of problems in terms compatible with the belief system of Africans.

Involvement in Stokvels

The word *stokvel* is used to refer to a variety of traditional cooperative economic clubs established by Black South Africans (Lukhele 1990) that may be important resources for coping with economic hardship. Members of stokvels agree to contribute a fixed amount of money to a general fund on a regular basis (e.g., weekly or monthly) and decide collectively how to allocate the money. Each member may receive allotments on a rotating basis, receive funds in time of need, or take out a loan. Stokvels enable economically disadvantaged people to draw on the pooled resources of the community in order to make major financial purchases.

In addition to its economic role, a stokvel may function as a system of social support. According to Holness (1998), "without fail each [stokvel] meeting began with an earnest and emotionally charged prayer, punctuated with endless 'amens' and followed by a time of personal sharing" (24). The social support function of stokvels has evolved over time (Lukhele 1990). According to Lukhele (1990), Black women made stokvels a more integral part of the community.

> Black women began to use stokvels as a means of protection against police harassment. When a stokvel member was arrested, the others would help with the home and children until the member came out of jail. In this way, stokvels became more than just organizations for the circulation of money and evolved into comprehensive support systems for members in times of hardship. (8)

Stokvels exist in various forms in present-day South Africa. Some stokvels have developed into well-funded organizations that play a role in business development. They continue to be well utilized by Blacks in South Africa (South Africa Institute of Race Relations 1996). Figure 7.1 summarizes stress and coping factors salient in the lives of Black South Africans.

Stressors
 Poverty
 Housing shortages
 Exploitative labor practices
 Family strains, particularly related to migrant labor

Coping Resources
 Religiosity and spirituality
 Traditional health care providers
 Stokvels

Fig. 7.1. Stress and coping factors in the lives of Black South Africans

Methodological Considerations

Project Overview

In conjunction with researchers at the University of Witwatersrand in Johannesburg and staff members at the Medical Research Council of South Africa, a project was undertaken on the stress process among Black women living in a township. The purpose of the project was to examine the relationships among stress, religiosity, depressive symptomatology, and self-reported physical health problems (see Copeland-Linder 2006 for a more complete description of the project). The project took place in 1996 in the township of Soweto near Johannesburg. The sample was obtained by using a systematic random-sampling technique. A sample of 172 women participated in the project (86% of original pool). The ages of the women ranged from 19 to 77 with a mean of 40.4 years. The mean education level of the women was standard 5 (equivalent to a sixth-grade education). The majority of the women were single. Thirty-eight percent of the sample reported that their income was unknown. The median annual household income reported by the remainder of the sample was R10,800, approximately $3,085 (at the time of the study). Structured interviews were conducted in the participants' homes. The women were interviewed about sources of stress, religiosity, mental health, and physical health problems. The women were offered a participation gift of R20 (20 South African dollars, the equivalent of 7 U.S. dollars at the time of the study).

Regression analysis was used to examine relationships between stress, coping, and physical and mental health. Overall, the findings indicate that stress is a significant predictor of self-reported health problems and depressive symptomatology. Religiosity served a protective function, although the protective role of religiosity varied depending on the source of stress, the facet of religiosity, and the outcomes of interest (depressive symptomatology and self-reported physical health problems).

Summary of Methodological Issues

The researcher faced four main methodological challenges while conducting research in South Africa. This section addresses the challenges faced and the strategies used to overcome them.

1. Involve key local assistants.

Involving local people in the research process is critical to the success of international research. Local people may serve as key informants who could be involved in a range of activities including the conceptualization of research constructs, the selection of measures, the implementation of the project, and the dissemination of the results. In stress research, key informants may be particularly helpful in identifying sources of stress and coping resources that are salient in a particular community. In the present study, the first stage of the project involved meeting with South African women who agreed to serve as informants. In addition to being members of the Soweto Township, the two women were experienced interviewers who were employed by the Medical Research Council of South Africa. They were compensated for their time spent on the study. The informants critiqued the preliminary interview protocol and provided valuable information regarding the cultural relevance and appropriateness of certain questions and concepts. In addition, the informants provided opportunities for the researcher to attend religious services and interview a traditional healer in order to gain a better understanding of the complexity of religious phenomena in South Africa.

2. Use data from ethnographic interviews to modify research measures.

One challenge of conducting research among Blacks in South Africa is that there are so few measures of psychological constructs that have been developed specifically for this population; therefore, scale development among Blacks is a research priority. If measures developed on U.S.

populations are used in South Africa, it is imperative that researchers investigate their appropriateness and modify them accordingly. In the present study, preliminary ethnographic interviews were conducted with a sample of 15 women from Soweto (who were not included as respondents in the main study) in order to increase the understanding of common stressors and the utility and subjective meaning of coping resources (e.g., religiosity) among Black South African women. The interview consisted of a variety of open-ended questions related to stressors and religiosity. Data obtained from the interviews were used to modify the quantitative measures used in the larger study. For example, the item related to "serious financial problems" was exchanged for more specific concerns such as "unable to afford necessities for children, such as food or school uniforms" and "unable to pay the bills." Items such as "having to work with a prejudiced coworker" and "having to live in an unsafe neighborhood" were added to the stress scale as these were reported in the preliminary interviews.

3. Address translation issues by using the multilingual interviewer approach.

There are 11 official languages spoken in South Africa. The translation issues that one may encounter vary depending on whether research is conducted in areas where one language is spoken versus areas where many different languages are spoken. In parts of South Africa where the populations are homogeneous in terms of language and ethnic origin, researchers have translated questionnaires into the local language of the area and then back-translated to English. However, in township areas such as Soweto, the labor forces draw on workers from all parts of the country; thus, many languages are spoken. In areas such as this, the practice has developed for multilingual interviewers to work from an English questionnaire and translate the interview into the language that the interviewee chooses (Becklake et al. 1987). During training sessions, multilingual interviewers come to agreement on how questions will be translated into the various languages. According to Becklake and colleagues (1987), "This approach is much preferred by the interviewers who believe it is more likely to yield valid information" (607). The multilingual-interviewer approach has been used in large-scale population surveys in South African townships (e.g., Daponte 1995), as well as other studies conducted in South Africa (e.g., Barbarin and Richter 1999; Dawes et al. 2005).

The absence of "pure" forms of standard languages in Soweto is another reason why some researchers do not translate questionnaires into a standard African language. For example, in Soweto frequent interactions among speakers of many languages have resulted in colloquial speech that is not a pure form of any of the official languages spoken in South Africa (Barbarin and Richter 1999). Thus, interviewers adapt the language of the interview to conform to the dialects and colloquial speech of residents in Soweto.

The multilingual interviewer approach was used in the present study. During interviewer training, two interviewers collaborated to improve the clarity of the interview questions for the Soweto population. The interviewers examined every question and decided how it would be translated into the various languages. The majority of the interviews were conducted in the Zulu, Sotho, or Tswana language.

There is an obvious disadvantage to employing a multilingual interview approach. Despite careful interviewer training, such a method leads to increased opportunities for human error in terms of the consistency in which questions are translated across languages. This method may be particularly problematic for open-ended questionnaires or in-depth ethnographic interviews and less problematic for closed-ended, structured questionnaires. The strengths of the multilingual approach may outweigh its limitations when used in areas such as Soweto where many ethnic groups and languages are represented.

4. Address sampling challenges in township areas.

Understanding the unique structural characteristics of townships is important for sampling. There is a housing shortage in Soweto. The formal housing structure in this area consists primarily of four-room brick structures. As new residents migrated to this area they often made shacks out of corrugated iron and placed them adjacent to or behind these brick structures. The corrugated iron shacks are considered separate housing units; some yards have one or more corrugated iron shacks. In the present study a standard mapping technique was used to obtain a systematic random sample. The neighborhood or zone that was chosen for this study consists of approximately 2,000 households. A map of the zone was obtained, and the households were randomly selected by marking every tenth yard. A yard refers to the plot of land on which a home(s) was built. In the event that no one answered in the target yard, the interviewers were told to go to the yard to the right of the target yard. If no one answered there, they were to go to the yard on the left of the target yard. Because multiple adult women often live in one yard, an additional sampling technique that involved using a table of random numbers was used to select the target woman. The names of all women 19 years or older who lived in the yard were included in the random selection. Once a woman was selected, she was enrolled in the project. Interviews were scheduled at the participant's convenience.

Lessons Learned

1. Be aware of the context in which the research is embedded.
2. Incorporate sociocultural context into study design.
3. Involve key informants in all aspects of the research, from conceptualization to dissemination of findings.
4. Select culturally appropriate measures; use ethnographic data to modify measures and pilot new items.
5. Address translation issues.
6. Attend to sampling challenges and train interviewers accordingly.

Conclusions

The stress process among Black South Africans is an important topic of research. Future research in this area should use longitudinal data, and it should combine qualitative and quantitative measures to allow for more incisive analyses of the processes or mechanisms by which coping resources facilitate well-being. Research in an international context can be challenging but rewarding. The lessons presented in this chapter are meant to inspire others to conduct research in this important area of study.

NOTE

1. In South Africa, the term *Black* is sometimes used to describe a number of different groups. In this chapter, *Black* refers to people of African descent.

REFERENCES

Anderson, N., and S. Marks. 1988. Apartheid and health in the 1980's. *Social Science Medicine* 27:667–68.

Barbarin, O. A., and R. Richter. 1999. Adversity and psychosocial competence of South African children. *American Journal of Orthopsychiatry* 69:319–27.

Barbarin, O., and R. Richter. 2001. *Mandela's Children.* New York: Routledge.

Becklake, M., S. Freeman, C. Goldsmith, P. A. Hessel, R. Mkhwelo, K. Mokoetle, G. Reid, and F. Sitas. 1987. Respiratory questionnaires in occupational studies: Their use in multilingual workforces on the Witwatersrand. *International Journal of Epidemiology* 16:606–11.

Behr, G. M., and C. W. Allwood. 1995. Differences between Western and African models of psychiatric illness. *South African Medical Journal* 85:580–84.

Blaauw, P. F., and L. J. Bothma. 2010. The impact of minimum wages for domestic workers in Bloemfontein, South Africa. *SA Journal of Human Resource Management* 8 (1), Art. #216. http://sajhrm.co.za.

Bureau of Democracy, Human Rights, and Labor. 2007. South Africa. Country Reports on Human Rights Practice 2006. http://www.state.gov/g/drl/rls/hrrpt/2006/78758.htm. Accessed May 11, 2007.

Cock, J. 1987. Trapped workers: Constraints and contradictions experienced by Black women in contemporary South Africa. *Women's Studies International Forum* 10:133–40.

Copeland-Linder, N. 2006. Stress among Black women in a South African township: The protective role of religion. *Journal of Community Psychology* 34:577–99.

Daponte, B. O. 1995. *Results from the 1995 Soweto population survey: Estimates of the population of towns in Soweto.* Sandton: Human Rights Institute of South Africa.

Dawes, A., Z. de Sass Kropiwnicki, Z. Kafaar, and L. Richter. 2005. Corporal punishment of children: A South African National Survey. Save the Children Sweden.

Dlamini, P., and M. Julia. 1993. South African women and the role of social work: wathint' abafazi wathint' imbokodo (provoke women and you've struck a rock). *International Social Work* 36:341–55.

Dressler, W. W. 1991. *Stress and adaptation in the context of culture.* Albany: State University of New York Press.

Fang, C. Y., and H. F. Meyers. 2001. The effects of racial stressors and hostility on cardiovascular reactivity in African American and Caucasian men. *Health Psychology* 20:64–70.

Gonzales, N. A., and L. S. Kim. 1997. Stress and coping in an ethnic minority context. In S. A. Wolchick and I. N. Sandler, eds., *Handbook of children's coping: Linking theory and intervention,* 481–511. New York: Plenum.

Hickson, J., and M. Strouss. 1993. The plight of Black South African domestics: Providing the ultraexploited with psychologically empowering mental health services. *Journal of Black Studies* 24:109–22.

Holness, L. 1998. Women's piety and empowerment: An observer's understanding of the Methodist Women's Manyamo Movement. *Journal of Theology for Southern Africa* 98 (July): 21–31.

Jones, J. 1995. Health care in South Africa: The people's view. *South African Medical Journal* 85:1252.

Keller, E. J. 2005. The challenge of enduring and deepening poverty in the New South Africa. University of California, Los Angeles International Institute website, http://www.international.ucla.edu/article.asp?parentid=24414. Accessed May 9, 2007.

Kessler, R. 1997. The effects of stressful life events on depression. *Annual Review of Psychology* 48:191–214.

Kiernan, J. 1995. African traditional religions in South Africa. In M. Prozesky and J. de Gruchy, eds., *Living faiths in South Africa,* 15–27. New York: St. Martin's Press.

Klugman, B., and R. Weiner. 1992. *Women's health status in South Africa.* Johannesburg: Women's Health Project.

Leibbrandt, M., I. Woolard, A. Finn, and J. Argent. 2010. Trends in South African income distribution and poverty since the fall of Apartheid. OECD Social, Employment and Migration Working Papers, No. 101, OECD Publishing.

Lukhele, A. K. 1990. *Stokvels in South Africa: Informal savings schemes by Blacks for the Black community.* Johannesburg: Amagi Books.

Magwaza, A. S., and K. Bhana. 1991. Stress, locus of control, and psychological status in Black South African migrants. *Journal of Social Psychology* 131: 157–64.

Perlin, L. I. 2010. The life course and the stress process: Some conceptual comparisons. *Journal of Geronotology: Social Sciences* 65B (2): 207–15.

Pearlin, L. I., and C. Schooler. 1978. The structure of coping. *Journal of Health and Social Behavior* 19:2–21.

Prozesky, M. 1995. Introduction. In M. Prozesky and J. de Gruchy, eds., *Living faiths in South Africa,* 1–15. New York: St. Martin's Press.

Reader's Digest Association South Africa. 1994. *Illustrated history of South Africa.* Cape Town: Reader's Digest Association South Africa.

Richter, L. M., D. Yach, N. Cameron, R. D. Griesel, and T. De Wet. 1995. Enrollment into birth to ten: Population and sample characteristics. *Pediatric and Perinatal Epidemiology* 9:109–20.

Rogoff, B., B. Radziszewska, and T. Masiello. 1995. Analysis of developmental processes in sociocultural activity. In L. Martin, K. Nelson, and E. Tobach, eds., *Sociocultural psychology: Theory and practice of doing and knowing,* 125–49. New York: Cambridge University Press.

Seedat, S., D. R. Williams, A. A. Herman, H. Moomal, S. L. Williams, P. B. Jackson, L. Myer, and D. J. Stein. 2009. Mental health service use among South Africans for mood, anxiety and substance use disorders. *South African Medical Journal,* 99:346–52.

Senekel, L., and M. Stevens. 1996. Approaches to care. In M. Goosen and B. Klugman, eds., *The South African women's health book,* 451–70. Cape Town: Oxford University Press.

Shepherd, A. 1994. The task ahead. *Africa Report* 39:38–41.

Slavin, L. A., M. L. Rainer, M. L. McCreary, and K. K. Gowda. 1991. Toward a multicultural model of the stress process. *Journal of Counseling and Development* 70:156–63.

South African Institute of Race Relations. 1996. *South African survey, 1995–1996.* Johannesburg: South African Institute of Race Relations.

Spangenberg, J., and C. Pieterse. 1995. Stressful life events and psychological status in Black South African women. *Journal of Social Psychology* 135:439–45.

Statistics South Africa. 2004. Census 2001—Primary Tables South Africa: Census '96 and '01 compared. Statistics South Africa. www.statssa.gov.za. Accessed May 11, 2007.

Swartz, L. 1998. *Culture and mental health: A Southern African view.* Cape Town: Oxford University Press.

Swartz, L., R. Elk, A. F. Teggin, and L. S. Gillis. 1983. Life events in Xhosas in Cape Town. *Journal of Psychosomatic Research* 27:223–31.

Thomas, L. E. 1999. Under the Canopy: Ritual process and spiritual resilience in South Africa. Columbia: University of South Carolina.

Turner, R., and W. Avison. 2003. Status variations in stress exposure: Implications for the interpretation of research on race, socioeconomic status, and gender. *Journal of Health and Social Behavior* 44, no. 4: 488–505.

Turton, R. W., and B. Chalmers. 1990. Apartheid, stress, and illness: The demographic context of distress reported by South African Africans. *Social Science Medicine* 31:1191–1200.

Wilson, F., and M. Ramphele. 1989. *Uprooting poverty in South Africa.* Cape Town: David Philip.

Yach, D., N. Cameron, N. Padayachee, L. Wagstaff, L. Richter, and S. Fonn. 1991. Birth to ten: Child health in South African in the 1990s. Rationale and methods of a birth cohort study. *Pediatric and Perinatal Epidemiology* 5:211–33.

8 | Methodological Considerations in the Study of Work and Occupations: The Case of Domestic Workers in New York City

Sherrill L. Sellers, Colwick M. Wilson, and Michelle Harris

One of the best examples of the gendered division of labor—the degree to which some tasks in a society are assigned based on one's sex—is domestic labor. Viewed primarily as belonging to the female domain, domestic work has increasingly become associated with low-wage work for immigrant women from the developing world. Recent scholarship on domestic servants has explored some of the political and economic factors that influence this global trend (Hondagneu-Sotelo 2001; Palmer 1989). Hondagneu-Sotelo (2001), for instance, notes that Latinas are the group most likely to perform domestic work in California. She explains the phenomenon as a function of U.S. labor demands, increasing immigration restrictions on Latin American countries that favor service work and transformations in women's understanding of family relationships—most specifically, parenting. Increasingly, U.S. families are able to purchase from domestic servants the work that was once performed by wives and mothers.

While these explanations seem reasonable, can they also describe the conditions that influence other ethnic groups who gravitate toward domestic work in the United States? Specifically, how do English-speaking West Indian domestics in New York make sense of their work experience? How do issues of race, nationality, culture, and gender influence that experience?

These questions become pertinent when one contextualizes the history of black domestic workers in the last century. In the first half of the twentieth century, immigrant women in the North and U.S.-born black women in the South provided a ready supply of low-cost domestic help. In 1900 nearly 44% of employed black women were domestic workers; by 1930 the figure had risen to 54%, and it reached its zenith in 1940 when 60% of native-born black women in the United States worked as domestic servants.

Black women dominated the domestic work occupation until the Civil Rights Act of 1964 opened opportunities for them to leave domestic service. Through the process of occupational succession, immigrant women of color were recruited for undesirable jobs vacated by native-born black women (Foner 2000). With recent demographic shifts toward Latina and Caribbean immigrant women, Romero (2002) suggests that "the racial and ethnic stratification that marked domestic service at the turn of the century persists today."

For instance, in New York, more than 20% of domestic workers were born in the Caribbean (U.S. Census 1992). These numbers account for a sizable subpopulation of mostly black, English-speaking female domestics, hailing from several different countries (e.g., Jamaica, Trinidad, Guyana, Antigua, and Barbados). Without question, one would expect this group of workers to be heterogeneous, including culture, immigration status, and reasons for entry into the field. While understanding and describing these differences is important, placed in the larger context of the occupational experiences of racial minority groups, and the ways in which gender might condition the assessment of occupational achievement, research on domestic work becomes richer and more nuanced.

This chapter integrates theoretical discussions of work and occupations with field experiences of interviewing domestic workers in New York City while employing the values promoted in empowerment research models as a guide to overcoming challenges presented in working with a socially vulnerable population. It provides specific recommendations for recruiting and retaining low-wage workers, a hard-to-reach population, in a research study, some cautionary notes about analysis of survey data, and it addresses the tensions between advocacy and research that may arise when studying hard-to-reach populations.

The chapter is organized into three sections. The first offers a brief review of the classic and contemporary research on domestic work. The second describes the Domestic Workers Project (DWP) that included a survey, in-depth interviews, and focus groups. Three methodological issues are identified—recruitment, sampling, and data-collection strategies. The last section presents a series of challenges and approaches for successfully conducting research with a hard-to-reach population. Each section concludes with a summary and a discussion of methodological implications.

Research Review

In the United States, domestic work rose to national attention in the early 1990s. Zoe Bird, then President Bill Clinton's nominee for attorney general, withdrew her nomination because she had hired undocumented domestic help and failed to pay social security and unemployment insurance. Next, the "British Nanny" captured national attention when parents accused a family caregiver of harsh treatment, which led to the death of their young child. Recently, Linda Chavez, a George W. Bush nominee, withdrew her name from consideration as secretary of labor because, somewhat ironically, she had failed to follow the federal labor laws related to hiring domestic help. National attention focused on the employers; missing from these high-profile stories were the perspectives of the employees—the domestic workers.

Taking a modernity perspective, it was predicted that domestic work as an occupational role would decline and virtually disappear (Coser 1973). Instead, domestic work is a growth occupation. The rise in two-income households created both a need for and sufficient income to afford household help. In port-of-entry cities, such as Los Angeles and New York, middle-class families have come to depend on the low-wage labor of domestic workers to maintain high standards of housework and child care (Palmer 1989).

Although domestic work has not disappeared, its nature has changed. In the past, domestic work tended to be full-time, full-service work. Now, some domestic workers focus exclusively on housework, while others provide only human care work in the form of elder or child care. A substantial minority of domestic workers combine these types of labor. In the United States, there also has been a shift to greater autonomy for some domestic workers. Housework has shifted from live-in work in one employer's home to day work with multiple employers. The shift provides domestic workers with more autonomy, and it makes the employer-employee relationship more transparent (Romero 2002).

Child and adult/elder care has not witnessed the same transformation, since many middle-class families seem to prefer the freedom a live-in nanny provides. Elder care is one of the fastest growing areas of domestic work and is perhaps unique to contemporary U.S. society. Individuals sandwiched between the needs of children and aging parents are spurring demand for this type of labor (Ibarra 2000). Ibarra notes that house-cleaners and human care workers seem to be at opposite ends of the domestic work spectrum, with cleaning being viewed as skilled work, while human care work is devalued as "unskilled, easy, and 'natural.'"

The demography of domestic workers has also changed. During the first half of the previous century, domestic work served as an occupational stepping-stone for white immigrant women into white-collar jobs. They performed domestic work for a short period, then experienced upward mobility by moving on to more prestigious occupations or marrying upwardly mobile white men (Dudden 1983; Katzman 1978). By contrast, until the mid-1960s, black women were trapped in domestic service, sometimes with generation after generation of mothers, daughters, sisters, and nieces working for the same family (Clark-Lewis 1994; Palmer 1989). Specifically, in the post–Civil War South, blacks were the traditional servant caste (Anderson and Bowman 1953). In the early twentieth century, black migrants from the South were also heavily concentrated in domestic work in the North. In fact, domestic service and other related employment such as laundry work and cooking were virtually the only occupations open to black women before World War I.

Currently, immigrant women increasingly perform domestic work. Yet, the experiences of immigrant women of color have been largely ignored in the empirical literature (Chow 1996), although during the last two decades of the twentieth century there was an increase in the number of studies focusing on this group. For example, Romero (2002) and Hondagneu-Sotelo (1994, 2001) studied women of Mexican descent, Chow (1996) examined the distinctiveness of Asian Americans, Glenn (1986) provided analysis of three generations of Japanese women as domestic workers, and Grasmuck and Pessar (1991) explored Dominican immigrants.

Little attention has been paid to the experiences of English-speaking Caribbean domestic workers. One exception is Shellee Colen's (1989) study of West Indian domestic workers in New York. Colen describes how a number of nannies are "working for their green card" and have expectations of moving out of domestic service into white-collar work (1989). It is an empirical question whether domestic work will be a ladder of upward mobility for these workers.

Theoretical and Methodological Implications

From the brief review of research above, several theoretical and methodological implications can be drawn. Significant theorizing on the place of domestic work in the U.S. occupational structure suggested that domestic work would disappear as an occupational role (Wilson and Wilson 2000). Instead, domestic service is a growth occupation and an emerging subject for research. Classic studies examined the experiences of women of European descent, often immigrant or rural women who came to the urban areas to improve their job and family prospects. A central question is whether models developed for European immigrant groups can be applied to the new waves of immigrant women of color who have assumed the domestic worker role. Although recent interest in domestic work has focused on the employers and tax concerns, many of the newer studies use qualitative techniques to examine the experiences of these women of color. A major challenge in conducting this research is how to work with a "hidden" or "hard-to-reach" population. Domestic workers are often socially, economically, and politically vulnerable and may therefore be marginalized from mainstream middle-class structures and resources. These factors present unique methodological challenges, many of which stem from the social distance between researchers and participants. The study described below used an empowerment research model that sought to acknowledge and address the power differential. In empowerment research, participants are viewed as active collaborators who should benefit from the research at least as much as the research team (Small 1995). With an empowerment approach, we found it possible to conduct methodologically rigorous research while also providing support for domestic workers' advocacy efforts.

To illustrate some of the challenges faced and lessons learned in successfully gaining access to and information about the experiences of immigrant women of color who were employed in domestic service, we share our experiences with the Domestic Workers Project principal investigator, Dr. Colwick Wilson.

Description of the Study

The Domestic Workers Project (DWP) occurred in two phases. The first phase involved a survey with mostly closed-ended questions. The second phase involved in-depth interviews and focus groups. This multimethod strategy aimed to capitalize on existing qualitative work while extending analysis of survey data. In this way, the study was able to examine not only standard objective measures of work and occupation but also questions of meaning and interpretation of the work experiences of English-speaking domestics.

In Phase I of the DWP, 102 English-speaking domestic workers living in the New York City area participated in face-to-face interviews. Respondents originated from seven Caribbean countries, including

Trinidad and Tobago, Jamaica, St. Lucia, and Guyana. (We note that Guyana is geographically located in South America; however, its linguistic, cultural, ethnic, and sociopolitical history is tied to the English-speaking Caribbean region.)

Most of the sample had a high school education (53%); over half (56%) were single, and 57% of the respondents were live-in workers. Respondents reported that the typical day included washing and ironing (88%), making beds (86%), cleaning the house (85%), and cooking (60%). Employers were often white married couples with more than one child. The average weekly salary was $276, ranging from a low of $70 to a high of $440 per week. Respondents reported working an average of 10 hours a day, 5 days a week. Compared to day workers, live-in workers reported slightly longer workdays and were more likely to be undocumented. Slightly over two-thirds of the respondents felt satisfied with their jobs; however, over 78% also reported that they would prefer a different type of job in the future.

Phase II involved in-depth interviews and focus groups with 40 participants from Phase I. Several themes were apparent in this section of the study. Participants in this phase of the study described relationships to employers that could only be hinted at in the structured interviews. For example, one recurring theme was the tension around "the list." Although most participants expressed a level of job satisfaction, employers' efforts to control the worker and her work environment through listing the day's tasks was a source of considerable irritation. Domestic work was viewed by those who performed it as skilled labor such that workers should have the autonomy to organize the work as they deemed necessary.

Phase I: Face-to-Face Survey

Recruitment and Sampling

Recruitment and sampling are perhaps the biggest challenges to research with hard-to-reach populations. Jarrett (1993) notes that personal contact with members of the community is an important tool. She suggests that impersonal strategies, particularly from individuals outside the community, are less likely to be successful in gaining access. Individuals considered to be from outside the community may be perceived as lacking legitimacy. Further, potential participants may be concerned that the researcher will devalue or exploit them for personal gain.

To encourage participation in the DWP, the research team asked church and community organization members, friends, colleagues, and relatives who knew domestic workers to serve as the initial contact between the interviewer and the interviewee. Whenever a contact provided information about a domestic worker, the principal investigator systematically requested that the contact person make a formal, face-to-face introduction of the prospective interviewee to one of the researchers involved in the project. However, this strategy was very time-consuming and threatened to extend the field period; therefore, telephone introductions were implemented. Whether by phone or face-to-face, the key to reaching domestic workers, and perhaps other hard-to-reach populations, is to establish a network of contact people to do formal introductions. This strategy helps to establish credibility and to build trust between the researchers and prospective respondents. It is also important to describe the potential benefits, direct or indirect, of participation in the research.

Although meetings were initiated by the research team, the respondent directed the content and flow of the formal introduction. This is consistent with the emphasis that participatory research places on empowering research participants and allowing them to be actively involved in shaping the research process (Small 1995). In the case of the DWP, this initial meeting facilitated relationship building by offering potential participants the opportunity to voice their concerns about how their information and experiences might be used and to have these concerns addressed by the researchers. The vast majority of potential interviewees asked specific questions about confidentiality. Questions included: Who gets the study information? How public will the results be? How might the interview and resulting manuscripts affect their employment? Where will the interview be conducted? Who will be present at the time of the interview? Attending to these concerns was a necessary and important step in gaining permission to conduct the interview.

Data Collection

Most of the interviews occurred in a respondent's home. Respondents coordinated a time when two or three workers could be interviewed at the same location. Each participant was interviewed individually while the others occupied themselves in unrelated activities, such as cooking, eating, or watching television. While it was requested that only the interviewees be a part of the interview, the husband and other family members or friends were often present and in a few cases attempted to influence participants' responses. In later interviews, the researchers delicately requested that family members not be present during the interview. Other interviews occurred at a community center that focused on adjustment issues of English-speaking Caribbean immigrants. The remaining interviews were conducted in churches where study participants were members.

Workers in low-wage occupations may be more difficult to reach than workers in other occupations. In the case of the DWP, structural factors such as work hours and place of employment presented substantial barriers to participation. It was particularly important to be sensitive to these matters in order to increase participants' willingness and ability to participate. For the researchers, the data collection process required substantial personal contact at varied hours. Almost 60% of the sample had live-in positions, so interviews had to be conducted on weekends or very early on Mondays before the workweek began. Weekends provide cherished time for the workers to be with family or friends and at church activities, which presented significant obstacles to the scheduling of interviews. Understandably, few were willing to be interviewed during their weekday lunch break.

Respondents were also hesitant to be interviewed because the principal investigator for the project, who was also the primary interviewer, was male while all of the respondents were women. Both the PI and respondents had some initial concerns about the gender differences. For participants, the specific concerns were related to employer ire. The workers would not allow the interviewer to walk with them on their way to work for fear that their employer or a friend of their employer might see the two together and assume an ongoing liaison. The PI was conscious of employee vulnerability and was also concerned that participants would shy away from more gender-specific questions, such as sexual harassment, with a male interviewer. A number of strategies were employed to help minimize the negative impact of these problems. These included employing female interviewers, gender matching of interviewer with interviewee when requested, and interviewing participants in the homes of friends and confidants.

It is difficult to gather survey data from those engaged in domestic work activities (workers and their employers) in part because information is often provided only to individuals close to those involved (Richardson 1999). In DWP, additional participants were sampled using a snowball technique. At the end of each interview, the interviewers asked respondents for no more than five names of women who might be interested in participating in the study. The PI randomly selected from the five names to lessen the chances of the sample clustering along family, kinship, or friendship lines. The randomizing served to reassure respondents that the study was nonselective in its recruitment.

A drawback of the snowball sampling approach is that it is very time consuming and labor intensive. However, this field strategy offers considerable advantages in gaining access to potential participants. The interviewer was able to explain the rationale of the survey and to begin establishing rapport with the potential respondent. The formation of a trusting relationship between the respondent and the interviewer increased the respondent's willingness to disclose information and allowed her to be confident that her responses would remain confidential. In addition, the research team's prior experience in the community helped to reduce respondents' distrust and fear of reprisal from employers and/or governmental authorities. For example, one of the interviewers was a community leader who had worked extensively with the English-speaking West Indian community and was known by some of the participants or by their family members and/or friends. Another interviewer was tied to the religious community of immigrant West Indians in New York City and was an invaluable resource in accessing potential respondents from churches in the area. Also, the PI was connected to one of the major universities in New York, and this stamp of approval provided another dimension of credibility and heightened perceptions of the importance of the study.

In the first phase of the DWP, no incentives were provided to the participants, and it appeared incentives were not necessary. Because of the focus on building a trusting relationship between researcher and participant, as well as the media attention on issues of domestic work (e.g., Zoe Bird), participants were very interested in describing their experiences as domestic workers. Several participants were surprised and pleased that a professional researcher was interested in their stories.

Unlike prior research, the DWP adopted a quantitative approach in the first phase. The survey primarily contained closed-ended questions, many from standard measures of job satisfaction, well-being, and occupational stress. It took between 90 minutes and 2 hours to administer; 102 individuals completed the surveys. An open-ended question concluded the questionnaire by asking, "If there was anything else you would like mentioned, please write it below." Slightly over 30% of respondents added comments.

At the height of the data collection process the interviewing team comprised three female interviewers and two male interviewers, including the PI. Concern about the influence gender might have on the interview led to the addition of an item that assessed impact of interviewer's gender. Respondents were asked "Did it make a difference that I was a (man/woman)?" Very few said yes. When the interviewer was male, it appeared that a few respondents had some hesitations early in the interview, but this discomfort dissipated midway through the interview.

Although each respondent answered that she felt comfortable with a male interviewer, and initial responses to the question suggested that it did not make a difference, analysis of open-ended questions indicated that gender of the interviewer did matter. When the interviewer was female, respondents were more likely to tell stories, describe an experience in vivid detail, and talk openly about the pain of being away from their own children. Female interviewers, therefore, seemed to elicit richer qualitative responses.

In the quantitative phase of DWP, several lessons were learned that are displayed in the box.

Lessons Learned from the Quantitative Phase of DWP

- Establish a network of contact people to do formal introductions.
- Describe the direct and indirect benefits of participation in the project.
- Be prepared to address issues of confidentiality.
- Be aware of time constraints potential participants may face.
- Consider matching on race and gender. Gender concordance was important in the qualitative component of the DWP.

Phase II: Focus Groups

Participants were asked if they would be interested in follow-up discussions, and the vast majority of respondents (97 out of 102) agreed to participate in in-depth interviews and focus groups. This mixed-methods approach was selected to further clarify the information received from the face-to-face survey interviews. The Phase II follow-up discussions were conducted six months after completing the survey. After the respondents from Phase I were contacted and verbal consent was given, participants were selected from that group based on age, length of stay in the United States, length of time working as a domestic worker, and formal level of education. Forty-six participants were selected from the 97 who expressed their willingness to be interviewed a second time. Because focus groups drew from the same pool as the survey, it was felt that a monetary thank-you would be appropriate. Focus group participants and key informants each received $20 for their involvement in this phase of the study. Further, in order to remove some of the potential barriers to participating in the in-depth interviews, respondents were given mileage or transportation reimbursement, child care was provided if necessary, and snacks for the respondent and their children were available.

On average, the focus groups and in-depth interviews ranged from one to three hours. Many participants saw the research as an opportunity to gather with friends who were also domestic workers. Often participants remained after the formal group process was completed to socialize and share experiences of life and work as immigrant domestic workers. Invariably, respondents reported making contact with their friends prior to attending the focus groups to ascertain who was attending and to clarify the process associated with their selection. The atmosphere was partylike, yet researchers had no difficulty collecting valuable data. In fact, the relaxed atmosphere seemed to allow discussion to flow freely.

Methodological Challenges and Lessons Learned

Conducting research with socially vulnerable populations brings a variety of challenges. This brief description of DWP suggests several methodological issues that researchers may face. What follows is a discussion of the most important lessons learned as a result of this project.

Sampling: Be Cognizant of the Structural Constraints and Unique Barriers to Participation

Sampling techniques (such as snowballing) that target these populations may be less conducive to generalization but are necessary in order to reach and provide information on underresearched groups. Participation in a study requires effort on the part of participants that may not be readily apparent to researchers. There are a number of barriers to participation including social distance between interviewer and respondent, fear of deportation, encroaching on the limited time off, and the possibility of employer displeasure. In addition, recent events have placed immigrants and undocumented workers in the national spotlight. The heightened scrutiny and perpetual fear of governmental authorities makes recruitment more difficult. Researchers must be aware of these constraints and barriers and develop strategies, such as those used in the DWP, to deal with them.

Recruitment: Establish Trust and Assure Confidentiality

Perhaps more than ever before, researchers must take care in entering communities. Community contacts are essential to recruitment efforts. Researchers must emphasize forming relationships with respondents that foster trust and encourage participants to take an active role in shaping the research. Vulnerable populations may be weary of being exploited for someone else's professional gain, but if researchers are clear in communicating their collaborative intent and ensuring that the research will be used to directly and/or indirectly benefit the respondents they may be more likely to agree to participate.

Certificates of Confidentiality from the government may also facilitate recruitment. A Certificate of Confidentiality aims to protect the privacy of the participants and is based on a federal law that states a person may not be compelled in any federal, state, or local civil, criminal, administrative, legislative, or other proceedings to identify the subjects of research covered by the certificate. Thus, the certificates help minimize risks to participants by adding an additional level of protection for maintaining confidentiality of private information, especially important if a researcher seeks to obtain identifying information that could harm participants.

Data Collection: Mode Matters

Mail surveys and telephone interviews are often less costly than face-to-face interviewing. However, the face-to-face mode has the added benefit of encouraging participation by building trust between researcher and participant. Although some research suggests that in face-to-face structured interviews participants may be less likely to report undesirable attitudes or behaviors (Krysan et al. 1994), it is possible to minimize this threat to validity. Paper-and-pencil self-administered questionnaires or computer-assisted self-interviewing technology have helped to decrease the likelihood of social desirability bias (Aquilino 1994; Turner et al. 1998) by increasing participants' perception of anonymity on sensitive topics. We found that initial efforts to build trust and establish rapport were effective at reducing the likelihood of socially desirable responses.

Data Collection: Use a Short Time Frame between Data Collections to Reduce Sample Attrition

Retention of hard-to-reach populations may be facilitated by limiting the time between data collection activities, maintaining contact with respondents, and building trust within the community from which participants are drawn. Cultivating these relationships will take time, yet the reward of rich data and positive community relations are worth the effort.

Interviewers: Rapport Building Is Essential

The DWP faced two interviewer-related challenges—gender differences between interviewers and respondents, and participants' initial distrust of the research enterprise. Interviewers were trained not to go straight into the interview. Instead, in their initial introductions, interviewers began with small "but important" talk. This discussion was guided by the respondents and often centered on the study. The two reoccurring themes were legal status and confidentiality. Participants were interested in who would review information and whether employers in particular had access to the interview data. This small important talk also highlighted the limited knowledge we have on how respondents understand issues related to informed consent.

Related to DWP specifically, and to hard-to-reach populations more generally, what became increasingly important was the interviewers' entrée into the community. This stamp of approval from known community members and friends was perceived as more legitimate than the remote "authority" of an institutional review board. However, institutional permission and documentation were viewed as authentication of the credibility of the interviewers. While institutional consent through IRB is mandatory and necessary, participants in this study were more concerned about issues of trust as they relate to the interviewers.

Interviewer: Race and/or Gender Concordance May Be Important

There is considerable discussion about the importance of matching interviewer and participant on race and/or gender (Hatchett et al. 2000). Findings from DWP seem to indicate that matching on gender makes a difference in the richness of open-ended responses but had little impact on the closed-ended survey.

Questionnaire Design: Standard Measures of Occupational Experience May Not Be Adequate

When investigating work and occupational experiences of U.S.-born and immigrant blacks, standard measures of occupations may require modification. For example, in order to generate occupational rankings Dressler (1988) and Parker and Kleiner (1966) replaced published rankings of occupations with rankings developed by informants drawn from the black community. Because their occupational opportunities have been severely restricted, it is quite possible that black Americans have devised other standards by which to measure a "good job" (Kirschenman and Neckerman 1991). Employment discrimination may foster an attitude toward occupations that may be distinctive from that of the majority group. For instance, Higginbotham (1985) suggests that black parents often taught their children that "there is no such thing as a lowly occupation," and "do the best you can, whatever you do." It is possible that because racial discrimination restricts occupational spheres, self-worth may be less tied to type of employment (Sellers 2000).

Mixed Methods: Use Both Quantitative and Qualitative Data

Mixed methodological strategies offer a more comprehensive picture of workers' experiences, and careful consideration of the order of data collection may yield more nuanced findings. Much of the prior research on domestic workers has used qualitative techniques. The DWP reversed this tradition, beginning with a quantitative survey before conducting in-depth interviews and focus groups. This approach enabled researchers to compare and contrast results from the more structured interviews with the nonstructured, free-flowing, open-ended discussions characteristic of the qualitative design. Participants appeared more willing to share their experiences during the qualitative interviews since they had developed a positive relationship in the earlier survey interview.

Incentives: Careful Consideration of What Is Appropriate Is Necessary

The role of incentives has become somewhat controversial; some institutional review boards have expressed concern that high incentives may be coercive. Studies with hard-to-reach populations may be especially vulnerable to this concern, since many of these populations are economically vulnerable. The DWP found that incentives were not necessary but provided an important thank-you to the participants in the second phase of the study. Monetary incentives may be less appropriate than gift baskets, phone cards, or other personalized items. Somewhat paradoxically, because these populations have received limited research attention, incentives may be unnecessary and may dampen participants' enthusiasm as the incentive may be viewed as "payment" for participation. Nonetheless, it is essential to find ways to acknowledge participants' time and effort. The key lessons learned are summarized in the box.

Summary of Lessons Learned

Sampling and Recruitment
- Be aware that establishing trust is of paramount importance.
- Be cognizant of unique barriers to participation.
Data Collection
- Know the strengths and limitations of chosen mode.
- Reduce attrition through short time frames between collections.
- Carefully consider incentives.
- Review standard survey items for cultural appropriateness.
Interviewers
- Consider matching on respondent race and gender.
- Establish rapport via small "but important" talk.

Conclusions

Housework is intensely private, yet it is linked to larger public issues, social-structural tensions, and wider social, economic, and cultural pressures (Cash, Sellers, and Claps 2005; Hochschild 1989). Paid domestic work draws immigrant women into the labor market and transforms the home into a place of work. Throughout U.S. history, the relationship between race, gender, and work has been contentious, fraught with stereotypes, contradictions, and conflicts (Amott and Matthaei 1991; Sellers 2000). Domestic work is at the intersection of capitalism, immigration, gender, and race. For the most part, U.S. employers of domestic workers have been wealthy or middle class, white, and female. Domestic workers have predominantly been women from socially marginalized or oppressed groups. Researchers who study domestic work must grapple with these divided, often competing, interests.

The epistemological foundation of most social science research has been logical positivism, a school of thought that maintains that knowledge is derived from observation and logical inference (Popper 1965). The principle of objectivity, of standing away from the human subject, presents special challenges to researchers collaborating with hard-to-reach populations. These populations are often hard-to-reach because they are marginalized from mainstream (and usually middle class) systems and structures. The ideal of a neutral, disengaged investigator may need to give way to alternative research paradigms and mixed modes of research. Balancing research requirements and advocacy/intervention needs is a particular challenge when studying vulnerable populations. DPW demonstrates one model for accomplishing this important goal. We found it possible to combine rigorous academic research while supporting advocacy efforts on the part of domestic workers in New York. Our research stance was that it is potentially unethical to conduct research "on" a vulnerable population without addressing the real-life circumstances of the participants. Our work has been used to inform the ongoing advocacy efforts of Domestic Workers United, a research and advocacy organization based in New York.

A central tenet of action-oriented research is its emphasis on empowering people who participate in the studies rather than solely benefiting researchers and academics. This applies to the entire research process from the study's conception and design to the dissemination of findings. For instance, Domestic Workers United has tapped into the research expertise of DWP. As such, the Domestic Workers United report was guided not only by the notion of involvement on the part of domestic workers themselves in the research project but also by the intent that the participants should benefit from the findings at least as much as the researchers do (Small 1995). Research can lead to policy and program interventions. For researchers, it is important to develop principles that connect one's research with policy and practice (Weiss 1986). Principles to consider are outlined in the box.

Principles for Connecting Research to Policy and Practice

- Develop a clear understanding among all involved in the research process as to what the research can and cannot provide.
- Make strategic judgments about where to publish research findings.
- Be clear about the distinction between action and research.
- Note to all involved in the study that advocacy may not be the primary function of the research.
- Recognize that fair and balanced reporting of research findings may go a long way to improving conditions.

This chapter has briefly examined one aspect of work and occupation. Other issues such as occupational stress, career mobility, labor force participation, and impact of globalization on work (Parrenas 2001) require additional study and may be informed by the methodological issues raised in this chapter. Research with hard-to-reach populations (such as domestic workers) presents important methodological challenges and opportunities. The DWP is one example of efforts to expand the research that examines work experiences and occupational achievements of people of color in more nuanced, culturally appropriate ways.

REFERENCES

Amott, T., and J. Matthaei. 1991. *Race, gender, and work: A multicultural economic history of women in the United States.* Boston: South End Press.

Anderson, C. A., and M. J. Bowman. 1953. The vanishing servant and the contemporary status system of the American South. *American Journal of Sociology* 59:215–230.

Aquilino, W. 1994. Interview mode effects in surveys of alcohol and drug use: A field experiment. *Public Opinion Quarterly* 58:210–40.

Cash, S., S. L. Sellers, and M. Claps. 2005. Money equals time: Influence of poverty status on hours spent doing housework. *Journal of Poverty* 9, no. 2: 89–109.

Chow, E. N. 1996. Family, economy, and the state: A legacy of struggle for Chinese American women. In S. Pedraza and R. G. Rumbaut, eds., *Origins and destinies: Immigration, race, and ethnicity in America,* 110–24. New York: Wadsworth.

Clark-Lewis, E. 1994. *Living-in, Living-out: African-American domestics in Washington, DC, 1900–1940.* Washington, DC: Smithsonian Institution Press.

Colen, S. 1989. Just a little respect: West Indian domestic workers in New York City. In E. Chaney and M. Garcia Castro, eds., *Muchachas no more: Household workers in Latin America and the Caribbean,* 171–94. Philadelphia: Temple University Press.

Coser, L. 1973. Servants: The obsolescence of an occupational role. *Social Forces* 52:31–40.

Domestic Workers United. 2006. http://www.domesticworkersunited.org/home iswheretheworkis.pdf. Accessed May 4.

Dressler, W. 1988. Social consistency and psychological distress. *Journal of Health and Social Behavior* 29:79–91.

Dudden, F. 1983. *Serving women: Household service in the nineteenth-century America.* Middletown, CT: Wesleyan University Press.

Foner, N. 2000. *From Ellis Island to JFK: New York's two great waves of immigration.* New York: Russell Sage.

Glenn, E. N. 1986. *Issei, Nisei, war bride: Three generations of Japanese American women in domestic service.* Philadelphia: Temple University Press.

Grasmuck, S., and P. R. Pessar. 1991. *Between two islands: Dominican international migration.* Los Angeles: University of California Press.

Hatchett, B., K. Holmes, D. Durna, and C. Davis. 2000. African Americans and research participation: The recruitment process. *Journal of Black Studies* 30, no. 5: 664–75.

Higginbotham, E. 1985. Race and class barriers to black women's college attendance. *Journal of Ethnic Studies* 13:89–107.

Hochschild, A. 1989. *The second shift.* New York: Avon Books.

Hondagneu-Sotelo, P. 1994. Regulating the unregulated? Domestic workers' social networks. *Social Problems* 41:50–64.

Hondagneu-Sotelo, P. 2001. *Domestica: Immigrant workers cleaning and caring in the shadows of affluence.* Berkeley: University of California Press.

Ibarra, M. 2000. Mexican immigrant women and the new domestic labor. *Human Organization* 54, no. 4: 456–64.

Jarrett, R. L. 1993. Focus group interviewing with low-income minority populations: A research experience. In D. L. Morgan, ed., *Successful focus groups: Advancing the state of the art,* 184–201. Newbury Park, CA: Sage.

Katzman, D. 1978. *Seven days a week: Women and domestic service in industrializing America.* New York: Oxford University Press.

Kirschenman, J., and K. M. Neckerman. 1991. We'd love to hire them, but . . . : The meaning of race for employers. In C. Jencks and P. E. Peterson, eds., *The urban underclass.* Washington, DC: Brookings Institution.

Krysan, M., H. Schuman, L. Scott, and P. Beatty. 1994. Response rates and response context in mail versus face-to-face surveys. *Public Opinion Quarterly* 58, no. 3: 381–99.

Palmer, P. 1989. *Domesticity and dirt: Housewives and domestic servants in the United States, 1920–1989.* Philadelphia: Temple University Press.

Parker, S., and R. Kleiner. 1966. *Mental illness in the urban Negro community.* New York: Free Press.

Parrenas, R. 2001. *Servants of globalization: Women, migration, and domestic work.* Palo Alto, CA: Stanford University Press.

Popper, K. 1965. *Conjectures and refutations: The growth of scientific knowledge.* New York: Harper and Row.

Richardson, C. 1999. *Batos, bolillos, pochos, and pelados: Class and culture on the south Texas border.* Austin: University of Texas Press.

Romero, M. 2002. *Maid in the USA.* New York: Routledge.

Sellers, S. 2000. *Dreams delivered, dreams deferred: The mental and physical health consequences of social mobility among black American men and women.* Unpublished doctoral dissertation, University of Michigan, Ann Arbor.

Small, S. A. 1995. Action-oriented research: Models and methods. *Journal of Marriage and the Family* 57:941–55.

Turner, C. F., L. Ku, S. M. Rogers, J. H. Lindberg, J. H. Pleck, and F. L. Sonenstein. 1998. Adolescent sexual behavior, drug use, and violence: Increased reporting with computer-assisted survey technology. *Science* 280:867–73.

U.S. Census Bureau. 1992. *Statistical abstracts of the United States, 1990.* Washington, DC: U.S. Census Bureau.

Weiss, C. 1986. The circuitry of enlightenment: Diffusion of social science research to policymakers. *Science Communication* 8, no. 2: 274–81.

Wilson, C., and L. Wilson. 2000. Domestic work in the United States of America: Past perspectives and future directions. *African American Research Perspectives* 6, no. 1. Retrieved April 20, 2007, from http://www.rcgd.isr.umich.edu/prba/perspectives/Winter2000/cwilson.pdf.

PART III | Strategies for Obtaining National Data
with African Americans, Caribbean
Blacks, and Black Churches

9 | The National Survey of American Life: Innovations in Research with Ethnically Diverse Black Samples

James S. Jackson, Cleopatra Howard Caldwell,
Myriam Torres, and Julie Sweetman

The National Survey of American Life (NSAL) is part of the National Institute of Mental Health's (NIMH) Collaborative Psychiatric Epidemiology Surveys (CPES) initiative that included three major nationally representative studies—the NSAL, the National Comorbidity Survey Replication (NCS-R), and the National Latino and Asian American Study (NLAAS). These studies were designed to examine the mental health status of diverse racial and ethnic groups living in the United States. The NSAL focused on black Americans, with a unique feature being specific attention to ethnic diversity within the black community. It includes samples of African Americans and Caribbean black adults and adolescents.

The NSAL builds upon the National Survey of Black Americans (NSBA), a study initiated over 25 years ago at the Institute for Social Research, University of Michigan. The NSBA was launched in 1979 as the first national probability sample of more than 2,000 noninstitutionalized black adults living in the continental United States (Jackson 1991). It is recognized as a landmark study that provided both conceptual and methodological innovations for conducting research in black communities. The NSBA has served as a fertile training ground for numerous scholars and is the cornerstone study of the Program for Research on Black Americans (PRBA). The book *Life in Black America* (Jackson 1991) is a compilation of findings from this study.

Three waves of longitudinal data were collected with the original NSBA participants in 1989, 1997, and 1999. In addition, a study of multigenerational families focusing on younger and older generations linked to the original NSBA participants was conducted in a 1979–80 study called the Three Generation National Survey of Black American Families (Jackson and Hatchett 1986). This study was designed to comprehensively assess the nature of relationships across multiple adjacent generations within black families (Taylor, Chatters, and Jackson 1993).

All of these data sets, including the CPES data sets, are available for public use through the Inter-University Consortium for Political and Social Research (ICPSR)[1] at the Institute for Social Research. ICPSR is the world's largest computerized social science data archive.

From a methodological perspective, the NSBA contributed to a better understanding of how to identify a national black sample, construct research questions with attention to cultural context and meaning, engage in skillful data-collection techniques with blacks, and provide strategies for interpreting results from a cultural perspective. This methodological information has been published in numerous documents over the years (Caldwell et al. 1999; Jackson 1991; Jackson and Hatchett 1986; Jackson, Tucker, and Bowman 1982). A wealth of substantive scholarly publications also has been produced based on NSBA data sets. A copy of the list of publications is available at http://www.umich.edu.isr/rcgd/prba.

One substantive focus in the NSBA was the mental health of black Americans. Over the years a number of advances have been made in approaches to studying this topic as well as in other areas relevant to blacks, such as discrimination and health. In addition, the importance of immigration among blacks cannot be ignored as a critical factor in American life. Consequently, the NSAL was conducted from February 2001 to June 2003 to build on our experience with the NSBA to broaden the scientific understanding of *Life in Black America in the 21st Century* with particular emphasis on risk and protective factors associated with mental health and well-being among ethnically diverse groups of black people. This chapter focuses on several conceptual and methodological innovations in the NSAL as a way of sharing lessons learned in conducting a study with nationally representative samples of African American and Caribbean black populations across multiple generations living in the United States. It also describes how we were able to link family members in a follow-up study abroad. We specifically focus on the significance of examining ethnic diversity in the black community, the NSAL sampling strategy and sample, the use of random probes with diverse ethnic groups, the use of supplemental surveys as a strategy for obtaining additional data, and a way to identify multigenerational samples.

Ethnic Diversity in the Black Community

Although important commonalities exist, there are considerable ethnic variations within the black population. Blacks from the Caribbean, for example, constitute the largest subgroup of black immigrants in the United States, accounting for two-thirds of the more than 2 million black immigrants in the country (Rong and Brown 2002). The Caribbean black population from English-speaking islands grew substantially throughout the twentieth century after the Immigration Act of 1965 ended the quota systems that previously limited levels of immigration to the United States from non-European countries (Jacobson 1998). Despite this diversity, few studies of black mental health address the mental-health consequences of within-group ethnic variation.

From a theoretical perspective, Warner and Srole's straight-line assimilation theory of European immigrants is frequently used to explain economic and mental health outcomes for immigrants. It assumes that immigrant groups enter this country at an economic and psychological disadvantage, but the longer they stay, the more they will assimilate and eventually gain upward economic mobility and better psychological adjustment (Harker 2001; Waters 1994). Previous studies, however, indicate no differences between immigrant and native born individuals when demographic factors are controlled (Harker 2001; Vega and Rumbaut 1991). This pattern of economic mobility and psychological adjustment has not been consistent among black immigrants.

Other theories have been offered to account for the often downward social mobility and psychological distress observed among black immigrants (e.g., segmented assimilation, Portes and Rumbaut 1996; intergenerational conflict, Waters 1994, 1996). According to Rong and Brown (2002), black immigrants can be characterized as either "triple disadvantaged" or the "model Black." The triple disadvantaged assumes the burden of race, origin, and socioeconomic status of being black in America. That is, they face the additional challenges of the blocked economic opportunity structure (e.g., lack of jobs, limited job mobility, low wages), which has implications for their living conditions (e.g., residential segregation) and challenges regarding their psychological well-being based on experiences with discrimination and racism just as native African Americans. In contrast, the model black comes to this country with advantages. For example, under the immigration selection process after 1965, certain careers were privileged for entry into the country (e.g., Caribbean nurses), which gave them middle-class status. These blacks were viewed by whites as model blacks because they were able to achieve socioeconomic and educational success quickly (Waters 1994). All of these issues have implications for ethnic identification, parent-child relationships, and the adaptation of subsequent generations of immigrant children. Interestingly, most available studies suggest expectations for similar or better psychological well-being for nonwhite immigrant adolescents than for native-born adolescents, regardless of demographic background (Harker 2001).

While African Americans have been the primary focus of most racial stress research, studies that include ethnically diverse black samples typically do not distinguish between ethnic groups (Tseng 2004). There is evidence to suggest that the way in which Caribbean blacks appraise and cope with the stress of racial discrimination varies by their level of identification with their ethnic heritage as well as their level of assimilation into American society (Waters 1994). Studies that assess Caribbean blacks' experiences with racial discrimination show that African Americans and Caribbean blacks perceive racial discrimination fundamentally differently because most Caribbean blacks immigrate from countries where social class matters more than race (Rong and Preissle 1998).

In examining gender differences in perceptions of racial discrimination, researchers have argued that not all members of subordinate groups are equally targeted. Sidanius and Pratto (1999) suggest that in a racial hierarchy, subordinate males as opposed to females will be the primary targets of discrimination. Thus, African American and Caribbean black males may perceive more incidents of racial discrimination than their female counterparts. Yet, previous findings regarding gender differences are mixed.

This brief review has demonstrated the significance of examining ethnic and gender variations within the black population. It should be noted that the limited available research on the mental health of ethnically diverse black populations was an impetus for conducting the NSAL.

NSAL Samples: Strengths and Challenges of Complex Survey Designs

The NSAL, which is a nationwide survey of the African American, Caribbean black, and non-Hispanic white adult populations, is based on a stratified, multistage area probability sample of the noninstitutionalized civilian population in the 48 contiguous states. It provides a comprehensive study of black Americans with an emphasis on mental disorders, stressors, and risk/resilient factors (Jackson et al. 2004). A national probability sample of households was drawn based on adult population estimates and power calculations for detecting differences in African

American and Caribbean black adult samples, using the African American sample as the primary core sampling base for the study. Size measures based on African American occupied housing units, rather than total occupied housing units in the United States, were used for sample selection of 64 primary sampling units (PSUs). A total of 56 of these primary areas overlap substantially with existing Survey Research Center national sample primary areas. The remaining eight primary areas were chosen from the Southern region of the country to represent African Americans proportionally according to their national distribution. From these 64 PSUs, 456 segments (blocks or block groups) were selected with probabilities proportional to the size of the African American population (Jackson et al. 2004). Caribbean black households were drawn from two subsamples. The first consisted of households in the 456 African American segments. In order to achieve the expected sample size for Caribbean black households, an additional eight primary sampling areas were selected in five states (Connecticut, Florida, New Jersey, New York, and Massachusetts) and the District of Columbia, which contain more than 80% of the Caribbean black population in the United States. From these eight PSUs, 86 segments with the highest proportion of Caribbean black households were selected. The non-Hispanic white sample was a stratified disproportionate sample of adults living in households located in the census tracts and blocks in 1990 that had a 10% or greater African American population. The NSAL weights were designed to correct for disproportionate sampling, nonresponses, and population representation across selected sociodemographic characteristics for African Americans, Caribbean blacks, and whites.

Only African American and Caribbean black adolescents were included in the supplemental adolescent study. Every household that included a black adult participant (18 years and older) was screened for an eligible adolescent (13 to 17 years old). Adolescents were selected among households using a random selection procedure at the household level. If more than one adolescent was eligible for the study, up to two adolescents were selected based on the sex of the first selected adolescent. That is, if a female was initially selected, then a male would be selected as the second adolescent in the household. The NSAL adolescent sample was weighted to adjust for variation in probabilities of selection within households, nonresponse rates for households, and nonresponse rates for individuals. The weighted data were poststratified to approximate the national population distributions for sex (males and females) and age (13, 14, 15, 16, and 17) subgroups for black youth.

In-home personal interviews were conducted with 6,082 adults[2] ($n =$ 3,570 African Americans, $n = $ 1,621 Caribbean blacks, and $n = $ 891 whites) and 1,170 adolescents ($n = $ 810 African Americans, $n = $ 360 Caribbean blacks). The age of the respondents ranged from 18 to 94 for adults (Mean = 43.6, s.e. = .21) and 13–17 for adolescents (Mean = 15.0, s.e. = .04). The majority of Caribbean blacks in the sample (74.2%) were from six countries (Jamaica, Haiti, Trinidad and Tobago, Guyana, Barbados, and Puerto Rico). Sex distributions among the African American (adults = 44% male, 56% female; adolescents = 50.4% male, 49.6% female) and Caribbean black samples (adults = 50.9% male, 49.1% female; adolescents = 45.1% male, 54.9% female) were relatively equal.

Data were collected using a computer-assisted personal interview (CAPI) to ensure respondent privacy when answering questions and to provide direct data entry. The final response rate was 72.3% among adults (African Americans = 70.7%, Caribbean blacks = 77.7%, whites = 69.7%) and 81% among adolescents (African American = 80.4%, Caribbean blacks = 83.5%). Details of the methodology used for NSAL have been previously described (Jackson et al. 2004), including the sample design, weighting, and variance estimation (Heeringa et al. 2006; Heeringa et al. 2004).

Lessons Learned

- The sampling frame developed for the NSBA provides a useful tool for determining the distribution of black households in the United States. For the NSAL, the sample was updated using the 1990 census. The sample has been used as the basis for other national studies, including a study of black churches described in chapter 12 (Caldwell) of this book.
- African American and Caribbean black households are not distributed in the same way throughout the United States. Most African Americans live in the South, followed by the Northeast, Midwest, and the West. Overwhelmingly, Caribbean blacks live in the Southeastern and Northeastern portions of the country.
- It is very costly to sample Caribbean blacks; therefore, oversampling in highly clustered areas was an important strategy used for efficient sampling. However, since clustering resulted in an increase in standard errors, care had to be taken to be sure that appropriate weights and standard error correction measures were

developed to reflect the correct distribution and population characteristics.

- Working with a sampling expert was required to obtain scientifically credible nationally representative samples of ethnically diverse populations through appropriate weighting for each ethnic group. A number of factors had to be taken into consideration in determining the type of design variables and weights needed (e.g., nonresponse, poststratification) to work with complex survey data.
- The quality of data collection is also critical to the success of any research investigation. As the first national study of African American and Caribbean black populations, a number of issues were encountered. Chapter 10 by Hastings, Kromrei, and Caldwell (this volume) describes some of these challenges and how they were addressed.

The Use of Random Probes in the NSAL

When making statistical comparisons across diverse groups (i.e., ethnicity, gender, age), there is always a risk that these groups will understand and interpret the same survey questions in different ways. Thus, "disparities" in the resulting data could indicate true variation among populations being studied, or they could instead reflect inconsistencies across groups in the interpretation of question meaning and, thus, the measurement of various constructs (Jackson, Tucker, and Bowman 1982). This is particularly likely to occur when respondents differ from researchers in cultural characteristics, level of education, or life chances (Schuman 1966). The random probe technique, as developed by Schuman (1966) and used in the NSBA and NSAL, is an efficient and cost-effective method for examining the fit between respondents' answers to questionnaire items and their personal conceptualization of study concepts.

We gathered data to determine the level of continuity or discontinuity in interpretations of selected terms and concepts in the NSAL. After answering particular questionnaire items, respondents were given standardized open-ended follow-up probes, such as "Could you tell me what you mean by [RESPONSE]?" This elicited a more detailed description of respondents' thought processes and definitions of the terms and concepts we were interested in understanding. The probing process offers insight into responses given to questions where meanings, especially cultural meanings, may be unclear. For example, the question "How spiritual are you?" may mean something different to each respondent.

Prior to the start of the NSAL data collection, ten closed-ended questionnaire items were selected for use in a modified version of Schuman's random probe technique. Items chosen covered a variety of topics including religiosity, spirituality, mental and physical health, work, family, ethnicity, discrimination, and views on social and economic issues. These items were chosen for random probing based on the value of their overall contributions to research over time and because they included general language that might be interpreted in different ways. Figure 9.1 presents the questionnaire items we used in the random probe procedure along with the specific probe for each item. The ten questionnaire items produced a potential pool of approximately 60,820 closed-ended responses to probe (6,082 respondents × 10 items). Each respondent was randomly preassigned to receive one of the ten random probes during his or her interview. Thus, this random probe procedure provided a 10% sample of the total pool, or approximately 6,082 probed elaborations. Each of the 10 probes was administered to approximately 608 respondents. This number was lower for whites because one of the probes was explicitly for African American and Caribbean black respondents. Use of the CAPI system for data collection allowed for complete randomization of the probe administration ensuring an unbiased application of random probes across all respondents and across all questionnaire items designated for probing.

NSAL 10 Random Probes (Each R gets ONE probe)

1. **B18.** How religious would you say you are—very religious, fairly religious, not too religious, or not religious at all?

    B18_rp: Could you tell me what you mean by [RESPONSE TO B18]?

2. **B19.** How spiritual would you say you are—very spiritual, fairly spiritual, not too spiritual, or not spiritual at all?

    B19_rp: Could you tell me what you mean by [RESPONSE TO B19]?

3. **C8.** How would you rate your overall physical health at the present time? Would you say it is excellent, very good, good, fair, or poor?

    C8_rp: Could you tell me what you mean by [RESPONSE TO C8]?

4. **C8b.** How would you rate your overall mental health at the present time? Would you say it is excellent, very good, good, fair, or poor?

C8b_rp: Could you tell me what you mean by [RESPONSE TO C8b]?

5. **D10.** (working) and **D28.** (not working) How would you feel if a (son/daughter SAME SEX as R) of yours had your job as a regular, permanent job? Would you say very satisfied, somewhat satisfied, somewhat dissatisfied, or very dissatisfied?

   D10_rp / D28_rp: Could you tell me what you mean by [RESPONSE TO D10 or D28]?

6. **E5.** Would you say your family members are very close in their feelings toward each other, fairly close, not too close, or not close at all?

   E5_rp: Could you tell me what you mean by [RESPONSE TO E5]?

7. **SC21.** Have you ever in your life had a period lasting several days or longer when most of the day you felt <u>sad</u>, <u>empty</u> or <u>depressed</u>?

   SC21_rp: Probe for a YES response: Could you tell me what you mean by sad, empty or depressed?

   Probe for a NO response: When I asked you about being sad, empty or depressed, what did that mean to you?

8. **G2.** (Blacks only) Which would you say is more important to you—being <u>black</u> or being <u>American</u>, or are both equally important to you?

   G2_rp: Could you tell me what you mean by *being* [RESPONSE TO G2]?

   H23c_cb. (Caribbeans only) Which would you say is more important to you—being <u>black</u> or being from (COUNTRY IN H23a_cb IF ONE COUNTRY GIVEN, OTHERWISE, COUNTRY IN H23c_cbl), or are both equally important to you?

   H23c_rp: Could you tell me what you mean by *being* [RESPONSE TO H23c_cb]?

9. **G6.** (African Americans & Whites) On the whole, do you think most white people want to see blacks get a better break, or do they want to keep blacks down or don't they care one way or the other?

   G6a_cb. (Caribbeans only) On the whole, do you think most white people want to see black Americans get a better break, or do they want to keep black Americans down or don't they care one way or the other?

   G6_rp / G6a_cbrp: Could you tell me what you mean by [RESPONSE TO G6 or G6a_cb]?

10. **H37.** What about your views on social and economic issues like help for the poor? Where would you place yourself on this scale?

    H37_rp: Could you tell me what you mean by [RESPONSE TO H]?

Fig. 9.1. Questions used in the NSAL random probe procedure

Data collected via the random probe procedure can be analyzed in two ways, quantitatively and qualitatively. To analyze the data quantitatively, coders predict the closed-ended responses from the probed responses after reading individual responses to the probes, resulting in a dichotomous code of accurate or inaccurate prediction. Then, using Schuman's (1966) recommended five-point scale on the probed responses, coders assess the degree of fit or congruence that exists. Points from 1 to 5 are given to each respondent based on the predictive ability of his or her response to the probe. The point values can be averaged across all respondents who received a probe for a particular questionnaire item. The overall level of understanding of a particular closed-ended item can be evaluated based on this information.

Codes can be developed based on the substantive content of responses to each probe to evaluate the random probe data qualitatively. The distribution and variation of responses within these codes can be compared to the researchers' original intent and meaning for the questionnaire items. Lack of congruence between researchers' intended meanings and respondents' interpretation of the items can be evaluated. If there are considerable discrepancies in perceived meaning, the researcher must decide on an acceptable course of action. The original closed-ended questionnaire items will be difficult to meaningfully interpret without revisions, knowing that discrepancies exist in the researchers' intent and the respondents' interpretation.

Both quantitative point values and qualitative codes can be used to assess potential differences in question interpretation and meaning across various groups of respondents (i.e., ethnicity, gender, age). For the NSAL, it will be particularly important to assess interpretations of probed questions across ethnic groups. African Americans, Caribbean blacks, and whites may bring diverse cultural perspectives to their interpretation of specific questionnaire items. If these racial and ethnic groups have different understandings of the terms and concepts used in the probed questions, this factor will be taken into account when conducting analyses with these closed-ended questionnaire items. Further, recognizing ethnic differences in terms and concepts will be catalytic in the refinement of future question wording and new research areas. This type of information will be instrumental in increasing cultural competence in survey research.

Lessons Learned

- Questionnaire items may have different meanings to research participants with different backgrounds. This is especially true for subgroup differences stemming from cultural experiences, gender socialization, and socioeconomic position. It is vital to test for variations in interpretations of question meanings across subgroups in studies, especially with multiple racial or ethnic groups. Discrepancy in meaning from the researchers' original intent is another critical concern. If differences are found, corrections must be made to ensure that study results will be meaningful.
- Simple procedures can be used to test for question meaning before or during a study. The random probe procedure developed by Schuman and used successfully in both the NSBA and NSAL is one such procedure.
- The selection of which questions to probe can be challenging. It is best to select questions that have the potential for multiple meanings, those that are critical for the study in terms of accuracy across groups, and those that may not have been used previously with the research population.

Supplemental Surveys as a Way to Extend Studies

As with most research investigations, there is never enough time to ask all the questions researchers would like to ask during data collection. The NSAL was no different. Although the average length of the adult interview was two hours and thirty minutes, and the adolescent interview averaged one hour and forty-five minutes, numerous issues were not covered. Concerns about time constraints, costs, and respondent burden prohibited lengthening the questionnaires. Because we felt it was important to obtain some of the information omitted from the initial interview, we used the strategy of requesting supplemental data from adult respondents and from the parent or primary caretaker of the adolescents using a self-administered mail survey that could be completed at any time after the initial interview had been completed. Cooperation for this survey was requested following the initial interview, and an address sheet was prepared and sent to the study office by the interviewer for those who agreed to participate. The supplemental questionnaire was then sent to the respondent. All respondents received a $50 incentive for their initial interview. Those who completed the supplemental interview received an additional incentive of $25. This section describes the procedure and results of the NSAL supplemental surveys, including lessons learned from this process.

The NSAL Reinterview Survey

All NSAL adult respondents had an opportunity to complete a supplemental self-administered mail survey. We called this phase of the study the NSAL Reinterview. A 40-page questionnaire was developed containing questions that had been eliminated from the initial questionnaire. The overall response rate was 56.5% ($n = 3,438$); 59.9% for African Americans ($n = 2,137$), 42.9% for Caribbean blacks ($n = 695$), and 68.0% for whites ($n = 606$). In general, the demographic distributions of reinterview respondents did not differ from those of the main NSAL sample. The largest differences were among response rates for the three ethnic groups. When compared to those who did not respond, individuals most likely to complete the reinterview survey were female, unemployed, and more educated, and had participated in the original NSAL interview after September 11, 2001. The reinterview survey weights took these differences into account.

Weighting the Self-Administered Reinterview Mail Survey. There are several challenges to effectively using the NSAL reinterview data. These include handling nonresponses and maintaining the national representativeness of the sample. We describe the process of weighting the data to address these concerns. Modified versions of the NSAL weights were created for use in analyses involving variables from the NSAL reinterview survey. These weights were created by multiplying the original NSAL weights by an additional factor, adjusting for nonresponses in the reinterview survey. To account for the issue of nonresponses, we conducted a logistic regression analysis to predict the likelihood of a reinterview response using all 6,082 NSAL adult respondents.

We included demographic predictors that are typically used in such analyses; however, we also included predictors that were relevant for our specific samples and the historical context for the study. The predictors for the final logistic regression model were ethnicity; gender; education; work status; age; home ownership; foreign-born versus U.S.-born; whether the respondents' initial NSAL interview took place after September 11, 2001; participation in the NSAL Clinical Reappraisal interview (a reliability and validity study of the CIDI, a mental disorders measure); count of chronic health conditions; length of initial NSAL interview; respondent prayer and other religious behaviors; respondents' assessment of his or her weight; financial hardship, respondents' birth order; welfare receipt status; respondent impatience during the initial NSAL interview; and respondent suspicion about the initial NSAL interview. Several interactions also were included in the model.

Predicted probabilities of responding to the reinterview survey were calculated and, for those who responded, the inverse of this probability was multiplied by the original NSAL weights. This figure was then divided by the mean of the new weights. All nonrespondents to the reinterview survey received a weight of zero. The final weights developed for the reinterview survey should always be used for analyses involving any variables from the reinterview, regardless of their status as independent or dependent variables. This ensures that the reinterview survey sample size is not reduced and that the national representativeness of the sample is maintained. With appropriate weighting of the data, the 3,438 participants in the reinterview survey provide additional data that expands the amount of information available in the original study in very meaningful ways.

The NSAL Parent Survey

Another unique feature of the NSAL is that it includes a parent/primary caretaker component that obtained data to situate the adolescent within a family context. This "Parent Survey" makes dyadic or family-level analyses possible. Regardless of whether or not the adolescents' parent/primary caretaker was in the NSAL adult study, he or she was invited to complete a separate questionnaire about his or her child(ren). This questionnaire included information about family processes (e.g., family functioning, monitoring, discipline, support, and conflict), childhood mental disorders for the adolescent, and the primary caretakers' mental health functioning and family history data (if not obtained in the adult study). This information was solicited in the same way as the reinterview survey.

The response rate for the Parent Survey was 65.0%. Weighting the data for this component of the NSAL was less challenging than that for the reinterview survey because the parents/primary caretakers are attached to the adolescents and are not an independent sample. Thus, the weights for the adolescent sample can be applied in dyadic analyses.

By using the reinterview procedure, we obtained additional information about a number of topics that otherwise would have been missed. Systematic follow-up efforts would have been necessary to increase the response rates obtained, especially for the Caribbean black sample. Nevertheless, corrections were possible through statistically weighting the data, which strengthen the final data sets for purposes of data analyses.

Lessons Learned

- Self-administered, mail-in reinterview surveys are a cost-effective way of obtaining additional data from participants in a research investigation.
- The mail-in survey approach often results in lower response rates than face-to-face interviews. Additional incentives and systematic follow-up procedures should be planned from the beginning to improve upon the typically low mail survey response rates.
- A sampling consultant is needed to appropriately weight the sample for reinterviews to account for nonresponses and to maintain the representativeness of the initial sample.
- Determining who is likely to respond to a follow-up survey has been the focus of considerable previous research. Chapter 11 by Wolford and Torres (this volume) discusses our approach to longitudinal data collection with the NSBA.

An Approach for Identifying Three-Generation Family Lineages

One area of research that is underrepresented in the scientific literature for blacks is multigenerational family studies. This is a significant oversight because family context provides the basis for depth of knowledge in almost every aspect of life from birth to death. It contributes to understanding predetermined genetic and social influences on outcomes that have implications for quality of life. Researchers interested in conducting multigenerational studies are often deterred by a lack of funding and limited information on effective strategies for obtaining efficient multigenerational samples. Here we discuss a novel sampling procedure to determine whether NSAL participants were part of three-generation family lineages and ways in which we were able to gather information for a cross-national multigenerational study.

The initial NSAL interview effectively ascertained whether or not participants in each of the ethnically diverse samples (i.e., African American, Caribbean black, white) were members of three-generation family lineages, that is, if the respondent had at least two adjacent generation members 13 years of age or older at the time of the interview. The family relationships eligible were currently living grandparents, parents, children, or grandchildren. This method, called the Family Network Sampling Procedure (FNSP), was used effectively in the NSBA in preparation for the subsequent Three Generation National Survey of Black American Families (Jackson and Hatchett 1986). The same procedure was used in the NSAL in preparation for a follow-up multigenerational study that crossed U.S. borders to reach participants' family members living in the Caribbean. This study is called Family Connections across Generations and Nations (FCGN). It was funded by the National Institutes of Health (NIH) for the purpose of examining how geographic barriers and distance affect the social networks of individuals in multigenerational families, and how country of residence influences physical and mental health.

The FNSP allowed us to quickly see which NSAL respondents were eligible for the multigenerational study. Since only 66.6% of the NSAL respondents were members of a three-generation lineage, sample selection costs were greatly reduced; only respondents known to be eligible were contacted for the multigenerational study. Figure 9.2 provides the complete set of FNSP questions used to identify respondents eligible for the three-generational family study.

The questions in figure 9.2 resulted in the identification of up to five adjacent family generations. Very few queries were necessary to obtain this information. It was possible that some respondents who were eligible when interviewed would no longer qualify because of deaths, since two to three years had transpired between the NSAL and the FCGN. The actual proportion of ineligible respondents, however, was relatively low because most of those who were eligible had multiple family triads (a group of three adjacent family linkages) to choose from. For example, a total of 17% of the eligible respondents had four or more adjacent generation lineages, thereby broadening the possibilities of selection. Twenty-one percent of those who had a parent and an eligible child also had a direct lineage grandparent. An additional 15% had at least one child and grandchild lineage to make them eligible for the multigenerational study.

We developed a series of rules for inclusion from the questions in

J6.
a) How many living grandparents do you have?   _____
b) How many living parents do you have?   _____
c) How many children do you have that are 13 years old
    or older?   _____
d) (ASK ONLY IF R HAS CHILDREN 13 YEARS OLD OR OLDER):
    How many grandchildren 13 years or older do you have?   _____

J7. INTERVIEWER CHECKPOINT (SEE **J6**)
    ❏ 1. IF **J6a** IS GREATER THAN "0" <u>AND</u> **J6b** IS
          EQUAL TO "1"   **GO TO J8**
    ❏ 2. ALL OTHERS   **GO TO J10**

J8. Is it your mother or your father who is alive?
    1—Mother
    2—Father

J9. Is at least one of the parents of your (MOTHER/FATHER IN **J8**) alive?
    1—Yes
    5—No

Fig. 9.2. The Family Network Sampling Procedure

figure 9.2 to select available triads for each respondent. To be eligible for the FCGN, study respondents had to be 13 or older, speak English, and reside in a contiguous familial triad. Special attention was given to determine if the triad was contiguous (see fig. 9.2, questions J8 and J9). This was closely monitored in the case of a respondent who had children and grandchildren. In addition, respondents had to reside in an eligible country. Family members of NSAL respondents living in Caribbean countries were given a known probability of selection based on available data that produced an international multigenerational sample. Due to inaccurate contact information and challenges inherent with third-world infrastructure, our methods yielded a smaller sample than anticipated. Nevertheless, the methodological approach taken proved valuable for identifying three-generation families.

Lessons Learned

- Conducting multigenerational studies as a follow-up to another research project is a useful strategy for expanding opportunities for conducting this type of research. The Family Network Sampling Procedure (FNSP) is a cost-effective way to gain access to information necessary to determine if a respondent is eligible for a follow-up multigenerational study.

- It is not possible to select an international multigenerational sample including Caribbean black families in the same way that one would select a multigenerational sample for blacks in the United States. Cultural differences and societal infrastructure, such as lack of road maps, street signs, and house addresses, to name a few of the problems, have to be taken into consideration when embarking on international data collection.
- Determining appropriate incentives for international research also can be difficult unless a member of the research team is familiar with local culture and customs. It is critical to establish research partnerships in international locations to assist with understanding local customs. Chapter 7 by Copeland-Linder and chapter 8 by Sellers, Wilson, and Harris, both in this volume, provide good examples of conducting research with international populations.

Conclusions

This chapter highlights several unique aspects of the NSAL, offering lessons learned in the hope of stimulating future research that builds upon our experiences with securing nationally representative samples of African American and Caribbean black adults and adolescents. We addressed both conceptual and methodological issues that should be considered when conducting research with ethnically diverse black samples focused on conceptualizing ethnic group similarities and differences, selecting and weighting the samples, probing for question meanings, extending the samples through follow-up surveys, and providing a strategy for tracking multigenerational family members to the Caribbean to produce an internationally representative sample that is unique in its own right.

Conducting research with ethnically diverse populations is critical because of changing immigration patterns from the Caribbean and Africa, diverging socioeconomic conditions, shifting black family structure, and disparities in social indicators of health and well-being, including living conditions and access to services. The incorporation of blacks of Caribbean descent in the NSAL will facilitate comparative empirical analyses of issues never before addressed due to limited conceptualizations of heterogeneity of experiences across ethnic groups within the black population and the limited sample sizes of previous research. We hope additional research projects will utilize procedures and lessons learned from the NSAL to expand the research base about black populations and to improve methodology to be used to conduct culturally competent research within black communities.

NOTES

1. ICPSR is located at the Institute for Social Research at the University of Michigan. It is a repository for a number of national data sets that are available for public use in different formats. The website is http://www.icpsr.umich.edu.
2. For ease of presentation, all numbers for sample sizes are not weighted; however, all means, standard errors, and percentages are weighted to reflect the complex survey design and probability sampling of the NSAL.

REFERENCES

Caldwell, C. H., J. S. Jackson, M. B. Tucker, and P. J. Bowman. 1999. Culturally-competent research methods in African American communities: An update. In R. Jones, ed., *Advances in African American psychology,* 101–27. Hampton, VA: Cobb and Henry.

Harker, K. 2001. Immigrant generation, assimilation, and adolescent psychological well-being. *Social Forces* 79:969–1004.

Heeringa, S. G., M. Torres, J. Sweetman, and R. Baser. 2006. *Sample design, weighting, and variance estimation for the 2001–2003 National Survey of American Life (NSAL) adult sample. Technical report.* Survey Research Center of the Institute for Social Research at the University of Michigan.

Heeringa, S. G., J. Wagner, M. Torres, N. Duan, T. Adams, and P. Berglund. 2004. Sample designs and sampling methods for the collaborative psychiatric epidemiology studies (CPES). *International Journal of Methods in Psychiatric Research* 13:221–40.

Jackson, J. S., ed. 1991. *Life in Black America.* Newbury Park, CA: Sage.

Jackson, J. S., and S. J. Hatchett. 1986. Intergenerational research: Methodological considerations. In N. Datan, A. L. Green, and H. W. Reese, eds., *Intergenerational relations,* 51–75. Hillsdale, NJ: Lawrence Erlbaum.

Jackson, J. S., M. Torres, C. H. Caldwell, H. W. Neighbors, R. Nesse, R. J. Taylor, S. J. Trierweiler, and D. W. Williams. 2004. The national survey of American life: A study of racial, ethnic, and cultural influences on mental disorders and mental health. *International Journal of Methods in Psychiatric Research* 13:196–207.

Jackson, J. S., M. B. Tucker, and P. J. Bowman. 1982. Conceptual and methodological problems in survey research on Black Americans. In W. T. Liu, ed.,

Methodological problems in minority research, 11–39. Chicago: Pacific/Asian American Mental Health Research Center.

Jacobson, K. C., and L. J. Crockett. 2000. Parental monitoring and adolescent adjustment: An ecological perspective. *Journal of Research on Adolescence* 10:65–97.

Portes, A., and R. Rumbaut. 1996. *Immigrant America: A portrait.* Berkeley: University of California Press.

Rong, X. L., and F. Brown. 2002. Socialization, culture, and identities of black immigrant children. What educators need to know and do. *Education and Urban Society* 34, no. 2: 247–73.

Rong, X. L., and J. Preissle. 1998. *Educating immigrant students: What we need to know to meet the challenges.* Thousand Oaks, CA: Corwin Press.

Schuman, H. 1966. The random probe: A technique for evaluating the validity of closed questions. *American Sociological Review* 31:218–22.

Sidanius, J., and F. Pratto. 1999. *Social dominance: An intergroup theory of social hierarchy and oppression.* Cambridge: Cambridge University Press.

Taylor, R. J., L. M. Chatters, and J. S. Jackson. 1993. A profile of familial relations among three-generation Black families. *Family Relations,* special issue: *Family diversity* 42:332–41.

Tseng, V. 2004. Family interdependence and academic adjustment in college: Youth from immigrant and U.S.-born families. *Child Development* 75:966–83.

Vega, W. A., and R. G. Rumbaut. 1991. Ethnic minorities and mental health. *Annual Review of Sociology* 17:351–83.

Waters, M. C. 1994. Ethnic and racial identities of second-generation black immigrants in New York City. *International Migration Review* 28, no. 4: 795–820.

Waters, M. C. 1996. Ethnic and racial identities of second-generation black immigrants in New York City. In Alejandro Portes, ed., *The new second generation,* 171–96. New York: Russell Sage Foundation.

Waters, M. C. 1999. *Black identities: West Indian immigrant dreams and American realities.* Cambridge: Harvard University Press.

10 | Conducting Quantitative Research with African American and Caribbean Black Adult and Adolescent Populations: Strategies for Training Interviewers from Experiences with the National Survey of American Life

Julia F. Hastings, Heidi Kromrei, and
Cleopatra Howard Caldwell

In this chapter we describe a process to successfully incorporate cultural traditions, appropriate responsiveness, and adaptations in communication style for interviewer training for data collections within Black communities. Examples are offered from the National Survey of American Life (NSAL) to provide guidance for improving participation rates of African American and Caribbean Black populations through culturally sensitive interviewer training strategies. We summarize the transitions between multiple NSAL interviewer trainings and provide lessons learned as guidelines for future interviewer training. The chapter is organized around three areas: (1) recruiting interviewers, (2) cultural adaptations to the interviewer training methods, and (3) interviewing skills with African American and Caribbean Black adolescents.

Background

Based on the 30-year history of the research conducted at the Program for Research on Black Americans (PRBA), we have learned the significance of incorporating culturally sensitive questions, employing indigenous community interviewers, and attempting to engage both the interviewer and respondent in the goals of the study for successful data collection (Caldwell et al. 1999). Few research studies devote serious attention to the mechanics of improving survey data quality for persons of color (Carton and Loosveldt 1999; Johnson et al. 2002). Johnson et al. (2002), for example, conducted a comprehensive literature review of survey administration strategies focused on improving participation rates. Of the studies reviewed, only 26 identified implementing new sampling techniques to capture the nonrespondents as a strategy to increase research participation among persons of color (58–61). References to other potential strategies, such as focusing on the interviewer training process, were not discussed. Research on data collection, however, generally suggests a positive relationship between the substance of interviewer training and the quality of responses obtained (Fowler and Mangione 1990; Groves and McGonagle 2001).

Typical outcome measures for data collection research are whether questions were read exactly as written, whether appropriate probing techniques were used, and the accuracy with which interviewers recorded answers (Fowler and Mangione 1990). The empirical evidence suggests a one-to-one relationship between the content and quality of interviewer training and the ability of interviewers to solicit cooperation (Groves and McGonagle 2001). Still, this literature omits any discussion of race or specific cultural characteristics of the study populations and demographic characteristics of the interviewers (Schuman and Hatchett 1974). To approximate cultural characteristics for racial groups, surveys generally use colloquialisms that are not layperson friendly (Fowler and Mangione 1990). Fowler and Mangione (1990) suggest that a significant portion of interviewer training time should be spent creating an environment that facilitates effective communication between the interviewer and the respondent.

Overview of the NSAL

The NSAL presented a rich opportunity to focus on the interviewer training process as a critical strategy for successful data collection within Black communities because it is a large national survey of ethnically diverse Black populations that include both adults and adolescents. It builds on the signature study of the Program for Research on Black Americans (PRBA), the National Survey of Black Americans (NSBA) (Neighbors and Jackson 1996). This pioneering study introduced a number of methodological innovations for conducting research with Black Americans, including the Wide Area Screening Procedure (WASP) for identifying Blacks who lived in areas with few other Blacks (Caldwell et al. 1999). As a follow-up study to the NSBA, one of the primary goals of NSAL was to utilize contemporary methodological advancements to gather the best data possible about the physical and mental health, as well as the structural and economic conditions, of diverse groups of Americans, with a particular focus on African Americans and Caribbean Blacks.

The survey instrument included specific assessments of mental disorders, stress, coping, neighborhood characteristics, religion, social support, and work. The NSAL field operations offered a unique opportunity to capture the complex process necessary to formally train racially and ethnically diverse interviewers from around the nation to gather highly structured data from African American and Caribbean Black adults and adolescents, in that the team of research investigators was Black, but the subcontracted training staff was not. This chapter describes how the researchers and training staff interacted to address a number of challenges that arose during interviewer training in order to ensure that high-quality and meaningful data were gathered for the study.

As background, the NSAL is a national area probability sample based on a race-stratified screening procedure to determine where the sample would be obtained (Jackson et al. 2004). Trained interviewers completed face-to-face interviews with 6,082 adults (3,570 African Americans, 1,621 Caribbean Blacks, 891 Non-Hispanic Whites) and 1,170 adolescents aged 13–17 years old (810 African American, 360 Caribbean Black) for a total of 7,252 participants from across the nation.

Interviewer Training Issues

Interviewer training with standardized protocols reduces participant response variation due to differences in interviewer administration of the survey questions (Groves and McGonagle 2001). The standardized approach ensures question wording is identical for each interview, requiring interviewers to ask each question uniformly. Further, probes for unclear participant responses are standardized as well. Basic and study-specific approaches served as two types of standardized interviewing training techniques (Groves and Cooper 1998).

Although interviewers today are highly trained (Camburn, Gunther-Mohr, and Lessler 1999; Fowler and Mangione 1990; Jackson 1991), other forms of bias can exist in well-designed and executed surveys. We discuss the bias associated with locating, hiring, training, and retaining interviewers that are the same race as the respondents. Though the census data shows that African Americans are highly concentrated in many geographical areas and sparsely distributed in others (Jackson and Hatchett 1986; Johnson et al. 2002), researchers may mistakenly believe that matching the race and SES of the interviewer with potential respondents in as many situations as possible will not be difficult. What NSAL's experience showed was that available African American and Caribbean Black interviewers were usually a mix of well-educated, professionally trained individuals and educated persons looking to transition their professional focus. Thus, we were forced to recognize the social distance or perceived personal or SES dissimilarity between the interviewer and respondent that might contribute to respondent refusals, quality of responses, and/or high interviewer turnover rates.

Other interviewer characteristics matter as well. Groves and Cooper (1998) explained that interviewers who are self-confident obtain higher response rates. Therefore, strategies to increase response rates should include interviewer training that focuses on strengthening interviewers' confidence level via highly professional, thorough, and culturally sensitive training techniques. Studies that do not pay particular attention to how interviewer characteristics influence response rates among African Americans and Caribbean Blacks generally collect data that poorly describe contemporary life (Jackson and Hatchett 1986).

We assert that it is not only important to systematically train interviewers in a standardized fashion but essential to adapt these procedures to reflect cultural nuances associated with the target population and the interviewers in training. The NSAL trained 260 interviewers, and its training methods were designed to provide a culturally sensitive environment that was conducive to reducing bias and gaining the highest response rates possible across multiple ethnic and generational groups. We summarize the lessons learned from four NSAL training sessions for interviewers. Through feedback from interviewers at each training session, the training staff was able to revise training methods after gaining valuable insight into essential considerations necessary for successful interviewing training.

Interviewer Recruitment Strategies

The initial problem with recruiting interviewers was figuring out where we could find potential African American and Caribbean Black interviewers. To address this issue we borrowed heavily from a hallmark tactic of ethnographic research—utilizing the richness of natural communities (Fetterman 1998; Smith 2005; Spradley 1980). This was the most appropriate response for the NSAL research team because the selected interviewers would administer the survey instrument in their own or similar communities and would most likely know how to gain access to local community members because of their understanding of the norms and behaviors within these neighborhoods. No interviewer training would be able to "teach" this inherent knowledge.

Through understanding the reciprocal relationship between potential interviewers and their communities, the NSAL research staff recruited interviewers through press releases in national Black newspapers, website advertisements, flyers posted in places frequented by African Americans and Caribbean Blacks such as barbershops, hair salons, community centers, and churches, and word of mouth. By recruiting interviewers from communities where our sample was drawn, the NSAL was introduced as a study *for* African American and Caribbean Black communities. Although our interviewer recruitment strategies attracted some community members who did not end up becoming interviewers, what they learned about NSAL provided us with free word-of-mouth advertising. Free publicity proved invaluable to the study because it naturally facilitated a positive reciprocal relationship between the study interviewers and the potential respondents.

Our interviewer recruitment strategy, though recommended, is not without limitations. Specifically, we found ourselves constantly dealing with communication issues. Words and expressions hold different values and meanings across regions and professions. Many NSAL interviewers were retired teachers, community leaders, social workers, homemakers, graduate students, and persons between employment positions. Our interviewers learned how to be more effective communicators with respondents where social distance could have been a factor, by developing a personal style that blended the professional language taught in training and community speech that would create the most conducive interview environment. The approach to gaining consent prior to conducting an interview could vary based on the unique characteristics of a community. Recruiting indigenous interviewers acknowledged the importance of understanding and valuing critical aspects of communication style and community life that might not be obvious to persons who do not reside within a particular community. African American and Caribbean Black communities across the nation have both similar and unique characteristics that must be appreciated in order to achieve meaningful data collection.

NSAL Interviewer Training Methods

Interviewer Training through a Cultural Lens

Interviewers for the NSAL were trained at four different training sessions over the course of fourteen months: January 2001, March 2001,

October 2001, and March 2002. On average, each training session lasted two weeks. Training sessions followed a lecture format and used small practice groups called *round robins.* All interviewers were trained to gather data on laptop computers using computer-assisted personal interviewing (CAPI) software for survey instrument administration. For interviewers needing supplemental assistance with understanding how to use the laptop computer controls and software, additional study periods and technology sessions were held during the evening hours. These training protocols were followed for both adult and adolescent surveys.[1]

Several African American and Caribbean Black cultural traditions, practices, and orientations were increasingly woven into NSAL interviewer training. For example, NSAL increasingly considered the dietary needs of many African Americans. Each break within the training schedule included foods such as butter- and salt-free popcorn, fresh fruit, and fruit juices. With a particular focus on dinner options, we learned that allowing choices between vegetarian and meat meals was inconsiderate of many African American and Caribbean Black health concerns. We immediately learned from the first training that options such as rare roast beef or a stuffed mushroom did not take into account persons who did not eat red meat or had to watch their salt intake. As training progressed, healthier food options included baked chicken, steamed vegetables, pasta, and fruit.

African American and Caribbean Black cultures are a diverse and complex blend of many original cultures from all corners of the globe. The cultural aspects incorporated into interviewing training were: (1) establishing collective study investment and shared skill learning; (2) building relationships between study and training staff and new interviewers; and (3) developing appropriate communication styles. Employing African American and Caribbean Black interviewers requires an emphasis on gaining cooperation or in-group identification with the task at hand to develop a reciprocal and equitable contribution from all participants. For example, as training progressed the research investigators emphasized that the interviewers represented the "life blood" of the investigation. Not only did the interviewers appreciate their acknowledged importance, they also began to share their past interviewing experiences with others who did not have equivalent experience. This public emphasis on the skills that new trainees brought to the NSAL training increased NSAL's credibility as a legitimate project seeking to improve conditions of Blacks across the nation. Further, the public acknowledgments augmented personal buy-in on the part of the interviewers and provided evidence that research studies from university institutions do not intend harm. The research investigators envisioned

---

Day 1
- Overview of the job and objectives of the two-day training
- Review the interviewer's manual, pledge of confidentiality, and statement of professional ethics
- What is a survey?
- Communicating with the respondent: Question reading, clarification, and feedback
- Components of interviewing: Probing and recording
- Diversity and sensitivity with interviewing respondents as well as interacting with peers and supervisors
- Laptop basics
- Round robin practice with scripts

Day 2
- Cover sheet overview and household screening exercises
- Tracking the selected respondent
- Sampling and procedures
- Administrative aspects and evaluation procedures
- Introduction to refusal aversion/conversion and role play with commonly heard objections
- Getting paid: Reporting your time and expenses
- Putting it all together: Questions and answers

Fig. 10.1. General Interviewer Training Content

that when African American and Caribbean Black interviewers understood the benefits of their labor, they would be more likely to make concerted efforts to complete interviews.

The purpose of general interviewer training (GIT) is to establish a consistent method for administering surveys. NSAL training emphasized standard general interviewer training techniques followed by lectures and exercises that demonstrated study-specific goals and techniques. Small discussion (round robin) groups were utilized to facilitate interviewing practice, including reading the questions aloud and the use of standardized probing techniques. All trainings occurred in Ann Arbor at a facility near the University of Michigan. To limit variation across training sessions, similar materials were used throughout. Figure 10.1 provides an illustration of the two-day GIT agenda.

Organizational Issues with GIT

If researchers do not conduct the interviews personally and choose to subcontract with another agency to conduct training sessions, as we did in the

NSAL, be aware of organizational issues. Among the problems in the first GIT process was the rapidly spread misperception on the part of training interviewers about who conceptualized NSAL and the commitment of the training staff. The subcontracted interviewer agency learned that the NSAL research investigators needed to directly and consistently influence the interviewer training process. Though the subcontracted agency employed experienced team leaders (TLs) and regional field managers (RFMs), the first cohort of newly hired interviewers developed misperceptions because all but one of the GIT training staff was White and the majority of NSAL interviewer trainees were African American. Because of this, many interviewer trainees believed the study was not designed by African American and Caribbean Black investigators and that the training staff would not be directly impacted by the outcomes of the research. Both of these interviewer concerns were untrue. In situations where there is not enough sensitivity to the racial and power imbalance between trainers and newly hired interviewers, misunderstandings regarding the study focus, goals and intent for data use can develop. Such misperceptions can create a highly volatile training situation if not addressed.

To address these problems the NSAL principal investigator, Dr. James S. Jackson, summarized the project objectives as well as facilitated a discussion about diversity in the workplace and in the field. Dr. Jackson's lecture at the second training replaced a session presented by the National Field Team staff that was rated very poorly by the first group of newly hired interviewers. As training sessions progressed, the subcontracted interviewer training agency recognized that it was critical to respond to the highly racialized situation by introducing more of the NSAL African American and Caribbean Black coprincipal investigators to the interviewer cohorts on the first day of GIT. This was not how they typically conducted trainings. PRBA postdoctoral research fellows were also introduced to the interviewers and assisted in conducting the round robin groups. These strategies were very effective in dispelling misconceptions about the project and reducing some of the initial discomfort felt by both interviewers and trainers.

Based on these experiences, it is clear that all interviewer trainings should have evaluations following each training day to monitor trainee concerns (see appendix 1). We used our interviewer training session evaluations to immediately learn about any difficulties. For example, one comment that struck the project research investigators was, "The GIT staff needs to have more diversity and sensitivity training interviewers. . . . I feel there should have been more African American GIT trainers."

Another suggestion to improve the training was to have the project research investigators "available" to discuss concerns. Largely due to the initial interviewer evaluations, we learned that a portion of interviewer trainees were uncomfortable with the training style of a few of the training staff. To acknowledge that the interview comments were taken seriously and to utilize talented African American seasoned interviewer experiences, a few of NSAL's best interviewers were promoted to trainers.

A different evaluation observed, "Allow trainees a chance to put new information into immediate practice." Another comment regarding the presentations stated, "I found . . . comments to many people to be condescending, patronizing, and offensive. I hear . . . that e-mail directions were beyond this group's understanding and they would 'never get it.'" These comments emerged from the racial imbalance between the training staff (mostly White) and the interviewer trainees (mostly African American and Caribbean Black). Clearly, if researchers do not pay attention to these dynamics, misinterpretation of research intent and study content become entangled within heated emotion.

No matter the research subject matter, we suggest the most effective manner for collecting data within African American and Caribbean Black communities is to utilize the talents of experienced African American and Caribbean Black interviewers and to match people with similar racial backgrounds to train and supervise persons with less interviewing experience. Since GIT's value lies in its structured procedure to train highly competent interviewers and provide a sound understanding of the principles of social science research, handling these issues is worth considerable effort.

Staffing the third and fourth GITs with outstanding previously trained interviewers was a very promising lesson learned. The new trainers were all very familiar with the study materials and technology and had many real-life experiences to share with new hires. All of the GIT trainers (except the RFMs) were African American. Many had been promoted to administrative duties (Field Coordinator, TL) due to their high level of productivity and professionalism. We found that by promoting an experienced African American team leader to the "lead trainer" position, many frustrating situations were avoided. The lead trainer's presence was strong and assertive, yet warmly received by the trainees. We actively addressed frustrations from both interview trainees and trainers by adopting training norms (use of question cards, need to be on time, etc.) and trainee responsibilities (see table 10.1). Though at times the training norms and trainee responsibilities were acknowledged with resentment and feelings of condescension, we found by openly discussing the rules most people felt heard and tensions were reduced. Including a strong and experienced African American lead trainer was a crucial component in improving the training design.

We also learned that the presence of PRBA postdoctoral research fellows allowed the training interviewers to see that NSAL served as an opportunity to help the next generation of researchers. Integration of the postdoctoral research fellows was instrumental in providing a context for the project when questions arose (particularly when questions pertained to issues of race) and in helping keep interviewers on task during an extensive schedule of training activities.

When thinking of the power imbalance between the people conducting the training and the people being trained, many times the trainees are persons who have had experiences of being poorly treated. Therefore, one offhand remark may trigger negative feelings. This is especially true considering the racial discrimination commonly experienced by African Americans and Caribbean Blacks. Without addressing the undercurrent of negativity among individual interviewer trainees and the training staff, no learning will occur. We strongly recommend providing an opportunity to discuss negative feelings openly and address any concerns immediately.

TABLE 10.1.   GIT Training Norms and Responsibilities

Training Norms	Training Responsibilities
• Cell phones are not allowed in training rooms. • Pagers are not allowed in training rooms. • No beverages are allowed on tables with the laptop computers except approved containers. • No questions will be addressed during the presentations. • ALL trainees are expected to be on time to training sessions.	• Be courteous to others. • Criticize ideas not people. • Be on time—tardiness will not be tolerated. • Wear your name tag at all times. • Note questions on any topic and address them during the wrap-up at the end of each day. • Questions for any trainer or staff member should be addressed during a break, on lunch, or during the wrap-up at the end of each day.

Lessons Learned by Revising GIT Methods

- Hire experienced African American/Caribbean Black interviewers as trainers.
- Talk openly about culturally charged topics.
- Make time to hear questions and concerns from project members.
- Encourage the project director to:
  - lecture on project and workforce diversity
  - provide a summary of the research project
- Develop smaller training groups for new interviewee interaction.
- Ensure the presence of African American research staff at all GIT sessions.

Study-Specific Training

Study-specific training covers the information needed to understand and administer the study's survey instrument(s). This training builds on the information learned in general interviewing sessions by explicitly focusing on the research investigation and introducing specific techniques for interviewing. The box provides an example of NSAL's study-specific training agenda. The box describes a straightforward approach to instruct new interviewers on the project survey instrument. A specific example from NSAL focuses on reminding interviewers to use formal forms of address such as "Mrs. Washington" or "Mr. Sullivan" until the respondent invites the interviewer to address her or him differently, to demonstrate respect for each respondent and his or her contribution to the NSAL.

Another aspect of interviewer training focused on modeling effective communication techniques. Some of the round-robin sessions focused on the importance of the nonverbal communication behaviors suggested by Bailey, Nowicki, and Cole (1998), for example, when respondents nod their heads, roll their eyes, or make sounds referring to a yes or no. Many trainees wanted to accept the nonverbal responses but were reminded of the level of certainty they must gain before responses could be interpreted as question agreement or disagreement. As exemplified above, variations in communicating information represented another manner in which African American interviewers and respondents might achieve a better interview relationship and, subsequently, a completed interview.

Evaluations were also solicited from the interview trainees to monitor the study-specific training experience. Feedback from the study-specific trainings highlighted a number of important techniques that needed improvement. New interviewers suggested they should participate in more role-playing, limit "what if" questions to the end, and incorporate more audience participation in the questionnaire section presentations. Many stated that the most effective aspects of training were the hands-on activities during the round robins and mingling with the NSAL research investigators. A few even commented on wanting to visit the campus where the project offices were located. As described above, working with a training staff that resembled the interview trainees created the best atmosphere in terms of interpersonal interactions between trainers and new hires. Recounting the lessons learned in the field gave trainers more credibility with new hires, and the interviewers were grateful for the opportunity to learn from experienced NSAL Interviewers.

Specific Interviewer Training Content

- NSAL project overview and sample design
- Instrument overview
- Short mock interview in round robin teams
- Updating and communicating software
- Questionnaire presentation—living situation, health, and family discussion
- Round robin teams: practice with questionnaire on lecture topic
- Welcome banquet—training interviewers meet the project staff
- Instrument conventions: repeating question series, probing, random probes
- Questionnaire presentation—mental health section I
- Round robin teams: practice with questionnaire on lecture topic
- Questionnaire presentation—mental health section II
- Round robin teams: practice with questionnaire on lecture topic
- Questionnaire presentation—demographics
- Round robin teams: practice with questionnaire on lecture topic
- Adolescent questionnaire presentation
- Round robin teams: adolescent mock interview
- Interview observations
- Field procedures

Some of the training method revisions would not have been possible without the African American training staff. Their presence allowed for leadership that was inclusive of cultural norms that were acceptable, and even appreciated, by interview trainees. For example, the African American training staff was able to talk openly about reasons behind the training content's rigid order in a manner that reduced negative feelings. The explanations relied on the staff's ability to speak tactfully, yet respectfully in the learning environment. In general, we learned that the aspects found most helpful were seeing and talking with the NSAL research investigators, learning from each other's mistakes in the round robins, learning how to probe with different questions in the round robins, building confidence with computer skills and software utilization, hearing stories from trainers with field experience, and starting and ending sessions on time. We also learned that NSAL postdoctoral research fellows were able to promptly assist those who had computer problems. Last, the trainees recommended more computer training with handouts and time to allow them to develop a personal rhythm with reading a series of questions rather than one question at a time.

Interviewing Skills with African American and Caribbean Black Adolescents

We learned that translating the general interviewer training lessons to the adolescent sample required much more attention. Many questions arose about how to handle adolescents because they were not children but not legal adults. Several seasoned interviewers described their experiences of interviewing African American and Caribbean Black adolescents as being uncomfortable because many took on adult roles in the family and did not consider themselves as needing to be parented. Therefore, training new interviewers to accept this family role differential emerged as a discussion topic.

Adolescent interviewer training was developed with an interactive presentation style in mind. Interviewers were allowed to actively contribute by offering their experiences as the topical areas were covered. The training began with an overview of adolescence. The project investigators described the age range for the study as 13 to 17 years old and emphasized that one year made a huge difference in the way adolescents think. Those between 13 and 15 were described as fluctuating frequently between acting childlike and acting grown-up. Interviewer trainees were cautioned to allow frequent breaks in the interview for this age range and to provide time for the adolescents to collect their personal thoughts during the one hour and forty-five minute interview. Adolescents between 16 and 17 years of age were described as being able to sit longer, but with differences in attention span that might vary by gender. We emphasized the interviewer's need to be flexible because he or she might not know whether the adolescent had a learning disability, health problems, or mental health issues such as attention deficit disorder, or just was not interested in the interviewing experience. It was stressed that perhaps the monetary incentive to complete the interview was the single most important motivating factor to complete the interview. In addition to providing tips (see box), the session allowed project staff to quiet interviewer anxieties about talking to unrelated teenagers about sexuality. This was particularly relevant when they asked the question, "Have you ever been pregnant or fathered any children?" The interviewers were prepared to expect outbursts that could range from anger to laughter about the question. Last, all interviewers were cautioned about silence. Silence for adolescents is not always a sign of being stubborn or dismissive. The silence very well could represent reflective thinking about how to answer.

African American and Caribbean Black Adolescent Interviewing Tips

- Relax.
- Try to find a private location to conduct the interview (privacy issues).
- Allow the teen to read and answer the question silently (point to the answer on the laptop) if a parent or guardian insists on remaining within earshot.
- Employ a "warm-up" period (laughter eases tension quickly).
- Do not try to become "friends."
- Remain true to yourself or "keep it real."
- Suspend judgment.
- Avoid "I remember when . . ." phrases.
- Expect outbursts of emotion.
- Listening is a critical first step in keeping the interview going.
- Silence may be a sign of thoughtfulness.
- Encourage them to express how they are feeling.
- Be ready to hear opinions you may not agree with.
- *Above all else—be patient.*

The lead adolescent project coprincipal investigator and the research fellows for the adolescent sample provided the theoretical background for each questionnaire section, then concluded with general information about adolescent development and techniques to improve the completion of the interview. The project research investigators thought it very important to convey that each interview should begin with a relaxed attitude. The same cultural nuances noted for the adult sample would be important factors to remember with the adolescent sample as well.

Conclusions

In summary, we learned from many mistakes and successes over the course of training African American and Caribbean Black interviewers. Current approaches should involve training with regard to behaviors and skills needed to gain the cooperation of Black interviewers and study participants, use of instructional techniques that incorporate African American and Caribbean styles of interactive participatory learning, provision of opportunities for the interviewers to make suggestions about gaining access to communities, using trainers of the same racial or ethnic background, and ensuring the project research investigators are as intimately involved in the training process as possible.

Lessons Learned from Adolescent Interviewer Training

- When interviewing adolescents, interviewers must recognize that adolescents are not just little adults and often do not think like adults. They are developing human beings with ideas and opinions of their own as they begin the process of figuring out who they are as individuals. Be respectful and authentic as you build rapport with them.
- For in-home interviews, it is vital to interview the adolescent with a parent or another responsible adult present in the home for safety reasons. This does not mean that that person needs to be in the same room at the time of the interview.
- Privacy during an interview is critical, especially if parents are near by. Use strategies that will ensure privacy such as using a computer for responses, explaining the importance of privacy in the interview setting to parents, or having the adolescent write his or her answer. Some studies have even used telephone interviews for

sensitive portions of the questionnaire to ensure privacy. We used computers in the NSAL for this purpose.

- Reassuring the adolescent of the confidential nature of the interview is critical for developing rapport and for getting them to answer questions. This point cannot be emphasized enough with adolescents.
- Don't be surprised if the adolescent is not available at the time that they agreed to be interviewed. Sometimes other priorities take precedent over completing an interview, even when they are being paid as an incentive. We found that working with parents to secure the adolescent interview was an important part of the process.
- Perhaps the most interesting piece of advice was that no matter what is stated in the text, each interviewer should expect the unexpected. Clearly, each adolescent interview will be different, each an experience unto itself.

NOTE

1. Although the training described is based on a national study, the techniques are applicable to regional and local studies as well.

REFERENCES

Bailey, W., S. Nowicki, and S. P. Cole. 1998. The ability to decode nonverbal information in African American, African and Afro-Caribbean, and European American adults. *Journal of Black Psychology* 24, no. 4 (November): 418–31.

Caldwell, C. H., J. S. Jackson, M. B. Tucker, and P. J. Bowman. 1999. Culturally-competent research methods in African American communities: An update. In R. Jones, ed., *Advances in African American psychology,* 101–27. Hampton, VA: Cobb and Henry.

Camburn, D. P., C. Gunther-Mohr, and J. T. Lessler. 1999. *Developing new models of interviewer training.* Paper presented at the International Conference on Survey Nonresponse 1999, Portland, OR.

Carton, A., and G. Loosveldt. 1999. *How the initial contact can be a determinant for the final response rate in face-to-face surveys.* Paper presented at the International Conference on Survey Nonresponse 1999, Portland, OR.

Fetterman, D. M. 1998. *Ethnography.* 2nd ed. Thousand Oaks, CA: Sage.

Fowler, F. J., and T. W. Mangione. 1990. *Standardized survey interviewing.* Newbury Park, CA: Sage.

Groves, R. M., and M. P. Cooper. 1998. *Nonresponse in household interview surveys.* New York: John Wiley and Sons.

Groves, R. M., and K. A. McGonagle. 2001. A theory-guided interviewer training protocol regarding survey participation. *Journal of Official Statistics* 17, no. 2: 249–65.

Jackson, J. S., ed. 1991. *Life in black America*. Newbury Park, CA: Sage.

Jackson, J. S., and S. J. Hatchett. 1986. Intergenerational research: Methodological considerations. In N. Daton, A. L. Green, and H. W. Reese, eds., *Intergenerational relations*, 51–75. Hillsdale, NJ: Erlbaum Associates.

Jackson, J. S., M. Torres, C. H. Caldwell, H. W. Neighbors, R. Nesse, R. J. Taylor, S. J. Trierweiler, and D. R. Williams. 2004. The national survey of American life: A study of racial, ethnic, and cultural influences on mental disorders and mental health. *International Journal of Methods in Psychiatric Research* 13:196–207.

Johnson, T. P., D. O'Rourke, J. Burris, and L. Owens. 2002. Culture and survey nonresponse. In R. M. Groves, D. A. Dillman, J. L. Eltinge, and R. J. A. Little, eds., *Survey nonresponse*, 55–70. New York: John Wiley and Sons.

Neighbors, H. W., and J. S. Jackson, eds. 1996. *Mental health in black America*. Thousand Oaks, CA: Sage.

Schuman, H., and S. J. Hatchett. 1974. *Black racial attitudes: Trends and complexities*. Ann Arbor: Survey Research Center, Institute for Social Research, University of Michigan.

Smith, L. T. 2005. On tricky ground: Researching the native in the age of uncertainty. In N. K. Denzin and Y. S. Lincoln, eds., *The Sage handbook of qualitative research*, 85–107. 3rd ed. Thousand Oaks, CA: Sage.

Spradley, J. 1980. *Participant observation*. New York: Holt, Rinehart, and Winston.

11 | Adjusting for and Predicting Nonresponse in a Panel Survey of African Americans

Monica L. Wolford and Myriam Torres

There is no better method for determining the nature and direction of the causal flow than the observation of changes over time. No cross-sectional study can provide us with comparable information. Yet, the process of conducting longitudinal research presents a unique set of challenges. Two of these are the difficulties of maintaining a representative sample and compensating for the systematic loss of individuals over the course of the study. While even the random loss of respondents can create problems by eroding the power of analyses, many authors have noted that the most critical problem is the bias that the disproportionate loss of particular subgroups introduces into the analyses (Musick, Campbell, and Ellison 2001). The size of the bias depends primarily on the relationship between the sources of nonresponse (e.g., males) and response probabilities as well as the amount of nonresponse (Bethlehem 2002). Reducing this bias by increasing cooperation in the underrepresented subgroups will result in smaller biases and more accurate estimations.

This chapter focuses on the dynamics associated with longitudinal nonresponse in the National Panel Survey of Black Americans. We examine sources of systematic nonresponse in order both to compensate for it statistically through the use of weights and to develop better procedures for identifying respondents most likely to be lost at later waves to enable intensified tracking efforts.

The data used for these analyses are from the National Panel Survey of Black Americans (NPSBA), a survey of 2,107 black Americans (Jackson 1991). The first wave of the study was done in 1979–80. These respondents were followed up in three data collections in 1987–88, 1988–89, and 1992. NPSBA, better known as NSBA, is part of a major research project undertaken at the Institute for Social Research, Program for Research on Black Americans (PRBA) to collect and analyze national survey data on African American populations (Neighbors and Jackson 1996). This survey explored a range of topics including the role of religion and the church, physical and mental health, and racial attitudes.

The NPSBA has several unique attributes with regard to nonresponse across multiple waves of data collection. First, it is a national probability sample panel survey of African Americans. As such, it is one of very few surveys with the ability to inform us about nonresponse rates for all African Americans rather than only those living in highly concentrated areas. For instance, while the Americans' Changing Lives (ACL) study found that black informants had a higher second-wave response rate than other respondents, they attributed this to the manner in which blacks were oversampled, resulting in the skewing of the sample toward rural Southern blacks (Kalton et al. 1990). The relatively large number of black Americans in this study provides us with a strong base for talking about nonresponse even with considerable attrition.

Second, unlike many of the studies in which patterns of nonresponse have been examined, this is a study of an individual's attitudes. Proxy interviews or interviews from any of several sources such as those used in the Survey of Income and Program Participation (SIPP) could not be used in this study. This will result in some differences in the patterns of nonresponse as well as an attenuated response rate.

Third, the unusual time frames of the panel data present a challenge. The first wave of the study was collected through face-to-face interviews during 1979 and 1980. The National Survey of Black Americans was not designed as a panel study and therefore only very limited recontact information was collected. During 1987 and 1988 a second wave of data was collected using telephone interviews, to follow up respondents eight years later. Naturally, such a long period of time and limited recontact information led to considerable attrition. Of the original 2,107 respondents, 102 were known to have died and 935 were reinterviewed for an overall response rate of 47 percent (see table 11.1).

The third wave of data was collected one year later and 779 (84 per-

TABLE 11.1.   National Panel Survey of Black Americans: Response Rates

	N	% of Wave 1	Response Rate (%)
Wave I (1979–80)	2,107	NA	67.0
Wave II (1987–88)	935	46.6	46.6
Wave III (1988–89)	779	39.1	84.3
Wave IV (1992)	652	33.3	83.6

Note: Known deceased were eliminated from calculation of the response rate. NA = not applicable.

cent) of the second-wave respondents were reinterviewed. Eleven re-spondents were known to have died in the interim. The fourth wave of data was collected three years later during which time an additional 34 respondents died. Of the 779 respondents recontacted, 652 (84 percent) were interviewed (see table 11.1).

Finally, while this is a study of noninstitutionalized African American adults, tracking information did not allow for the exclusion from the sample frame of original respondents who had since entered an institu-tion. This has led to an underestimated response rate.

Sources of Nonresponse

In order to more effectively examine the sources of nonresponse, we must characterize the underlying processes leading to nonresponse. We began this procedure by assessing the indicators of nonresponse used in cross-sectional studies. These are general demographics such as region, urbanicity, gender, age, and ethnicity. Usually, this is all the information known about the respondent. When we are seeking to account for attri-tion in the later waves of a survey, however, there is an abundance of data about those who did not respond to subsequent data collections. The characteristics used successfully in the few longitudinal studies in which nonresponse has been examined were added to those from cross-sec-tional studies. These are presented here in the categories that theoreti-cally represent the primary sources of nonresponse.

Demographics

It is reasonable to assume that many of the dynamics that determine nonresponse in a cross-sectional survey would influence response rates in a longitudinal context. Generally, the data available about respondents in most cross-sectional surveys are limited to demographic data col-lected from an informant or extrapolated from census data. In addition, demographic indicators of the likelihood that a respondent will change residences and their facility with survey formats and understanding of research agendas must be considered.

Employment

Another important determinant of response rates is the nature of the re-spondent's employment situation. This goes beyond the mere presence or absence of employment, to include the nature of the job search for the unemployed and the stability of employment for those currently employed. Obviously, those respondents currently looking for work who find work in another locality are more difficult to trace. Similarly, people who lose their jobs are more likely to leave their original location. The type of employment and how people feel about that work may have an impact on their staying in the job as well as their willingness to continue to participate in the study.

Income and Assets

Financial stability and the resources to weather economic downturns should result in less movement among respondents.

Community Involvement

The degree of involvement the individual has with the community through interaction with neighbors, club memberships, important relationships with others, and civic activities should be related to both an individual's willingness to complete a survey and the likelihood of being locatable at recontact.

Topic of the Study

To some extent, we expect that the topic of the study would affect a respondent's willingness to continue to participate. Certainly, as a source of nonresponse this has the potential to be the most damaging to the viability of the data collected in later waves. The systematic loss of respondents with particular attitudes toward the topic under study introduces a severe bias into any longitudinal analyses.

Affective States

Finally, the individual's affective state and attitudes toward the survey should be related to their likelihood of participating in later waves. Kalton et al. (1990) reported that the interviewer's rating of the cooperativeness of the respondent was positively related to further participation. Negative emotional states such as self-reports of depression and tenseness had a negative effect on response rates. These effects are likely to be attenuated in studies with longer time spans between waves.

Analyses

Since theories of nonresponse are in the early stages of development and Lepkowski and Coupers's (2002) model of nonresponse did not address this particular population, all of the non–open ended items (approximately 1,200 variables) were given the opportunity to enter the analyses. Following the process outlined by Kalton, Lepkowski, and Lin (1985), the numerous social and demographic characteristics of the respondents measured in the study were reduced to those with highly significant bivariate relationships to nonresponse. Since a large number still remained, these were then reduced further to those that showed a significant relationship with nonresponse in multivariate analyses. While most work on nonresponse relies on examining the marginal distributions, O'Muircheartaigh (1989) notes that particular subgroups in the population are subject to the greatest attrition. We chose therefore to base the final analyses on the SEARCH algorithm, or Automatic Interaction Detector developed by Sonquist, Baker, and Morgan (1973). In this way, we were able to enter into the SEARCH command as joint predictors those variables with significant multivariate linear relationships with nonresponse along with categorical variables from the questionnaire and those variables deemed likely to have nonlinear effects.

Results

A total of 28 variables entered the final SEARCH analyses, which were run separately for each of the three waves. The analyses shown in table 11.2 are weighted to compensate for unequal selection probabilities and cross-sectional nonresponse at Wave I. It is clear that many subgroups do end up underrepresented in later waves. In particular, in Wave II the subgroup with one of the lowest response rates consisted of individuals who did not live in a family-owned home and whose household unit needed repair, who primarily desired good interpersonal relations and challenging work in a job, were male, and had either a very high or very low household income. This group had a response rate of 13.54%. In contrast, one of the groups in Wave II with the highest response rate were home owners with at least some college education, who were willing to cross party lines to vote for a platform that favored blacks, and who rarely missed work due to personal problems (87.80%).

Many of the characteristics that significantly predict attrition over the waves are demographic variables. Of those that are typically used to predict nonresponse in cross-sectional studies (region, urbanicity, gender, and age), only region was consistently nonsignificant. However, these variables clearly play a lesser role in predicting nonresponse across waves than other characteristics of the respondents.

The overwhelming predictor of nonresponse in all three waves was whether or not the respondent or their family owned their home, with

TABLE 11.2. Percentage of Variance in Nonresponse Explained Using SEARCH

	Wave II	Wave III	Wave IV
Demographics			
Home Ownership	3.19	4.33	3.60
Household Unit in Need of Repair	1.03	0.90	1.41
Education	1.07	1.03	0.00
Number of Persons in Household	0.50	0.00	1.52
R's Age	0.18	1.02	0.55
Living Three Generational Family	0.00	0.51	0.52
Urbanicity	0.31	0.38	0.23
Gender	0.77	0.00	0.00
Marital Status	0.00	0.43	0.00
Type of Dwelling	0.23	0.00	0.00
Work			
Occupation (9 categories)	0.55	0.65	2.30
Most Important Factor in a Job	0.77	0.44	1.50
Frequency of Absence from Work	0.44	0.99	0.37
Employment Search Status	0.00	0.00	1.75
Amount of 1978 Employed	0.00	0.64	0.00
Income and Assets			
Household Income	1.22	1.80	0.81
Personal Income	0.96	0.33	1.19
Interviewer's Estimation of Household Income	0.00	0.67	0.46
Paid Salary, Hourly, or Other Type of Wage	0.60	0.00	0.00
Community Involvement			
Frequency of Other Church Activities	1.14	1.41	0.69
Voted in Presidential Election	0.00	0.76	1.86
Main Romantic Involvement	0.43	0.00	0.00
Topic of Study			
Would Support a Black Political Party	0.00	0.51	0.45
Would Support a Black Platform	0.58	0.00	0.00
Affective States			
R was Suspicious–Open	0.24	0.75	0.00
R was Bored–Interested	0.25	0.45	0.00
R was Hostile–Friendly	0.00	0.00	0.56
Frequency of Feeling Depressed	0.30	0.00	0.00
Total variance explained	14.76	18.01	19.77

home owners consistently responding at a higher rate than renters and others. The next most important predictor across all three waves was the condition of the unit in which the respondent lived, as rated by the interviewer. This is primarily due to nonresponse among people who did not own their homes and whose residence was in need of repair.

Age showed a nonlinear relationship to nonresponse with middle-aged respondents most likely to respond to later waves. The level of education a person had achieved was strongly associated with nonresponse in the first two reinterviews, but not the third. Individuals with higher levels of education were more likely to respond than those with lower levels. This is the same pattern found in the ACL data at the bivariate level, though in that study it does not appear to have been significant in multivariate analyses (Kalton et al. 1990).

Not surprisingly, the nature of an individual's work, its steadiness, and their attitudes toward it were also important predictors of nonresponse. While we did not find a significant effect for employment status by itself, most of the items about working presume this information. Occupation, for example, was only collected for those working at the time. It is a strong predictor of nonresponse, with individuals who work in white-collar jobs most likely to respond while people in service work, craft workers, and the unemployed were least likely to respond. Intriguingly, the elements of a job, other than pay, that an individual considered to be the most important factor of a job were important predictors of nonresponse. Individuals who valued job factors such as working at their own pace, having good promotion opportunities, and good working conditions were the most likely to be retained.

The effects of both household and personal income on response rates tend to be nonlinear in this sample. Those with incomes near the median appear to be most likely to respond. The interviewer's estimate of the household's income, however, acts in a linear fashion, with respondents from households whose income appeared to be low reinterviewing less. In addition to the rate of pay, the manner in which one is paid has a small effect on nonresponse as well. Respondents who receive a salary or are paid by the unit of work done are more likely to remain in the study.

The strong positive impact on response rates of a respondent's attending activities at a church other than regular services seems to bear out the importance of the respondent's ties to the community in maintaining a sample over time. Similarly, both voting and being either married or having a main romantic involvement are positively associated with being reinterviewed.

We found only minimal effects for the topic of the study on reinterview rates. In addition, only two of the many items that relate to the centrality of being black to the individual were significant predictors of nonresponse. These were whether they were in favor of forming a black political party and whether they would cross party lines to vote for a candidate with the best platform for African Americans. Neither of these entered all three searches, however, nor did they account for much of the variance.

The affective component, while weak, did show some impact despite the period of time between waves. Respondents that interviewers rated as open, interested, and friendly were more likely to continue in the study. Conversely, respondents who reported often feeling depressed were less likely to be reinterviewed.

While the SEARCH technique has some advantages, the use of logistic regression to predict nonresponse is also common. Since SEARCH is designed to identify interaction effects, and logistic regression favors main effects, we have elected to present both here. The results of the stepwise logistic regressions are presented in table 11.3. Only the variables from the SEARCH that were significant predictors of nonresponse for at least

TABLE 11.3. Logistic Regression of Nonresponse

	Wave II		Wave III		Wave IV	
	B	S.E.	B	S.E.	B	S.E.
Owns Home vs. Rental Condition	−0.32***	0.06	−0.41***	0.06	−0.40***	0.06
Gender	−0.53***	0.13	−0.56***	0.13	−0.70***	0.13
Employment Search Status	−0.43***	0.06	−0.42***	0.06	−0.48***	0.06
Voted—Presidential Election	0.45***	0.12	0.44***	0.12	0.35***	0.12
Living Three Generation Family	0.36***	0.11	0.30***	0.12	0.39***	0.12
Frequency of Other Church Activities	0.11***	0.03	0.11***	0.03	0.12***	0.03
Employed Only Part of 1978	−0.49***	0.17	−0.54***	0.18	−0.60***	0.18
Interviewer's Estimation of Household Income	0.15***	0.06	0.13**	0.06	0.13**	0.05
Support for Black Platform	0.30**	0.12	0.26**	0.13	0.26**	0.13
Number of Persons in Household	−0.07**	0.03	−0.07**	0.03	−0.06**	0.03
Most Important Factor in a Job	−0.34**	0.15	−0.34**	0.16	−0.39**	0.16
Education	0.15**	0.07	0.14**	0.07	0.10	0.06
Personal Income	−0.08***	0.03	−0.05*	0.03	ns	
Urbanicity	−0.12*	0.07	−0.18***	0.07	−0.07	0.07
Frequency of Absence from Work	−0.10**	0.04	−0.02	0.04	−0.01	0.04
Paid Salary/Hourly Wage	0.39	0.35	0.44	0.37	0.68*	0.38
Model chi-square	258.1***		323.9***		455.3***	
Percentage predicted correctly	65.9%		69.6%		72.3%	

Note: B = standardized regression coefficient (beta). S.E. = standard error. ns = not significant.
* = < .10   ** = < .05   *** = < .01

one of the three waves were entered into the analyses; variables not significant in any of the waves were deleted. Almost half of the variables identified by SEARCH as predictive appear to act only through interactive effects. Of those that remained, the most notable are the changes in the significance of gender and the amount of time during the year previous to the study that the respondent was employed. Their effects were weak and inconsistent in the SEARCH but strongly significant in all three waves in the logistic regression. The state of the respondent's job search—whether or not he or she was employed, unemployed but looking for work, not actively looking but interested in working, or not interested in working—also increase in significance, but less dramatically.

Table 11.4 compares respondents reinterviewed with those who refused and those we were unable to recontact. Presented are the column percentages for the interviews and the three types of interview outcomes by some of the variables that accounted for the greatest variance in nonresponse. A clear pattern is visible in the effect of home ownership on the three types of outcomes. The proportion of home owners is similar in those interviewed versus those who refused, but dramatically different for those not found in the second wave. Though not shown here, this finding is repeated in the third and fourth waves. The same pattern is

TABLE 11.4. Interview Outcomes by NPSBA Wave II Predictors of Nonresponse (%)

	Interviewed	Refused	Lost
Owns Home vs. Rental Condition			
Owns Home	59.8	59.5	34.9
Rents—Good Condition	17.6	20.2	20.0
Rents—Minor Repairs	15.2	13.1	26.7
Rents—Major Repairs	7.4	7.1	18.5
Education			
0–11 Years	35.8	67.1	45.5
High School Graduate	33.1	24.4	31.8
Some College	18.5	4.9	16.8
College Graduate	12.6	3.7	6.0
Frequency of Other Church Activities			
Frequent	42.6	41.2	30.2
Not Frequent	25.6	31.8	22.2
Not Church Member	31.8	27.1	47.6
Voted in Presidential Election			
Voted	64.2	68.3	43.8
Did Not Vote	35.8	31.7	56.2
Total N	935	85	851

present for the state of the household unit. The percentage of people lost in tracking increases substantially for those living in units needing minor and major repairs.

In contrast to home ownership, whose effect as a predictor of nonresponse is primarily due to respondents who could not be located, people with low levels of education refuse to be reinterviewed at a much higher rate than others. Conversely, those who have had at least some college education rarely refuse.

The effect of having strong ties to the community should act through a sense of general civic obligation, the means to track individuals who leave the community, and the decreased likelihood that an individual will leave a community to which they have strong ties. The first dynamic should lead to a lower refusal rate, while the second two should decrease the number of respondents lost in tracking. Surprisingly, table 11.4 shows no impact on refusal rates for either frequency of involvement in church activities or voting. Both, however, substantially decrease the rates at which respondents are lost in tracking.

As indicated in the box, researchers planning to conduct longitudinal studies of black Americans can draw upon the findings from this study to address nonresponse.

Lessons Learned

- Respondents with certain demographic characteristics are more likely to be nonresponders. These include male gender, young or old age, lower levels of education, and very high or very low income.
- Owning a home (strongest predictor across the waves) and residence in need of repair are also strong predictors of nonresponse.
- Employment situations including being unemployed, employed in service sector, and expressing a desire for challenging work were also sources of nonresponse.
- Respondents who do not attend church regularly or who are unmarried/not romantically involved were more likely to be nonresponders.

Conclusions

Many of the findings presented here confirm the results reported by McArthur and Short (1985), Kalton et al. (1990), Harris-Kojetin and

Tucker (1998), Kalsbeek, Yang, and Agans (2002), and Lepkowski and Couper (2002). Even though the sample is a considerably different sub-population, home ownership remains extremely important to predicting nonresponse, as it was even for the CPS Study with only an eight-month interval between waves (Harris-Kojetin and Tucker 1998) and the Add Health Study of a population of adolescents (Kalsbeek, Yang, and Agans 2002). Extending this further is the importance of the condition of the dwelling unit for nonhomeowners. While this variable was not present in the other studies, it is reasonable to believe its impact reaches beyond the black population. Kalsbeek et al. (2002) also found that the length of time the household had resided at its current address was an important predictor of second wave recontact. Unfortunately, similar information was not collected in this study.

The level of education appears to be more critical for nonresponse among black Americans than in the American population as a whole (O'Muircheartaigh 1989). On the other hand, gender, urbanicity, and marital status are not as central to these analyses as they were to the analyses by Kalton et al. (1990), Harris-Kojetin and Tucker (1998), and McArthur and Short (1985).

The nature of the respondents' occupations and their attitudes toward and behaviors at work are predictors of nonresponse not addressed in previous studies. It may be that the unique employment conditions facing African Americans lead to very different dynamics on these dimensions. The importance to this population, however, is clear.

The strong relationship between household and personal income and nonresponse is consistent with the findings of Kalton et al. (1990). However, the nature of the relationship between income and nonresponse is less clear in this study, tending toward nonlinearity rather than the simple relationship found between low income and low response rates in the ACL data. This pattern is similar to what Uhrig (2007) found in a study of attrition in a British household panel study.

We also found variables related to the respondent's involvement in the community to be substantially related to nonresponse. This finding is consistent with Lepkowski and Couper's (2002) results that community attachment and social integration variables were significant predictors of recontact at later waves. The NPSBA tended to focus more on church-related and political activities than those reported for ACL (Kalton et al. 1990). This is, however, consistent with the broader, more political, and highly central role the church plays in the black community (Brown and Wolford 1993; Lincoln and Mamiya 1990).

While not major predictors in this study, variables central to the topic of the study did show some relationship to nonresponse in later waves. Despite the small size of the variance they account for, their relation to the topic of the study makes them important to account for. Similarly, the impact of the items relating to the affective state of the respondent, while small, remains important.

The relationships of the predictors to the three interview outcomes generally confirm the patterns seen in the work by Kalton et al. (1990). There are clearly different dynamics driving nonresponse due to refusal and nonresponse due to the difficulty of recontacting some respondents. Research conducted by Lepkowski and Couper (2002) used the ACL to ascertain differences in predictors of nonresponse due to location (lost) and refusals. Using 37 predictors of nonresponse, they found many differences in prediction patterns for both groups, which underscore the need to understand the nature of this better in order to reduce nonresponse in later waves of data collection.

While this chapter presents only the framework for a theory of longitudinal nonresponse, what we have discovered so far is useful for enhancing efforts to account for nonresponse. First, when developing a questionnaire, this framework identifies a range of important issues for nonresponse. Items should be developed to cover this range or modified to tap it more centrally. For example, besides including the traditional sociodemographic correlates of nonresponse, researchers should consider including interviewer observation questions such as assessing the condition of the housing unit and the respondent's level of cooperation during the interview.

Second, we now have a framework for highlighting respondents who are most likely to be lost. This allows us to target tracking efforts more economically. Finally, the adoption of this framework allows the analyst creating nonresponse weights to restrict the focus of his or her search to those variables already identified as associated with longitudinal nonresponse.

NOTE

This research has been supported by the National Institute of Mental Health (Grant no. MH48666).

REFERENCES

Bethlehem, J. 2002. Weighting nonresponse adjustments based on auxiliary information. In *Survey nonresponse,* ed. R. M. Groves, D. A. Dillman, J. L. Eltinge, and R. J. A. Little, 275–87. New York: Wiley.

Brown, R. E., and M. L. Wolford. 1994. Religious resources and African American political action. *National Political Science Review* 4:30–48.

Harris-Kojetin, B. A., and C. Tucker. 1998. Longitudinal nonresponse in the Current Population Survey (CPS). *ZUMA Nachrichten Spezial,* 263–72.

Jackson, J. S., ed. 1991. *Life in black America.* Newbury Park, CA: Sage.

Kalsbeek, W. D., J. Yang, and R. P. Agans. 2002. Predictors of nonresponse in a longitudinal survey of adolescents. *Proceedings of the Section on Survey Research Methods, American Statistical Association,* 1740–45.

Kalton, G., J. Lepkowski, and T. K. Lin. 1985. Compensating for wave nonresponse in the 1979 ISDP research panel. *Proceedings of the Section on Survey Research Methods, American Statistical Association,* 372–77.

Kalton, G., J. Lepkowski, G. E. Montanari, and D. Maligalig. 1990. Characteristics of second wave nonrespondents in a panel survey. *Proceedings of the Section on Survey Research Methods, American Statistical Association,* 462–67.

Lepkowski, J., and M. P. Couper. 2002. Nonresponse in the second wave of longitudinal household surveys. In *Survey nonresponse,* ed. R. M. Groves, D. A. Dillman, J. L. Eltinge, and R. J. A. Little, 259–72. New York: Wiley and Sons.

Lincoln, C. E., and L. H. Mamiya. 1990. *The black church and the African American Experience.* Durham: Duke University Press.

McArthur, E., and K. Short. 1985. Characteristics of sample attrition in the Survey of Income and Program Participation (SIPP). *Proceedings of the Section on Survey Research Methods, American Statistical Association,* 366–71.

Musick, M., A. Campbell, and C. G. Ellison. 2001. Strategies for sample attrition analyses in the National Survey of Black Americans. *African American Research Perspectives* 7 (1): 50–74.

O'Muircheartaigh, C. 1989. Sources of nonsampling error: Discussion. In *Panel surveys,* ed. D. Kasprzyk, G. Duncan, G. Kalton, and M. P. Singh, 271–88. New York: Wiley and Sons.

Sonquist, J. A., E. L. Baker, and J. N. Morgan. 1973. *Searching for structure.* Ann Arbor, Michigan: Institute for Social Research.

Uhrig, S. C. N. 2007. *The right end of attrition: Repeated nonresponse in the British Household Panel Study.* American Association for Public Opinion Research Annual Conference.

12 | Research with Black Churches: Lessons Learned from the Black Church Family Project

Cleopatra Howard Caldwell

Black churches are pivotal institutions in the lives of African Americans (Mattis and Jagers 2001; Taylor, Lincoln, and Chatters 2005). They have been embedded in the social, economic, political, health, and educational fabric of Black communities since the establishment of the first Black church in the eighteenth century (Billingsley 1999). Researchers and service practitioners now recognize the potential of Black churches for addressing the physical, social, and psychological well-being of African Americans through both their spiritual and community outreach missions. Previous research confirms the vital role Black churches can play in working with community-based researchers and service agencies in efforts to reach diverse African American populations (Caldwell, Greene, and Billingsley 1994; Eng and Hatch 1991; Hatch and Derthick 1992; Resnicow 2000; Williams et al. 1999).

With the many challenges facing African American communities today, especially with regard to health disparities and social concerns, the scholarly interest in the potential of Black churches as a base for research will only continue to grow. Thus, effective mechanisms for involving the Black church community in the scientific research process and service delivery must be identified. This chapter outlines conceptual and methodological challenges in conducting research with Black churches. Specifically, we describe a number of lessons learned while conducting the Black Church Family Project (Billingsley and Caldwell 1992; Caldwell, Greene, and Billingsley 1992).

The Black Church Family Project

With financial support from the Ford Foundation and the Lillie Endowment, Dr. Andrew Billingsley and his colleagues launched the Black Church Family Project (BCFP) to collect data from a nationally representative sample of Black churches. Telephone interviews were conducted with church representatives to identify and describe family-oriented community-outreach programs sponsored by Black churches that were designed to enhance the functioning of African American family and community life. The outreach programs of interest were those that included services for people who were *not* church members. Results from this study supported the significance of the community-outreach role of Black churches in meeting the needs of community residents (Billingsley and Caldwell 1991). We found, for example, that some of the outreach programs offered through Black churches were designed to assist with functions typically provided within the family. These included instrumental functions such as the provision of food, shelter, clothing, and health care. They also included expressive functions like imparting a sense of acceptance, self-worth, culture, and pride (Caldwell et al. 1992; Caldwell et al. 1995; Rubin, Billingsley, and Caldwell 1994).

We found that characteristics of the senior minister (e.g., age, seminary training, and community involvement) were determinants of whether or not a Black church engaged in community outreach programming or worked collaboratively with secular and other religious organizations to support African American families. Senior ministers were identified as key influences on whether or not churches operated community outreach programs (Caldwell et al. 1994). Thus, they were the power base of the church (Thomas et al. 1994).

Because this was a community-based participatory research project (Israel et al. 1998, 2005; Minkler and Wallerstein 2003) it was critical to establish a steering committee that included members with research expertise and community expertise in the nature of Black churches. Consequently, a 16-member steering committee was formed to guide the development of the BCFP. This committee included equal numbers of community representatives (i.e., ministers, church members, local leaders) and social science researchers charged with conducting a study of 1,500 randomly selected Black churches throughout the country. In addition, in-depth interviews were conducted within selected churches to gather more qualitative details of the role of the contemporary Black church in the lives of African Americans. The involvement of African American ministers in the project gave it credibility in religious communities and provided much-needed community expertise in every phase of the research process.

The BCFP was divided into two phases. Phase I was a 30-minute telephone survey of 755 randomly selected Black churches throughout the Northeast, North Central, and Western regions of the country for the purpose of gathering information on the history, structure, and support characteristics of Black churches across different denominations. Although this was originally designed as a national probability study, the study period ended before we were able to complete the data collection in the Southern region of the country. Despite this limitation, the scientifically rigorous conceptual and methodological approaches used in the BCFP can serve as models for future research with Black churches. The sampling frame developed for the study can be an especially useful tool for understanding the distribution of Black churches from regional and national perspectives.

Phase II focused on a carefully selected sample of 100 Black churches from around the country that operated exemplary family-support programs. Black churches in the Southern region of the country were a special focus of this phase to accommodate the lack of Southern churches in the 755 churches included in Phase I of the BCFP. Black churches in rural areas also were included in Phase II. Rural churches can present a different profile of religious participation than churches in urban areas because of the vast geographic region covered by a church and because one senior minister may pastor multiple churches. In-depth face-to-face interviews were conducted with representatives from each church including the senior minister, coordinators of community outreach programs, and program participants. In addition, direct observations of outreach programs in action were made. The results of the Phase II qualitative studies are reported in Dr. Andrew Billingsley's 1999 book, *Mighty Like a River: The Black Church and Social Reform.*

The two-phase approach to doing research with Black churches used in the BCFP allowed us to gain a tremendous amount of experience in working with different types of Black churches. In this chapter, we focus on several issues that may be useful for other researchers interested in working with Black churches. We begin by focusing on conceptual issues, including the definition of a Black church and the implications of using a specific definition. We then discuss a number of methodological issues to consider such as obtaining a random sample of churches, gaining access to the church, deciding whom to interview or work with within the church, and interviewer training. We incorporate lessons learned and recommendations for future research with Black churches throughout the chapter.

Conceptual Issues

One of the most challenging tasks in conducting research with Black churches is to define what will or will not be considered a Black church for the purposes of the research. In the BCFP, after much discussion, we defined a Black church as one with at least a 51% African American congregation and an African American senior minister. We also restricted our sample to Christian denominations and faith traditions because of the study's limited time-frame and budget. In talking with experienced Black church researchers such as Drs. C. Eric Lincoln and John Hatch, we identified a number of additional challenges in working with non-Christian faiths, such as the Nation of Islam, when using a telephone interview approach. In his extensive work with Black Muslims, Lincoln (1986) found that a more personal approach (e.g., face-to-face interviews) was necessary to engage this religious group in research because of their heightened mistrust of the academic research enterprise. We therefore

TABLE 12.1.   Denominations Included in the Black Church Family Project: Major Black Denominations Sampled

Major National Black Denominations
   National Baptist Convention, U.S.A., Inc.
   National Baptist Convention of America
   National Primitive Baptist Convention, U.S.A.
   Progressive National Baptist Convention, Inc.
   National Missionary Baptist Convention of America
   Church of God in Christ, Inc. (COGIC)
   African Methodist Episcopal Church (AME)
   African Methodist Episcopal Zion Church (AMEZ)
   Christian Methodist Episcopal Church (CME)
Other Black Faith Traditions
   Apostolic
   Holiness
   Pentecostal
Major National White Denominations
   Church of God, Anderson, IN
   Church of God, Cleveland, TN
   Episcopal
   Lutheran
   Presbyterian Church in America
   Presbyterian Church U.S.A.
   United Methodist
   Seventh-Day Adventist
   United Church of Christ (Congregational)
   Christian Church (Disciples of Christ)

began with the nine historically Black Christian denominations included in the Lincoln and Mamiya (1990) study and expanded to include large predominantly White denominations that had numerous churches that met our definition of a Black church (e.g., United Methodist, Presbyterian). At the advice of our religious community representatives, we then included other religious groups in an attempt to represent as many of the faith traditions important to African Americans as possible with Black churches as defined by study criteria.

Our operational definition allowed us to be selective as to which churches would be eligible for the study so that the focus of the study remained on Black churches and the needs of African Americans. Table 12.1 presents the denominations and faith traditions that were part of the BCFP. Consistent with the reality of African American religious participation, the majority of churches in the BCFP were from the Baptist denomination.

The operational definition of a Black church that we used also limited our ability to include some denominations that are important within African American communities, such as the Catholic Church, because it required the senior minister to be African American. Given the limited number of African American priests who are pastors of predominantly Black Catholic churches, it was not feasible to efficiently identify Black Catholic churches for the study. Thus, it is important to consider the implications of the definition of a Black church used in a study to make sure that the denominations and faith traditions of interest will be included. This is critical because there can be significant differences in denominational tenets, rituals, beliefs, and traditions that can have implications for research implementation and findings. For example, a study seeking to involve African Americans in specific types of stem cell research may have recruiting difficulties with potential participants from faith traditions that believe that life begins at conception; their religious doctrines would lead them to oppose research involving human embryos. Strong ideological differences are problematic for developing trusting working relationships among academic-church partnerships and for recruiting churches as research participants.

Lessons Learned—Planning Considerations

- Form a research steering committee composed of researchers and community representatives familiar with the denominations and faith traditions to be included in the study.

- Be aware of potential ideological conflicts that could derail working relationships as you conceptualize the study. *The Directory of African American Religious Bodies: A Compendium* by Dr. Wardell Payne (1991), from the School of Divinity at Howard University, is a useful resource for clarifying African American denominations and faith traditions. It will help researchers become familiar with a variety of African American faith traditions so that conflicts with specific religious tenets and beliefs can be avoided when selecting denominations and faith traditions to involve in research, especially research in the health arena.
- Use a definition of the Black church to provide boundaries for the research. Identify church doctrines and traditions that govern expectations for beliefs and behaviors to determine the potential influence they may have on the goals of the research.

For others considering how to conduct research with Black churches, the suggestions in the two nearby boxes are offered based on lessons learned from conducting the BCFP, with a specific focus on planning issues and conceptual issues.

Lessons Learned—Conceptual Considerations

- Form a research advisory committee to help clarify issues.
- Use available resources to determine distinctions between denominations and faith traditions.
- Become familiar with doctrines and beliefs of included faith traditions.
- Develop operational definition of Black church.
- Understand influence of exclusionary criteria based on definition.

Methodological Issues

Sampling

Our original goal was to obtain a national probability sample of 1,500 Black churches throughout the country in an effort to represent the diversity of churches operating family and community outreach programs to assist African Americans. This turned out to be a daunting task, with the most challenging issue being how to develop a plausible national sampling frame for Black churches. Legislation from the 1930s resulted in the separation of church and state; therefore, the federal government no longer collects systematic data on churches. To solve this problem, we assumed that Black churches were distributed in a similar manner as Black households. This allowed us to seek permission to use the basic sampling strategy developed for the National Survey of Black Americans, the first national probability sample of Black Americans ever conducted (NSBA; Jackson 1991). The NSBA sample was drawn according to a multistage area probability procedure designed to ensure that every Black household had an equal chance of selection for the study. Based on the 1970 distribution of the African American population, 76 primary sampling areas were selected to represent the nation. These areas were stratified by racial composition and geographic areas in four regions called "clusters": Northeast, North Central, West, and South (Taylor and Chatters 1988). The BCFP staff worked with researchers from NSBA and the Division of Survey Technology at the Institute for Social Research at the University of Michigan to design the sampling strategy and to randomly select Black churches for the sample.

The desired total sample size of 1,500 churches was allocated among the four geographic regions in proportion to the number of African American households in each region. A random sample of churches, stratified by denominations/faith traditions and urbanicity within each region, was selected from the 76 primary sampling areas. Most churches (75%) in the final sample ($N = 755$) were from large urban areas, with a smaller portion representing small urban or rural areas. The urban bias reflects the lack of Southern churches in the sample. The uncertainty in estimating eligibility and response rates for Black churches resulted in the use of a replicated sampling procedure. This procedure allows for the release of the sample for a particular area in smaller segments rather than using the entire sample selected at one time. Thus, specific numbers of churches were released as needed for a primary sampling area. In larger areas, segments of 100 churches were released at one time, while in smaller areas, segments as small as 50 churches were released at one time. The rationale for doing this was that we could decide when to release a new replicate based on how well the data collection was going in an area. In some areas, it was not necessary to release new segments because interviews were being completed as expected. In other areas the inability to contact a selected church or refusals to participate in the study contributed to the need to release new segments. This procedure has implications for achieving a better response rate for the study (Hess 1985), thus improving the scientific credibility of the study.

The final sample for the BCFP included 315 Northeastern churches, 320 North Central churches, and 120 Western churches. Although we reached our goal in obtaining the number of churches desired for each region, the overall response rate for the study was about 60% because of the number of nonresponses from eligible churches. At the time, we did not have a response-rate expectation for churches because most church studies did not select a random sample of Black churches, and sample response rates typically were not reported. The response rate for the BCFP is lower than the 70% frequently expected in a probability sample of households using a face-to-face interview approach, yet it does provide evidence that a relatively rigorous random sample of Black churches was obtained.

Identifying Black Churches

A major challenge in selecting a random sample of churches is the fact that there is no comprehensive listing of Black churches to form the sampling frame for a study. Consequently, it was necessary to compile information on the number of Black churches within each geographical region included in the study. Prior to conducting the BCFP we assessed current knowledge about the number of Black churches distributed throughout the country; the most conservative estimate was between 65,000 and 75,000 churches (Jacquet 1989; Melton 1988). The constantly fluctuating number of "storefront" churches prevalent in many African American communities, however, made it difficult to know the exact number of churches in any region of the country. In addition, the decision to conduct telephone interviews excluded churches without permanent addresses and telephone numbers. Thus, smaller churches that were mobile and likely to use answering machines rather than have a church secretary were underrepresented in the final sample for Phase I of the BCFP.

We used a number of creative approaches to identify Black churches within each of the primary sampling areas. As with the NSBA study (Jackson 1991), the Wide Area Screening Procedure (WASP) was used to identify Black churches in areas that were sparsely populated by African Americans. Specifically, we checked local telephone directories for church denominations included in the study for each site. A research staff person would then call several churches in each denomination in a predominantly White area to tell them about the study and ask if they knew of any Black churches in their area. A number of Black churches were identified in places sparsely populated with African Americans using this approach. In a few areas, we even identified several Black churches that had cooperated as part of the Underground Railroad during slavery and still existed in some predominantly White areas of the country. The fact that White key informants knew where Black churches were located in their area reflected what Dr. James Jackson and colleagues have identified as the high visibility of African Americans in geographically clustered areas with low population density for this group (Gurin, Hatchett, and Jackson 1989).

In addition to using the WASP approach, we received cooperation in identifying Black churches from a wide range of local organizations including church denominational headquarters, the National Urban League, the NAACP, mayors' offices, colleges and universities with African American studies programs and departments, and individual churches. By far, the best suggestion was to go to the national and local associations of Black funeral directors. There are very pragmatic reasons for funeral directors to have lists of Black churches, and this recruitment strategy proved to be quite successful.

Accessing Black Churches

Gaining access to Black churches is a major challenge for any outsider, regardless of race. The African American community in general has a basic mistrust of research, stemming, in part, from the misdeeds revealed based on the well-known study of syphilis in Black men in Tuskegee, Alabama, conducted by the U.S. Public Health Service (Jones 1981). We found, however, that having the support of the senior minister increased our chances of successfully engaging churches in research. Who should be interviewed within the church will depend upon the research focus and the type of data that will be collected, but in every case, the senior minister of the church is the person who initially must be contacted to obtain permission to do the study at the church.

Following the advice of our steering committee, we decided that we only needed a respondent who was familiar with the history of the church and knowledgeable about its outreach activities. Being cognizant and respectful of how busy senior ministers typically are, especially those that also may maintain full-time employment in addition to being the pastor of a church, we did not specify that the respondent had to be the senior minister of the church; rather, the senior minister could designate someone else from the church. In contacting the senior minister to obtain permission for the church's participation in the study, however, 72% of the senior ministers decided to respond to the 30-minute telephone survey, and a donation was made to the church for their participation.

Based on a comprehensive review of the role of clergy in Black churches related to mental health service delivery, Taylor et al. (2000) concluded that the senior minister is pivotal to the development and operation of church-based health and social programs. We also found that having contact with the senior minister was a vital strategy for engaging Black churches in research. Working with a prominent church member, however, was critical to gaining access to the senior minister.

Interviewer Training Issues

Training interviewers to work with religious people required special attention, especially because not all of our interviewers were religious themselves. Our preference was to hire older African American female church members as interviewers because they tend to be the workers of the church in general. By conducting the BCFP at a predominantly White university we were not able to hire all African American or religious interviewers. We therefore had to prepare our diverse interviewing staff to be culturally sensitive at multiple levels. From the religious perspective, it was important to instruct the interviewers in how to show appropriate deference to Black ministers because they have very high regard within African American communities, regardless of their educational background or financial status (Neighbors, Musick, and Williams 1999; Williams et al. 1999). Respecting all people was required, but older Black church people received special recognition during training due to their earned places of honor within the church (Taylor et al. 2000). Everyone was to be addressed by his or her known title (e.g., Reverend, Dr., Mr., Mrs., or Ms.) and last name unless told to do otherwise by the respondent.

We knew that the interviewers would be asked about their religious background and if they belonged to a church. Most of our interviewers could respond affirmatively to these questions, but a few who were not religious had to be prepared not to offend respondents. They were instructed to talk about their childhood religious upbringing in establishing rapport with the respondent if they had been socialized in a church.

If not, they were trained to speak briefly and honestly about their religious beliefs, while also being prepared to respectfully decline invitations to the respondent's church or have a prayer said for them if they found this offensive. This strategy worked well for avoiding long religious conversion conversations prior to the telephone interview. In fact, one of our best interviewers was an Irish, White male atheist who had been raised as a Catholic. He was able to gain the confidence of the respondents through honest responses to religious questions. During the project, he gained a fuller appreciation of religious people by interacting respectfully with respondents while remaining true to his own convictions. This made him an outstanding interviewer for the project. The bottom line is that honesty and respect are the best policies in preparing interviewers to work with religious respondents or anyone else who may have divergent views.

Lessons Learned—Interviewer Training Methods

- Matching on race may not always be possible, but it is critical to provide project-specific training that is culturally based and appropriate.
- Showing deference to the minister is vital.
- Foster an attitude of respect, particularly for older church members.

Interest in conducting research with Black churches has increased significantly over the past decade, yet most studies rely on small convenience samples. Randomly selecting churches (or church members) for participation in research has a number of benefits, including the ability to generalize findings. The boxes offer methodological suggestions for conducting research with Black churches with a focus on interviewer training issues and general methodological lessons learned.

Lessons Learned—Methodological Considerations

- Most major church denominations have listings of the churches that belong to their group. In contacting the different denominational headquarters included in this study, we found that some will provide a listing at no cost, while others charge a fee to obtain this information. Some also produce books of church listings, and the more technologically sophisticated headquarters can provide computer printouts with specific church information (e.g., race of senior minister, congregational size) based on the areas of interest.

- Although Baptist denominations have the largest number of Black churches, a concern when sampling Black Baptist churches using denominational lists is how to eliminate duplicate churches. This stems from the fact that a Baptist church can belong to more than one denominational group (e.g., Southern Baptist, Missionary Baptist, Primitive Baptist). This complicates the sampling process if cross-checks are not made to be sure that a church has not been counted more than once.

- The sampling frame developed for the BCFP was based on the original NSBA sampling frame. Dr. Jackson and his colleagues (2004) at the Institute for Social Research, University of Michigan have recently completed the data collection for the National Survey of American Life, which is a follow-up study to the NSBA. The sampling frame for African American households in this study is based on census data for the year 1990. This more recent sampling frame should be helpful as a starting point for estimating the distribution of Black churches in different areas of the country today. It is important to note that most of the primary sampling areas from the original sample remain relevant today.

- Listings of local telephone directories on the Internet should make it easier to identify Black churches by denomination throughout the country. Nevertheless, the Wide Area Screening Procedure remains one of the best strategies for identifying Black churches in predominantly White areas of the country.

- The influx of answering machines and voice mail has significant implications for identifying churches and conducting telephone interviews. We found that leaving a message about the study resulted in few return telephone calls from churches. Depending on the area of the country, leaving multiple messages on a church answering machine could become quite costly. Therefore, we adopted a policy of sending the senior minister a letter about the study, then following up with telephone calls at different times of the day as often as necessary to reach someone at the selected church. A total of ten callbacks was made unless there was a compelling reason to continue to call a particular church. As a last re-

sort, calls were made at 10:00 a.m. on Sunday morning, just before the 11:00 a.m. church service. This procedure worked well for
identifying a time that someone would be in the church office to
receive the recruitment.

Conclusions

Contemporary Black churches represent strong, independent, economically viable, well-respected, self-help institutions in African American
communities. They span a broad range of social classes and embrace a
wide range of denominational affiliations and faith traditions. Because
of their history and independence, Black churches can play a major role
in harnessing the resources of both the larger society and the African
American community to ameliorate some of the health and social issues
that continue to plague African Americans. The commitment of many
Black churches to addressing the needs of African Americans in today's
society make them a natural setting for conducting research and deliver-
ing services for African Americans from diverse backgrounds. Emerging
studies speak to the unrealized and powerful potential of Black churches
to engage in social reform through community-based research partnerships with universities and other secular organizations. Working with
Black churches, however, can be both rewarding and challenging. In this
chapter, we have offered a number of ideas for increasing the success of
future research with Black churches based on our experiences with the
Black Church Family Project.

REFERENCES

Billingsley, A. 1999. *Mighty like a river: The Black church and social reform.* New
York: Oxford University Press.
Billingsley, A., and C. H. Caldwell. 1991. The church, the family, and the school in
the African American community. *Journal of Negro Education* 60:427–40.
Billingsley, A., and C. H. Caldwell. 1994. The social relevance of the contemporary
Black church. *National Journal of Sociology* 8:1–23.
Caldwell, C. H., L. M. Chatters, A. Billingsley, and R. J. Taylor. 1995. Church-based
support programs for elderly Black adults: Congregational and clergy charac-
teristics. In M. A. Kimble, S. H. McFadden, J. W. Ellor, and J. J. Seeber, eds., *Aging, spirituality, and religion: A handbook,* 306–24. Minneapolis: Augsburg
Fortress.

Caldwell, C. H., A. D. Greene, and A. Billingsley. 1992. The Black church as a family support system: Instrumental and expressive functions. *National Journal of Sociology* 6:21–40.

Caldwell, C. H., A. D. Greene, and A. Billingsley. 1994. Family support programs in Black churches: A new look at old functions. In S. L. Kagan and B. Weissbourd, eds., *Putting families first,* 137–60. San Francisco: Jossey-Bass.

Eng, E., and J. W. Hatch. 1991. Networking between agencies and Black churches: The lay health advisor model. *Prevention in Human Services* 10:123–46.

Gurin, P., S. J. Hatchett, and J. S. Jackson. 1989. *Hope and independence: Blacks' response to electoral and party politics.* New York: Russell Sage Foundation.

Hatch, J., and S. Derthick. 1992. Empowering Black churches for health promotion. *Health Values* 16:3–9.

Hess, I. 1985. *Sampling for social research surveys, 1947–1980.* Ann Arbor: Institute for Social Research, University of Michigan.

Israel, B. A., E. Eng, A. J. Schulz, and E. A. Parker, eds. 2005. *Methods in community-based participatory research for health.* San Francisco: Jossey-Bass.

Israel, B. A., A. J. Schulz, E. A. Parker, and A. B. Becker. 1998. A review of community-based research: Assessing partnership approaches to improve public health. *Annual Review of Public Health* 19:173–202.

Jackson, J. S. 1991. *Life in Black America.* Thousand Oaks, CA: Sage.

Jackson, J. S., M. Torres, C. H. Caldwell, H. W. Neighbors, R. N. Nesse, R. J. Taylor, S. J. Trierweiler, and D. R. Williams. 2004. The National Survey of American Life: A study of racial, ethnic, and cultural influences on mental disorder and mental health. *International Journal of Methods in Psychiatric Research* 13:196–207.

Jacquet, C. H., ed. 1989. *Yearbook of American and Canadian churches, 1989.* Nashville: Abingdon Press.

Jones, J. H. 1981. *Bad blood: The Tuskegee syphilis experiment.* New York: Free Press.

Lincoln, C. E. 1986. *The Black Muslims.* Durham: Duke University Press.

Lincoln, C. E., and L. H. Mamiya. 1990. *The Black church in the African American experience.* Durham: Duke University Press.

Mattis, J. S., and R. J. Jagers. 2001. A relational framework for the study of religiosity and spirituality in the lives of African Americans. *Journal of Community Psychology* 29:519–39.

Melton, J. G., ed. 1988. *Encyclopedia of American religions.* 3rd ed. Detroit: Gale Research.

Minkler, M., and N. Wallerstein, eds. 2003. *Community-based participatory research for health.* San Francisco: Jossey-Bass.

Neighbors, H. W., M. A. Musick, and D. R. Williams. 1998. The African American minister as a source of help for serious personal crises: Bridge or barrier to mental health care? *Health Education and Behavior* 25:759–77.

Payne, W. 1991. *Directory of African American religious bodies.* Washington, DC: Howard University Press.

Resnicow, K., et al. 2001. A motivational interviewing intervention to increase fruit and vegetable intake through Black churches: Results of the Eat for Life trial. *American Journal of Public Health* 91:1686–93.

Rubin, R. H., A. Billingsley, and C. H. Caldwell. 1994. The role of the Black church in working with Black adolescents. *Adolescence* 29:251–66.

Taylor, R. J., and L. M. Chatters. 1988. Church members as a source of informal social support. *Review of Religious Research* 30:432–38.

Taylor, R. J., C. G. Ellison, L. M. Chatters, J. S. Levin, and K. D. Lincoln. 2000. Mental health services in faith communities: The role of clergy in Black churches. *Social Work* 45:73–87.

Taylor, R. J., K. Lincoln, and L. M. Chatters. 2005. Supportive relationships with church members among African Americans. *Family Relations: Interdisciplinary Journal of Applied Family Studies* 54:501–11.

Thomas, S. B., S. C. Quinn, A. Billingsley, and C. H. Caldwell. 1994. The characteristics of northern Black churches with community health outreach programs. *American Journal of Public Health* 84:575–79.

Williams, D. R., E. E. H. Griffith, J. L. Young, C. Collins, and J. Dodson. 1999. Structure and provision of services in Black churches in New Haven, Connecticut. *Culture Diversity and Ethnic Minority Psychology* 5:118–33.

PART IV | Research Involving Structural Issues
Focused on Families, the Mental Health
System, and the Media

13 | A Certain Kind of Vision: Revealing Structure, Process, and Meaning in African American Families

Andrea G. Hunter and Deborah J. Johnson

The methodological strategies that one uses reflect not only a desire to observe a specific unit, behavior, or process but also a settling on what one wants to reveal. Collectively, in our work there has been urgency about capturing a certain "angle of vision" that reveals nuances, variations, and the everyday experience and practice of African American family life. To "reveal something" is not a question of locating oneself in the family strength or deficit camps but rather of working beneath the cover of representation, discourse, and politics to understand more about how black life is lived, understood, and felt, and its implications for African American individuals, families, and communities. It is a stance that acknowledges the political and sociohistorical context in which knowledge generation occurs. African American family studies and its corollary in the developmental sciences have long been tied to public and political discourses about race and the representation(s) of the social and cultural life of blacks. It is no understatement to suggest that much of the classic work on African American families in the last century has sought to juxtapose the "facts" of black life against its representations in the American public imagination (Hunter 2006). The challenge here is not only methodological; it is also interpretive. Indeed, research methodology is an interpretive tool. The question is, How do we, who study African American families, use these tools in ways that will not obscure what we want to understand?

In this chapter, we illustrate how our methodological choices serve larger interpretive goals to reveal the nuances of African American family life that are evident but go unexamined, to highlight unheard (and sometimes silenced) voices that are witness to and express meanings that give coherence to black life, and to uncover cultural groundings. Using studies from the fields of child development and family studies as exemplars, we focus on core areas of family research including family structure and form, family process, and meanings. We write in a collective voice about shared insights, which are then illustrated by our individual work. In addition, through the use of first-person narrative and language that at times does not conform to the conventions of scientific writing, we give visibility to the subjectivity that underlies methodological choices. We conclude with a summary of lessons learned, and highlight the interpretive principles and methodological strategies that inform our work on African American families.

Interpretive and Methodological Strategies for Studying Structure and Process in African American Families

For much of its history, black family studies has engaged questions about the variation in families and what divergences from "normative" family models mean for the health and functioning of African American individuals (Hunter 2002, 2006). Scholars have also attempted to "write-in" aspects of the black experience (both culture and minority-based experiences) that were omitted from models and theories about the family. In our individual work we have focused on revealing the deep structure of culture and minority-based status that inform structure and process in African American families and have worked to develop culturally relevant conceptualizations of and methodological approaches to the family that reflect the everyday experiences of African Americans. Hunter, in her studies of family structure and living arrangements, has worked to represent the variety of ways people come together to create a family life and to infuse the interpretation of diverse families with a sense of cultural coherence. Using a community epidemiological approach as an exemplar, Hunter highlights how an emphasis on diversity and variations within a defined population, and a nuanced interpretive lens, can yield insights about African American families. Johnson, in her studies of parental racial socialization, has developed a variety of observationally based methodological approaches to examine the socialization processes through which African American parents prepare their children to cope with race. She highlights the importance of developing measures that are grounded in the cultural experiences and real-world challenges of African American children and families.

Cultivating a Sense of Cultural Coherence: Understanding Diversity and Variation in African American Families; Hunter Discusses Her Work on Family Diversity

When family scholars attempt to capture a representation of the family, they engage complex symbolic meanings and must find ways to make sense of a family terrain that is multidimensional and multilayered. I have worked to draw on representations of families that were organic to the population under study and struggled to develop ways of structurally organizing families that better revealed their everyday and mundane practices. With this approach, I do not directly tackle the question of symbolic meanings but rather view emergent family structures as a series of adaptations, compromises, and interlocking life struggles through which I may understand the variety of ways African Americans create family, which in turn begins to inform me about culture, meanings, and the exigencies of black life. Whether one targets parent-child dyads, multigenerational family lineages, the household, or kinship systems, each family site is connected, overlapping, and simultaneously engaged with other sites. No matter how narrow the lens, it is important to find ways to make the connections among family sites visible. Such an orientation can yield a great deal, particularly in the study of African Americans who are more likely than nonblacks to partner, raise, and bear children in arrangements that are both less institutionalized (e.g., cohabitation, nonmarital childbearing, informal adoption) and more often grounded in extended family traditions. Within families, individuals are at multiple locations via generational and kin positions (e.g., grandmother, mother, daughter, cousin). As individuals within family contexts are considered, it is important to address from whose eyes the behaviors, interactions, or processes of interest shall be viewed. This is not a question of who is reporting (although it can be) but rather from whose vantage point (e.g., household head, child, grandparent) in the family one looks. Viewing the family from multiple vantage points provides a more textured analysis of families and the impact of diverse family structures on behavior, interaction and process, and the well-being of family members.

The challenge, whatever the research problem, family site, or vantage point of interest, is to develop a strategy that allows one to hold on to the complexity of people's family lives. I have struggled with the problem of how to make sense of and meaningfully represent the variety of ways African Americans choose to live together using national survey data

(Hunter 1997), historical records (Hunter 1993, 2001), and community studies (Hunter and Ensminger 1992; Hunter et al. 1998; Pearson et al. 1990; Pearson et al. 1997). An exemplar is a number of studies based on the Woodlawn Longitudinal Study (Kellam et al. 1975), where colleagues and I have grappled with the conceptual and practical problems of working with diverse family households. Woodlawn, a largely poor black community in Chicago, was the site of a community epidemiological study of mental health focusing on a cohort of first-grade entrants and their families who were followed through the end of their high school years, culminating in a 30-year follow-up in middle adulthood. The family patterns in Woodlawn, not unlike many other urban and rural black communities, exposed the limitations of conventional conjugal-centric typologies of the family. Kellam and colleagues (1977) found 86 different combinations of adults living with Woodlawn children as they entered first grade.

To capture these diverse living arrangements, colleagues and I developed a typology that merged both a focus on parental systems (i.e., 1, 2, or no parents) and a rather detailed look at extended families, including adult and minor kin (Hunter and Ensminger 1992). This approach was taken for three reasons. First, we wanted to develop a typology that reflected the ways African Americans bridge conventional and alternative family patterns. Second, we wanted to call attention to two streams of work on family diversity. Studies of family diversity, primarily grounded on white families, have largely focused on derivatives of the nuclear family (e.g., step, blended families) with little attention to the presence or role of nonnuclear kin. In contrast, black family scholars have emphasized aspects of family life that have been excluded from conventional models, including multigenerational family relationships, malleability of household boundaries, and the role of fictive kin and parent surrogates. Finally, we wanted to highlight the fluidity of households that is overlooked by conventional approaches to studying children's families. In highlighting the diversity and fluidness in black children's families and households, we raised the question of whether the rate of female-headed households tells us enough about the variations in black children's family lives.

A subtext of these studies was to locate families and households within a broader "kinship space." Detailed typologies of extended family households (10 types) revealed different stories, e.g., married couples bringing in a sibling with children, grandparents opening their homes to their adult children and grandchildren. As Woodlawn children aged, these configurations shifted. Aunts and uncles were likely to move on, grandparents became less common, and nieces and nephews, the grand-children of the next generation, were now present. We were interested in how these diverse and shifting household configurations shape the par-enting and child care systems within households. For example, taking a closer look at parenting and extended family households, we examined the parental involvement of grandmothers living in multigenerational family households with their grandchildren (Pearson et al. 1990). We ex-plored how the prevalence of grandmothers' involvement in parenting and the configuration of activities they engaged in vary across diverse multigenerational family contexts. Although reliance on grandmothers is a well-worn cultural and family strategy for African Americans, the type and configuration of grandmothers' parenting activities were shaped by the constellation of other relatives in the household. We also illustrated the role of an assortment of kin who in nontrivial ways par-ticipated in parenting and child care. In this and other community stud-ies, we highlighted a variety of parenting models from parenting alone to multiple caregivers (Hunter et al. 1998; Pearson et al. 1997).

Across the Woodlawn studies, findings suggest that knowing the rate of female-headed households does not tell us enough about how black children's family lives may differ from (or converge with) conventional models of the family. We identified diverse parenting systems, multiple sites of family transitions, and endemic patterns of family change, many of which are invisible to conjugal-centered approaches to the family. In-deed, if we, as family scholars, are to understand African American fam-ily life, it is critical that we take on a conceptual lens that allows us to look at the diversity and fluidness of family life in complex ways. However, a central challenge is to find ways to preserve the complexity (and diver-sity) of African American families in the face of practical pressures for data reduction. There are three major strategies that I use to balance the need for rich detail with the practical need to collapse categories and summarize data. First, I work to retain an emphasis on descriptive analy-sis, even when quantitative and inferential data-analytic approaches are used. Second, I let the insights from thick description drive the decisions I need to make about data reduction. Finally, I move back and forth be-tween these two or more vantage points (e.g., the general and the specific) in my analytic and interpretive approach. What underlies this process is an attempt to connect with what makes family contexts quali-tatively different and culturally meaningful. This involves a kind of intu-itive element, a feeling about people and families, and above all it requires a willingness to let people speak about their own experience. Embracing this type of approach requires that one develop representations of families that are organic to the population under study and work to find ways to better reveal the everyday and mundane practices of families. It is also an approach that pushes the researcher to engage the question of what is it that one wants to reveal.

Revealing Cultural and Minority-based Status in African American Parental Socialization Processes: Johnson Discusses Her Work on Racial Socialization

Pushing against historical perspectives on black family dysfunction, the research on racial socialization has built upon behavioral and attitudinal approaches to parenting by shifting to an emphasis on how social stratification factors may impinge upon normative child outcomes. In early descriptive studies, African American parents acknowledged racial socialization as a feature of their parenting. These studies also revealed that most were explicitly involved in racial socialization processes (Spencer 1983; Holliday 1992). Often the goals of these socialization efforts were to have their children develop or strengthen skills to manage mundane experiences associated with devalued racial status and combat threats posed by hostile racial contexts (Hughes and Chen 1997; Stevenson, Reed, and Bodison 1996). The next generation of studies gave rise to the notion that parents could have many racial socialization orientations (race-based barriers, pride; non–race-based, humanistic; or individual efficacy). Moreover, it was shown across several studies that parental characteristics and experiences influenced parental racial coping orientations and race-related child outcomes (Hughes and Johnson 2001; Johnson 2001). However, parental socialization orientations and parental characteristics did not fully explain the variation in child outcomes, and processes that might link parent factors (i.e., individual characteristics, behaviors, processes) more comprehensively with child characteristics (i.e., personality characteristics, coping skills, behavior) were not on the radar screen. Conceptually, at that time, the field had pretty much defined itself by looking from immovable structure to structure, from independent variable to static outcome variable. For example, many studies assessed variation in the associations between parent characteristics and parental socialization strategy/orientation, or between parent characteristics and child outcomes, but rarely through process.

Consequently, I became more interested in process despite the importance of these earlier efforts emphasizing the more structural and descriptive elements such as numbers of racial coping strategies (RCSs) or age of children and RCSs used (Johnson 1988, 1996). Specifically, I was interested in revealing the tacit mechanisms that link characteristics of parents and children, parental racial socialization orientations, and child racial coping skills.

Studying a potentially volatile topic where the stakes were quite high for African American parents required new information that could be observed about parenting processes (Johnson 2001, 2005). Despite the pervasiveness of discrimination and shared experiences of prejudice among black parents in American society, these are not events that could be captured easily or captured in substantial numbers through naturalistic observation. The task devised was one that would most likely trigger parents' socialization behaviors in relation to a racially charged event. To enhance the observability of parents' and children's interactions around this issue, six open-ended child vignettes depicting some form of racial conflict were provided to a parent-child dyad. Two vignettes depicted a within-group conflict having to do with cultural authenticity (e.g., not "talking black"), and four vignettes depicted a between-group conflict where black/white conflicts were prominent (e.g., choosing black friends over white). Parents and children were left with decisions about who should start the process, how each vignette was to be solved, and in what manner of discussion; these interactions were videotaped. From coding and analysis of the videotaped interactions, I gained a reliable understanding of parenting style and microprocesses that either promoted or undermined parental goals around racial socialization. Since children's responses to the vignettes were obtained in an earlier session sans parents, comparing children's resolutions in parent/nonparent contexts would reveal the impact of parent oversight on child solutions and the relation between child solutions and parental childrearing strategies. Essentially, I could learn what's "in the box" and what might lie outside of it with respect to parental influences on child racial coping.

Initially with 12 families and later with 20 additional families, I learned that there was a lot more to predicting child coping than parent orientations or characteristics. Parent goals or philosophies for coping with race were subject to their negotiation style and ability to scaffold or build upon children's ideas and behavior. The use of negotiation strategies, scaffolding, and reinforcement provided a foundation for interaction that set the stage for children to develop a diverse set of RCSs. In addition, these modes of interaction seemed to supersede the imposition or extrication of race in the problem-solving process. That is, whether parents went about underscoring the impact of race or diminishing its impact in interactions with their child was less important than simply having a race-inclusive discussion. This approach revealed a distinction between the goals of socialization around race and the parental processes interacting with those goals.

African American parents must manage and sift through the effects of racism and discrimination; these additional burdens reflect fundamental inequities among families in our society. My research and similar studies by other scholars of color have helped the field to conceptualize parental racial socialization goals and processes as being a more complex and diverse set of parenting duties and experiences for African American families. A mixed-methods approach, infused with meaning rooted in social history and culture, helped to achieve this level of understanding. African American families remain focused on what most American parents are focused on, and that is the healthy development of their children and the provision of skills, social and otherwise, that will enable them to negotiate society effectively and to become productive members. With respect to racial coping, scholars observe the additional stressors and responsibilities that typify African American parenting. And African American parents recognize the unfairness of having to prepare their children to manage racism. Nevertheless, they do so because the cost of not doing so is too great. The underlying processes inherent in these socialization practices are revealed through the confluence of methods I selected and by interpretive strategies that consider culture, social positioning, and development.

Interpretive and Methodological Strategies for Exploring Meanings in African American Families

African Americans have a kind of presence in the American imagination, but it is a visibility that is painfully unrevealing. It is a rather curious "publicness" that, in the words of W. E. B. DuBois (1969), yields the African American with "no true self-consciousness, but only lets him see himself through the revelation of the other world" (45). In our research, regardless of the methodological approach taken, each of us has struggled to look beneath the veil to get at what black people's lives and experiences are like and to do so in ways that are meaningful and recognizable to the people we study. We believe it is also critical to find ways to just listen to how people interpret and understand their own lives. Qualitative methodology, in whatever form it takes, is fundamentally about listening and connecting with an interpretive position outside oneself. It is an approach that is powerful not only because it "gives" voice to respondents, but also because these voices have the power to transform us. Quite independently we have been drawn to work with African American men because of both their visibility and the muteness of their voices in social research. Using qualitative methodological strategies, we explore the meanings of and transformations in core social identities and family roles. Hunter describes a project that explores the meanings of manhood and the coming-of-age experiences of young African American men, and Johnson reviews a project that explores African American men's perspectives on fathering and reflections on their parenting experiences as intertwined with racial meaning. In both these exemplars, Hunter and Johnson highlight methodological and analytical strategies they have used to listen to voices that are often unheard (or silenced) and to share the power to assign meaning with those who have given their stories.

Transformations in Young Men's Lives: Sharing the Power to Assign Meaning; Hunter Discusses Her Work on the Meanings of Manhood and Coming of Age

The exploration of social identities in modernist and postmodernist traditions requires the juxtaposition of the self in relation to others, to social categorization, and to the meaning(s), language(s), and discourse(s) of identity and difference (Holstein and Gubrium 1994). Interrogating identity constructions at the intersections of race and gender (and social class) exposes tensions in interpretive practice and the ways identity and social categories are constructed via language and power relations. With colleagues, I have explored African American men's constructions of manhood across the life course, with an eye toward the collective generation of meaning, intersubjectivity, and the everyday practices that inform social identities (Hunter and Davis 1992, 1994; Hunter et al. 2006). Not unlike generations of men before them, young African American men's constructions of manhood have to do with a sense of integrity and strength of self, a core sense of responsibility, and social connections and obligations to family, community, and race (Hunter et al. 2006). These meanings of manhood are cast against a backdrop of race, social class, and place as young men confront and struggle with barriers to becoming the men they want to be. Indeed, the young men we spoke to are acutely aware of their visibility and vulnerability and how, in DuBois's (1969) words, they are viewed "through the revelation of the other world" (45). As one teenager candidly told us, "They think we come out the womb labeled, with an orange jump suit on and a number on our back."

A challenge for us, as scholars of black life, is to displace this "other world" interpretation and to listen to what individuals have to say about their lives. Qualitative methodologies privilege the interpretive voice of participants, and push the researcher to share the power to assign meaning. To do this requires researchers, at times, to follow the participants' story rather than their own and to use data-analytic strategies that preserve an interpretive role for the participants. In this and other studies, we have used a concept-mapping procedure (Trochim 1989) that is an example of a data-analytic strategy where respondents directly shape interpretation. Young men sorted the ideas that were generated by participants into categories that were conceptually similar resulting in a concept map on which we based our interpretations. However, despite our singular interests, it quickly became evident in our dialogues with young men that they chose to share stories that were beyond our primary research aim (i.e., social construction of manhood). One such story was young men's reflections on life without fathers, manhood, and coming of age; it was a compelling story of loss, survival, and redemption. We asked participants to tell us something about what they thought being a man means, and what they also told us was something about the type of men they wanted to become. As it happens, for adolescents father loss was an important interpretive bridge between ideology and identity.

To bridge the gaps between our own biographies and meanings and those of our participants, we must find ways to connect with the cultural and lived experience from which their stories emerge. The stories of the young men we spoke to were grounded in African American narrative traditions, ranging from Southern folk thought to hip-hop and rap. As we read the dialogues that young men had with each other and with us, and work with the interpretation of the concept maps, we do so understanding the importance of "concrete experience as a criterion of meaning" in core black cultural traditions and its importance in validating knowledge claims as a symbolic vehicle for theorizing and for creating new meanings (Collins 1991, 208–9; Gwaltney 1980). This is the analytic tradition in which my research and interpretive approach is also grounded. Thus, in this and other projects I reflect on a basic lesson from black Southern storytelling traditions. That is, a story once told has been given over to the retelling. While the integrity of the plot and narrative may be maintained, the next telling is necessarily infused with the insights that come from listening and making connections to one's own lived experience and wisdoms—it is a blending of insights. To do this, and do it well, you must respect the storyteller and the story told.

Transformations in Fathers' Lives: Listening to Unheard Voices; Johnson Discusses Her Work on African American Fathers

The literature on African American fathers, parenting perspectives, and socialization is scant at best, with but a few notable exceptions (for examples, see Allen and Conner 1997; Connor and White 2006; Storm et al. 2000). There is a growing literature focusing on special populations of African American fathers with unique problems, such as single parents, incarcerated fathers, or adolescent fathers. Another part of the literature on men and manhood also intersects with issues of fatherhood (e.g., Hunter et al. 2006), but does not explicitly focus on it. Much emphasis in research has been placed on economic provider role issues that often become the narrow lens through which black fathering is understood (Bowman and Foreman 1997). Moreover, the voices of black men across an expanse of fathering roles go largely unheard and unexamined.

My research concerns were threefold (Johnson and Davis 2001; Johnson and Livingston 2002): (1) the literature bypassed fatherhood; or (2) it emphasized special circumstances of African American fathers; or (3) the paradigms used to study black fatherhood did not reflect the depth of fathering experiences and perspectives. In this work, I push past narrow or negative perspectives of black fathers and attempt to highlight and specify diversity in fathering roles that have been masked by nuclear family–centered approaches to the black family that view fathers as largely missing.

Among all these disparate conceptual elements was the deafening silence of men's voices in research on fathers. Several factors associated with the typical data collection processes account for this; two issues have played a key role. First is the use of mothers as gatekeepers for fathers' experiences; that is, in the field we interview mothers about what fathers do or don't do, think or don't think—an approach that abandons and bypasses fathers' perspectives. The exclusive interrogation of mothers in order to understand black family life is less about mothers and more about the view that black fathers are thought to be largely unavailable or of little consequence to the positive development of their children. The other approach has been to interview fathers about parenting but use measures and surveys developed for gathering information about mothers or from mothers' perspective. Although these methods have yielded important findings, I felt the men themselves might have something more to offer and thus broaden the parenting picture. My critiques of the field made it necessary to take an approach that allowed men's own words to shape the work.

Rather than individual interviews, I used "directed focus groups" to enhance the process of discovery with respect to key issues in men's experiences, and their thinking about parenting. In the directed focus group method, I developed a core of nine topics to guide the discussions. The range of topics included child rearing, racial socialization, and community fathering. However, while it was important to achieve coverage of core domains, getting good data also meant flowing with the group's own interests and rhythms. I was fortunate to recruit African American fathers who were largely middle-aged men, with children whose ages spanned infancy to adulthood. Of concern as I began the study was conducting the focus groups without a male counterpart. This choice goes against convention in the field. Nevertheless, I discovered that on the topic of fathering, cross-gender facilitation was a strength. It was clear that in the context of discussion, the men attempted to develop a bridge to me as a woman, to increase my understanding of their view. There was no presumed shared thinking or language, and their explanations and descriptions were highly detailed. The other benefit was their comfort with sharing deep emotions around their fathering. Often in unbroken male space where hardship and relationships are discussed, one might expect some negative expressions of anger toward women (ex-wives or girlfriends); these expressions were sometimes touched upon but may have been minimized due to this gender-bridging process. Rather than using my gender as an excuse to vent, it became an opportunity to explain and share.

The use of a qualitative approach that emphasized structural and affective elements around fathering provided men an opportunity to express the full range of parenting experiences and their understanding of the fathering role. As a researcher and as a human being, I was humbled by the ways men were willing to share profoundly personal experiences.

I left each group with an enormous sense of respect for the unrecognized struggles of these men to engage the fathering role and to resolve the deep meaning of fathering. They also seemed to benefit a great deal from these sessions. First they related that "in the past no one had asked them about their thoughts on parenting," and they were grateful to be asked. Second, they often entered the focus group context cautiously but emerged from the process feeling good about sharing emotion-laden experiences and feeling less isolated in their thinking about race. They also found that they had common concerns about their child-rearing decisions and the challenges associated with parenting African American children.

Lessons Learned: Interpretive Principles and Methodological Strategies

In John Gwaltney's *Drylongso: A Self-Portrait of Black America* (1980), Ruth Shays, an elderly black woman, begins her narrative, "I think there is more talking *around* what black people are than there is talking *about* what we are" (27). Shays's words can be read as both a critique and cautionary tale for those who study black life. But what does it mean to talk about what black people are? We, in different ways, have asked what is evident but remains unseen—what have the fields of developmental science and family studies talked around. Using diverse research projects, we have illustrated how our emphasis on capturing a certain angle of vision has influenced our research questions, methodological choices, and interpretive strategies. Focusing on the three central prongs of family studies—structure, process, and meaning—we highlighted how one can work to reveal the nuances, variations, and everyday experience and practice of black family life. As we have worked to cultivate a certain angle of vision in our work, we have viewed methodology as an interpretive tool and tied our methodological choices to the question of what it is that one wants to reveal, and we remain mindful of the adage to respect the storyteller and the story told.

Conclusion

Table 13.1 summarizes some of the lessons we have learned from our work, with a focus on the interpretive principles and strategies that have

TABLE 13.1.   Lessons Learned: Cultivating an Angle of Vision to Reveal
Structure, Process, and Meaning in African American Families

Revealing Structure and Process
Interpretive Principles
- Understand what makes family contexts qualitatively different and culturally meaningful for African Americans
- Reveal the deep structure of culture and reveal cultural and minority status–based parenting processes as unique features of African American child rearing

Strategies
- Develop a conceptualization of the family that is organic to the population studied and that reveals the everyday and mundane practices of families
- Use multiple vantage points within the family to inform a textured analysis of behavior, interaction and process, and individual well-being across diverse family contexts
- Develop measures grounded in the experiences of the population that reflect real-world challenges of African American families and culturally resonate with this population
- Use observational methods for depth of understanding about family process and interaction, and family members' perspectives about meaning and their behavior
- Use insights from a thick description to inform decisions about data reduction, data analysis, and interpretation

Revealing Meanings and Unheard Voices
Interpretive Principles
- Displace "other world" interpretations of black life and listen to what individuals have to say about their lives
- Individuals are interpreters of their own experience and, as cointerpreters, share the power to assign meaning.
- Partner with participants based on mutual trust and respect and a commitment to reveal and value their stories
- Bridge the gaps between our own biographies and meanings and those of participants and connect with the cultural and lived experience from which stories emerge

Strategies
- To reveal aspects of the black experience that are invisible or distorted, use methods and analytical techniques that preserve the interpretive voice of participants
- Interpretive analysis should be informed by knowledge of culturally based narrative traditions, variations in language, and the ways of conveying meaning and making knowledge claims.
- Cultivate a critical awareness of one's interpretive and epistemological framework and the role of one's identity in the research process
- Develop protocols and measures that acknowledge the unique features of participants' cultural and lived experience
- Maintain a respectful engagement with participants throughout the research process

informed the research discussed in this chapter. Telling stories about African American life and looking for truths encourages us to mine inter- and multidisciplinary approaches and to be ever mindful of the interconnections among conceptualization, theory, method, and interpretation. We seek *how* to do this, so we may better understand *what* something really is. Furthermore, we are not only reporters of what we find but storytellers as well, not only because we must interpret what we find but also because in reporting results we offer causal plots and impose a narrative to make sense of what we find. This is not so very different from the storytelling traditions of our foreparents. Indeed, whether the work is qualitative or not, we tell stories about the dynamics of family life, of people's lives and the situations in which they live; we make inferences about their motivations, their psyche, and their behavior; and ultimately we offer cautionary tales to others about how their lives may unfold.

REFERENCES

Allen, W. D., and M. Conner. 1997. An African American perspective on generative fathering. In A. J. Hawkins and D. C. Dollahite, eds., *Generative fathering: Beyond deficit perspectives,* 52–70. Thousand Oaks, CA: Sage.

Bowman, P., and T. Forman. 1997. Instrumental and expressive family roles among African American fathers. In R. Taylor, J. Jackson, and L. Chatters, eds., *Family life in Black America,* 216–47. Thousand Oaks, CA: Sage.

Collins, P. H. 1991. *Black feminist thought.* New York: Routledge.

Connor, M. E., and J. L. White, eds. 2006. *Black fathers: An invisible presence in America.* Mahwah, NJ: Lawrence Erlbaum.

DuBois, W. E. B. 1969. *The souls of Black folk: Essays and sketches.* Chicago: Mc-Clug.

Gwaltney, J. 1980. *Drylongso: A self-portrait of black America.* New York: Vintage Press.

Holliday, B. 1992. Black maternal beliefs. Washington, DC. Unpublished manuscript.

Holstein, J. A., and J. F. Gubrium. 1994. Phenomenology, ethnomethodology, and interpretive practice. In N. K. Denzin and Y. S. Lincoln, eds., *Handbook of qualitative research,* 262–72. Thousand Oaks, CA: Sage.

Hughes, D., and L. Chen. 1997. When and what parents tell children about race: An examination of race related socialization among African American families. *Applied Developmental Science* 1:200–214.

Hughes, D., and D. J. Johnson. 2001. Correlates in children's experiences of parents' racial socialization behaviors. *Journal of Marriage and the Family* 63, no. 4: 981–95.

Hunter, A. G. 1993. Making a way: Strategies of southern urban Afro-American families, 1900 and 1936. *Journal of Family History* 18:231–48.

Hunter, A. G. 1997. Living arrangements of African American adults: Variations across age, gender, and family status. In R. Taylor, J. Jackson, and L. Chatters, eds., *Family life in Black America,* 262–76. Thousand Oaks, CA: Sage.

Hunter, A. G. 2001. The other breadwinners: The mobilization of secondary wage earners in early twentieth-century Black families. *History of the Family: An International Quarterly* 6:69–94.

Hunter, A. G. 2002. (Re)envisioning cohabitation: A commentary on race, history, and culture. In A. Booth and A. Crouter, eds., *Just living together: Implications of cohabitation for families, children, and social policy,* 41–52. Mahwah, NJ: Lawrence Erlbaum Associates.

Hunter, A. G. 2006. Teaching classics in family studies: E. Franklin Frazier's *The Negro Family in the United States. Family Relations* 55:80–92.

Hunter, A. G., and J. E. Davis. 1992. Constructing gender: An exploration of Afro-American men's conceptualization of manhood. *Gender and Society* 6:464–79.

Hunter, A. G., and J. E. Davis. 1994. Hidden voices of Black men: The meaning, complexity, and structure of manhood. *Journal of Black Studies* 25:20–40.

Hunter, A. G., and M. E. Ensminger. 1992. Diversity and fluidity in children's living arrangements: Family transitions in an urban Afro-American community. *Journal of Marriage and the Family* 54:418–26.

Hunter, A. G., C. F. Friend, S. Y. Murphy, A. Rollins, M. Williams-Wheeler, and J. Laughinghouse. 2006. Loss, survival, and redemption: African American male youth's reflections on life without fathers, manhood, and coming of age. *Youth and Society* 37:423–52.

Hunter, A. G., J. L. Pearson, N. Ialongo, and S. G. Kellam. 1998. Parenting alone to multiple caregivers: Child care and parenting arrangements in Black and white urban families. *Family Relations* 47:343–53.

Johnson, D. J. 1988. Parental racial socialization strategies of Black parents in three private schools. In D. T. Slaughter and D. J. Johnson, eds., *Visible now: Blacks in private schools,* 251–67. Westport, CT: Greenwood.

Johnson, D. J. 1996. *Father presence matters: Towards an ecological framework of fathering and child outcomes.* Monograph, LR-FP-96-02. Philadelphia, National Center on Fathers and Families.

Johnson, D. J. 2001. Parental characteristics, racial stress, and racial socialization processes as predictors of racial coping in middle childhood. In A. Neal-Barnett, ed., *Forging Links: Clinical/developmental perspective of African American children,* 57–74. Westport, CT: Greenwood.

Johnson, D. J. 2005. The ecology of children's racial coping: Family, school, and community influences. In T. Weisner, ed., *Discovering successful pathways through middle childhood: Mixed methods,* 87–100. Chicago: University of Chicago Press.

Johnson, D. J., and J. Davis. 2001. Fatherhood among middle aged African American men: Retrospective accounts of childrearing and transformative experiences. Symposium on Developmental and Intergenerational Issues in Fathers' Involvement in Children's Lives. American Educational Research Association, April 10–14, Seattle, WA.

Johnson, D. J., and J. Livingston. 2002. African American Fathering Experiences: Race, Parenting, and Socialization Messages. Biennial Meetings of the Society for Research on Adolescence, April 10–13, New Orleans.

Kellam, S. G., J. D. Branch, K. C. Agrawal, and M. E. Ensminger. 1975. *Mental health and going to school.* Chicago: University of Chicago Press.

Kellam, S. G., M. E. Ensminger, and J. R. Turner. 1977. Family structure and mental health of children. *Archives of General Psychiatry* 34:1012–22.

Pearson, J. L., A. G. Hunter, J. C. Cook, N. Ialongo, and S. G. Kellam. 1997. Grandparent coresidence and parental involvement in urban contexts. *Gerontologist* 17:50–67.

Pearson, J. L., A. G. Hunter, M. E. Ensminger, and S. G. Kellam. 1990. Black grandmothers in multigenerational households: Diversity in family structure and parenting involvement in the Woodlawn community. *Child Development* 61:434–42.

Spencer, M. B. 1983. Children's cultural values and parental child rearing strategies. *Developmental Review* 3:351–70.

Stevenson, H. C., J. Reed, and P. Bodison. 1996. Kinship social support and adolescent racial socialization beliefs: Extending the self to family. *Journal of Black Psychology* 22, no. 4: 498–508.

Storm, R. D., H. Amukamara, S. K. Storm, T. E. Beckert, P. Storm, and D. L. Griswold. 2000. Parenting success of African American fathers. *Journal of Research and Development in Education* 33:257–67.

Trochim, W. 1989. An introduction to concept mapping for planning and evaluation. In W. Trochim, ed., *A Special Issue of Evaluation and Program Planning* 12:1–16.

14 | Methods for the Study of Mental Health in African American Populations

Lonnie R. Snowden

Everyone concerned with the well-being of African American populations must attend to African American mental health. Mental health forms the basis for a personal sense of happiness and feeling of satisfaction. It facilitates successful performance of personally valued tasks and attainment of important personal goals (U.S. Department of Health and Human Services 1999).

But in ways that often are overlooked, mental health also affects the economic and social fate of individual African Americans and African American communities. Mental health facilitates performance of productive activities (U.S. Department of Health and Human Services 1999) and promotes formation of human and social capital (Coleman 1988). The ability of African Americans to optimize individual *and* community well-being is inextricably linked to African American mental health (Snowden 2003).

Former surgeon general David Satcher issued a report entitled *Mental Health: Culture, Race, and Ethnicity: A Supplement to Mental Health: A Report of the Surgeon General* (U.S. Department of Health and Human Services 2001). Subsequent reviews echo many of the supplement's conclusions (Snowden and Yamada 2005). The report consolidated what is known about African American mental health by reviewing the best available scientific evidence. Well-founded conclusions were drawn, several of which are restated below.

It is clear from the report that although much has been learned, much more remains to be learned. Conjecture is common. Important empirical observations occur but rarely are followed up in programs of study yielding cumulative knowledge. Questions addressed thus far cover a narrow band from a very wide spectrum. The research base must be enlarged.

Wide-Ranging Methods to Match Diverse Questions

How can we increase the amount of rigorous research on African American mental health? A starting point is to recognize that questions of interest span a wide range. It is widely recognized that research methods must be geared to research tasks—that the methods chosen for a study should be those best suited to theoretical and policy-related concerns motivating inquiry. Put another way, it is important to ensure that the choice of research methods is dictated by the research question at hand.

In studying African American mental health, diverse issues demand that the research program draw investigators and methods from many disciplines. To do otherwise would be to artificially restrict the range of methods and thereby give short shrift to important questions.

Effectiveness, Differential Effectiveness, and Cost Effectiveness

In *Mental Health: Culture, Race, and Ethnicity—A Supplement to Mental Health* (2001), the former surgeon general noted a lack of evidence on outcomes of care for African Americans receiving mental health treatment. The report called for more research evaluating the African American response to novel but standardized treatments as well as to care delivered under the usual conditions of community practice. The former kind of studies address *efficacy*—the impact of interventions studied under tightly controlled but artificial conditions—and the latter address *effectiveness in real-world conditions.*

A first step toward enlarging the body of research is to examine its underlying logic, especially as that logic applies to research with African American populations. Whether psychosocial or biomedical (Herbeck et al. 2004), interventions typically are promoted in something like a standard form. Although subject to variation at the discretion of clinicians, crucial elements define a core. The core is readily seen in treatments delivered following a manual constructed to standardize the intervention's key features.

Investigators rarely examine whether there are differences between African Americans and whites in intervention effectiveness, and few determine whether there are African American versus white treatment interactions. An underlying assumption is universalist. That is, an effective treatment touches on something fundamental and, as a matter of course, will be equally effective for everyone who receives it.

Arguing from a sociocultural point of view (Snowden and Yamada 2005)—and often in the name of cultural competence (e.g., Cross et al. 1989; Betancourt et al. 2003)—critics sometimes object to standard treatments. They assert that African American traditions and beliefs are such that standard treatments cannot achieve therapeutic objectives when used with African Americans. They claim that to be effective, treatment must take account of a distinctive African American sociocultural perspective, if not be designed entirely from that perspective. The position reflects a belief that African Americans suffering from mental illness will reject standard treatments or will try them to no avail, because the premises neglect the psychological makeup of African Americans and conditions of African American life.

Taking an empirical perspective on the issue reveals that both sides are making claims about what conditions are necessary for effective treatment, and that the real controversy is one of conflicting claims about effectiveness. As currently presented, however, several issues are entangled. Are standard procedures equally effective for African Americans and others? Are modified procedures effective in their own right? Are they more effective than standard procedures (Snowden 1996)?

Although rarely recognized, treatment effectiveness must be considered in other contexts. One is a context of resources: What financial commitment is required to achieve how much improvement? How might resources be otherwise expended? Just beyond effectiveness is the issue of cost effectiveness (Hargreaves et al. 1999).

Issues of cost effectiveness are sometimes inescapable when studying mental health treatment of African Americans. As will be discussed later, African Americans are overrepresented in high-need, multiproblem populations. For this reason African Americans often require several forms of assistance. It is important to evaluate effectiveness broadly, keeping in mind a wide range of potential consequences and possibilities for alternative uses of resources.

Cablas (1999) reported one of the few studies that examined the cost effectiveness of treatment separately delivered to African Americans. The investigators conducted a complex investigation that illustrates several important methodological concerns. Limitations are noted below, but the study stands as one of the most comprehensive and rigorous of its kind.

In samples of African American, Latino, and Vietnamese youth, Cablas compared the impact of a brokerage, strengths-based case-management intervention with that of usual care delivered by the county (outpatient psychotherapy and referral). Youth were randomly assigned to either the experimental or usual-care conditions. Both interventions emphasized what was described as cultural sensitivity in the provision of care.

Results were reported in terms of scores on a widely used measure of symptoms and social functioning, the Child Behavior Checklist (CBCL), and in terms of use and cost of mental health and juvenile justice involvement. Results pointed to an improvement for all groups in CBCL scores. However, analysis left important questions unanswered: For African American and other youth, how did differences in functioning translate into key social and monetary indicators? What resource levels were required to realize what kind of gains?

In keeping with aims of the intervention—which included engagement of 12–17-year-old youth from juvenile hall who met DSM-IV criteria for mental illness and exhibited mental health, social and educational, and substance abuse problems and were receiving ongoing mental health and supportive services—it was determined that African American youth showed an increased use of mental health treatment. In turn, they demonstrated an increase in mental health treatment-related costs. African American youth also demonstrated a decrease in juvenile justice involvement. They had 10 fewer juvenile hall days, on average, at 12-month follow-up. There was also a substantial decrease in average juvenile justice costs. The decrease in juvenile justice costs more than offset the increase in mental health costs.

The study had features that addressed special circumstances of African American life. It provided a core intervention and adapted the intervention to take account of African Americans' sociocultural needs. However, the nature of the adaptation was not specified in the only report of the study currently available. Better-described examples of adapted interventions have not yet appeared in the research literature. That this limitation is widespread underscores the importance of investigators indicating how interventions were translated to address an African American sociocultural orientation. The resulting information contributes to a theoretical understanding of what *sociocultural translations* means and how it might operate as well as facilitating replication.

The researchers did not take advantage of this modification of standard care to address an important question that might have been studied. They did not demonstrate the *necessity* of sociocultural accommodation by varying the conditions under which the intervention was provided and comparing adapted and standard versions.

The investigators examined effectiveness, as usually occurs in community-based randomized clinical trials (RCT), through analysis of change in scores on the Child Behavior Checklist. They went on to demonstrate that another important goal, linkage to ongoing mental health treatment, also was attained.

The broader assessment of impact included the cost analysis described above that showed an increase in the cost of mental health treatment but also showed that the increase was more than offset by savings in juvenile justice–related costs. The investigators thereby translated abstract, humanitarian gains into tangible terms. They provided information to advocate for continuing the program and created an opportunity for reinvestment into other areas of psychological and social need.

Mental Health Treatment and Social Adversity: Substitution and Complementarity

Cablas's study highlights another conclusion by the former surgeon general (1999) in his report that is often overlooked in studies of African American mental health. African Americans with mental health problems are especially likely to become members of high-need populations. For example, African Americans are overrepresented among mentally ill persons who are arrested and incarcerated (Cuellar, Snowden, and Ewing 2007). Because of this overrepresentation, providing high-quality mental health care to members of high-need groups might have a disproportionately beneficial impact on the African American population (Alegria, Perez, and Williams 2003).

Successful treatment of mental illness might improve the social standing of African Americans and, through improved psychological well-being and social functioning, decrease involvement in social services and the legal system. Cablas's study presented one approach to the issue of this interdependency between mental health treatment, social programs and systems, and documented intersystem effects. The issues can be and often are addressed with greater comprehensiveness and precision by other means.

Concepts and methods come from economics, where questions of offset are defined as problems in "substitution," or functional equivalence, of one kind of activity for another. Does outpatient mental health treatment reduce the chances that African Americans will use emergency services? The question translates into a hypothesis about substitution: Does outpatient treatment substitute for emergency service use?

Economists have recognized that substitution need not occur; indeed, activities sometimes augment instead of substituting for each other. Activities may serve as *complements* rather than as *substitutes*. Complementarity and substitution are opposites. "Substitutes are goods or services that may replace each other while complements are goods or services that augment the simultaneous use of one another" (Goldstein and Hogan 1988). Thus, it cannot be taken for granted that outpatient care reduces emergency care. Outpatient care might have no effect at all or might, by reducing the stigma associated with help seeking, actually *increase* the use of emergency care.

Substitution hypotheses often are tested in a multivariate regression framework. When designing substitutions studies, investigators develop comprehensive explanatory models, paying particular attention to the variables believed to function as substitutes.

Hypothesized substitution effects are evaluated according to a particular arrangement of variables. In a hypothetical study of whether outpatient mental health treatment offsets emergency room use, outpatient treatment would appear as an independent variable (X). Covariates in the model would include other variables jointly associated with outpatient treatment and emergency care, for example, age, gender, diagnosis, functional status, substance abuse, and others. The dependent variable in the model would be the variable substituted for, emergency room visits (Y).

Results from the analysis indicate whether substitution occurs, whether complementarity occurs, or whether neither occurs. These outcomes are expressed as a statistically significant and negative regression coefficient (e.g., as outpatient mental health treatment goes up, emergency room use goes down), a statistically significant and positive regression coefficient (e.g., as outpatient mental health treatment goes up, emergency room care goes up), and a regression coefficient that is not statistically significant (e.g., there is no association between outpatient mental health treatment and emergency room use).

Snowden (1998) tested a widely held belief that informal assistance (voluntary support networks) offsets formal assistance (specialty treatment) among African Americans coping with mental health problems. From national data he evaluated the association between assistance obtained from a friend, relative, or a religious figure with that obtained from a mental health center, a mental health specialist in private practice, a hospital-based mental health clinic, or an inpatient psychiatric hospital. The results revealed that friends, relatives, and religious figures served as *complements* to specialty mental health services: Persons seeking assistance from a friend or religious helper were likely also to seek it from a specialized professional source. The results further revealed that African Americans were more likely than whites to show this complementarity. The data indicated that African Americans using informal resources for assistance were *more* likely, not less likely, to use professional assistance.

Snowden's study illustrates methods for studying substitution and complementarity, but his findings have no bearing on whether substitution effects occur elsewhere. In view of research demonstrating that control of mental illness promotes better community functioning (U.S. Department of Health and Human Services 1999), it seems likely, for example, that mental health treatment could substitute for incarceration. This speculation remains only a hypothesis, however, a question for testing in further research.

From Individual to Environment: Economy and Community

Poverty is especially important to consider in conducting research on African American mental health. Poverty must be understood not only at individual and family levels but also at community and societal levels. Whether rural or urban, poor African Americans tend to live in areas of concentrated poverty, where accumulating social problems take on a life of their own (cf. McFate, Lawson, and Wilson 1995). Many poor neighborhoods suffer from few resources and considerable distress, disadvantages reflected in high unemployment rates, homelessness, high residential turnover, substance abuse, and crime (Wilson 1987). Development of generalized trust and informal mechanisms of social control, both components of collective efficacy, is hampered (Sampson, Randenbush, and Earls 1997). These neighborhood and community problems can exacerbate individual challenges to successful functioning associated with mental illness.

The economic well-being of African American people and communities must be understood within a wider societal context. An important but often overlooked aspect of that context is the economy. The state of the U.S. economy varies from region to region and over time. African Americans are especially vulnerable to regional distress and cyclical downturns: African Americans have "a greater likelihood of experiencing unemployment, and having a harder time finding reemployment" (Broman 1997, 166). Because they are insecurely attached to the labor market and have little wealth as a cushion, African American individuals and institutions are particularly sensitive to larger economic forces (Jaynes and Williams 1989).

Whether studying access, treatment, or improvement, it is important to consider the impact of social and material resources in explaining African American mental health. The scope of concern must include not only individual and family factors but community and societal factors as well. This wider context affects levels and types of stress to which vulnerable and mentally ill persons are exposed, treatment options available, and levels of support provided by people in situations where rehabilitative efforts are attempted.

Along with many conceptions and methods to study socioeconomic status (Williams and Collins 1995), several approaches now permit inclusion of economic and social indicators as regular features of research. One method is to include area level along with individual indicators of poverty. Using such methods, researchers assess the impact of poverty at the community or neighborhood level as well as at the level of the person or family.

Studying the impact of alcohol abuse on social, legal, health-related, and occupational functioning, Jones-Webb et al. (1997) considered whether study participants lived in a poverty neighborhood. They identified census tracts for African American, Latino, and white men from a national probability sample and determined which tracts had poverty rates higher than 20%. Following convention, these census tracts were designated as poverty neighborhoods. Survey respondents were classified as residents or nonresidents of poverty neighborhoods.

The investigators conducted multivariate analysis to determine how much residence in a poverty neighborhood predicted adverse consequences of alcohol consumption. For African American men more than white or Latino men living in a poverty neighborhood was detrimental. African American residents of poverty neighborhoods were found to be especially likely to suffer drinking-related difficulties, even after controlling for level of drinking and drinking-related attitudes and demographic factors, including personal socioeconomic standing.

Another approach permits researchers to focus on cyclical changes in the state of the economy and to link changing economic fortunes to rates of African American mental heath problems, treatment, and recovery. Time-series analysis allows investigators to test Jaynes and Williams (1989, 294) contention that "Blacks are acutely sensitive to expansions and recessions of business cycles."

Time-series methods focus on establishing covariation among time-varying events (Catalano, Dooley, and Jackson 1983). Often, social indicators serve as dependent variables (e.g., weekly admissions to the psychiatric emergency room). They are explained in terms of independent variables that vary over time. Some independent variables are single events, such as launching of a special program. Other independent variables are time-varying social indicators, such as unemployment claims assessed to capture downturns in the local or national economy.

When using time-series methods, units of analysis are not people but indicators observed at points in time. For example, if 104 weeks of psychiatric emergency admissions were examined on 500 persons per week, then $n = 104$. The methods are complex because time-varying observations lack independence and must be adjusted accordingly. They also require something of a reorientation in thinking. Thus, control variables are time-varying indicators as well and might include ecological influences on behavior like holidays and the weather.

Catalano, Snowden, and Shumway (2007) used time-series analysis to investigate a possible link between changing economic conditions and the frequency of African American involuntary civil commitment. As an indicator of economic security, the investigators used the number of initial claims for unemployment insurance in California filed over 156 months. Unemployment claims are a good indicator of the state of the economy, whether it is expanding or contracting, because to be eligible workers must have lost their jobs due to slack demand. Workers cannot file if job loss occurs for reasons unrelated to economic contraction, such as being terminated because of poor job performance. Eligible workers are largely employed full-time in relatively stable firms. Unemployment claims are closely watched as an indicator, and it is accepted that large numbers of claims point to a general loss of employment security in the labor market.

Catalano, Snowden, and Shumway (2007) argued that community tolerance declines during economic contraction because there is more insecurity and frustration in the community. Norms of acceptance and trust become strained, and deviant acts are less tolerated than previously. As a result, the number of persons considered dangerous to themselves and others, and ultimately subjected to involuntary civil commitment, would be expected to increase. The investigators further proposed that persons coerced into treatment during periods of economic distress might be functioning at a higher level than those coerced into treatment during times of economic prosperity. Finally, the investigators proposed that these processes become intensified when those involved are African American. They argued that African American acts of supposed deviance would be recognized more readily and tolerated less, resulting in a stronger association between economic contraction and involuntary commitment among African Americans.

Data linking unemployment claims, rates of involuntary commitment, and functional levels were analyzed using times-series analysis. The investigators sought differences between African Americans and whites in the strength of associations, controlling for trends, cycles, and other patterns of serial correlation that might induce spurious associations.

The results supported the hypotheses about African American men. The data indicated that during economic downturns there was more involuntary civil commitment, commitment occurred among persons who were functioning at higher levels than persons committed during better economic times, and this pattern fit African American men especially well.

Area-level coding and time-series analysis open the way to studying other important community and economic forces on African American mental health. The methods permit researchers to address community and economic determinants of symptoms and psychopathology, stress, support, and other aspects of social and psychological functioning where African Americans might be especially vulnerable or especially strong.

Application of Standard Measures to African American Populations: Cross-Cultural Validity

Sound measurement is a prerequisite for meaningful research on all populations and in all areas of research. Without procedures that assess what they are intended to assess, research-based evidence cannot be properly interpreted. This principle is enshrined in well-accepted psychometric standards of validity and reliability.

Special problems confront researchers who attempt to ensure that measures are as reliable and valid for African Americans as other populations, especially when, as is usually the case, they have been developed on populations other than African Americans. The problem has often been described under the rubric "cross-cultural validity" (cf. Snowden 1996).

Suspicions of cross-cultural invalidity come about because there sometimes are differences between African Americans and other groups in use of language and styles of communicating about personal problems, in community standards indicating how socially desirable such experiences are to acknowledge, and even in underlying categories by which the mind organizes thoughts and experiences.

Any of these differences can compromise assessment procedures that, when used with African Americans, might indicate something other than what was intended. Anthropologists have documented that certain symptoms have a special meaning to African Americans based on African American community traditions (Snow 1993). For this reason, African Americans appear to express some symptoms in accordance with distinctive idioms of distress.

It is, therefore, possible that African American symptom profiles might include distinctive elements. Unless African American–specific symptoms were included on standardized checklists, or if they were included but not properly categorized, African American mental health–related distress might be overlooked or misinterpreted.

Cross-cultural equivalence can be understood as a concern that measurement procedures evaluate equivalent underlying psychological and social constructs in African American and other populations. Some investigators have grappled with cross-cultural equivalence, demonstrating, for example, that key symptoms do not predict the presence of an underlying mental disorder equally well for African Americans and whites (Algeria and McGuire 2003). One psychometric for studying the issue is to study *factorial invariance,* the problem of assessing whether ostensibly equivalent factors point to equivalent underlying constructs.

Both in theoretical and methodological terms, factorial invariance has enjoyed a long history of attention from leading figures in factor analysis. For example, methodologists have invoked factorial invariance as an important consideration in understanding change. In this context the central concern is, "When the operations of measurement are the same, how can we be clear about whether or not these operations produce measures of the same attribute when they are used at different points over which change is to be recorded?" (Cunningham 1991, 107).

Horn (1991) illustrated the application of factorial invariance in an example from aging research. He proposed a hypothetical study in which three questions were asked to measure self-esteem: whether respondents believed themselves to be attractive, smart, and likable.

How important is each question in addressing the underlying construct, self-esteem? Horn proposed the following results from a hypothetical factor analysis conducted in two samples, one of younger persons and another of older persons. Attractiveness is most important (most heavily weighted) among 20-year-olds, whereas intelligence is most important among 60-year-olds. Sociability is equally important in both groups. He concluded, "These factor analytic results thus indicate that self-esteem is represented in a different way in the thinking of young and old people" (117). Similarly, factor analytic results can indicate how symptoms of distress are represented in a different way in the thinking of African Americans and whites.

Chow, Snowden, and McConnell (2001) assessed whether indicators of symptoms and social functioning might be represented differentially in samples of African Americans, Asian Americans, Latinos, and whites. They evaluated factorial equivalence of the BASIS-32, a widely used measure of symptoms and social functioning. Using LISREL, they sought to replicate across the groups a factor structure found for whites and similar to that reported by developers of the BASIS. The factor structure did replicate, giving preliminary reassurance that standard interpretation of the BASIS-32 was accurate for African Americans.

Confirmatory factor analysis is readily available to investigators who, if not themselves conversant with the procedure, can seek consultation from methodological specialists. Ultimately, investigators will have the capacity to routinely evaluate the cross-cultural validity of methods for assessing the social and psychological functioning of African Americans.

Lessons Learned

- African Americans with mental health problems are especially likely to become members of high-need populations.
- Whether studying access, treatment, or improvement, it is important to consider the impact of social and material resources in explaining African American mental health.
- Methods to study economic and social indicators of poverty now include several approaches to permit area-level along with individual or family indicators of poverty. Using such methods, researchers can assess the impact of poverty at the community or neighborhood level as well as at the level of the person or family.

- Area-level coding and time-series analysis open the way to study-ing other important community and economic forces on African American mental health.
- Suspicions of cross-cultural invalidity come about because there sometimes are differences between African Americans and other groups in use of language and styles of communicating about personal problems.

Conclusions

Diverse problems from a wide spectrum beckon investigators to study African American mental health. It is important to make inroads be-cause mental health and mental illness are central to the individual and collective well-being of African Americans. Recent developments, espe-cially the report *Mental Health: Culture, Race, and Ethnicity* by the for-mer surgeon general, have consolidated our understanding and pointed the way to new directions for future work.

An optimistic view of the future follows. The next generation of stud-ies will emphasize high-priority themes. Investigators will focus on the impact of interventions, paying particular attention to evaluating pro-posed adaptations to the sociocultural conditions of African American life. Their studies will consider differential effectiveness, comparing the response of African Americans and others to standard and adapted forms of intervention. They will increasingly take account of cost effec-tiveness, recognizing that considering resource expenditure is an impor-tant part of the equation.

Investigators will design studies that directly test trade-offs between participation in mental health treatments and programs and participa-tion in institutions of public support and social control. They will do so because they understand the importance of taking a broad perspective on African American problems and recognize that trade-offs between mental health and adverse experiences are sometimes possible.

More than in the past, investigators will come to examine community and societal contexts in which mental health problems occur and where solutions are implemented. The economic fate of African Americans will be studied and its role documented as a cornerstone for understanding mental health.

Research will improve in quality as investigators carry out methodological studies that upgrade our capacity for precision and rigor. The specter of differential validity, haunting researchers who have done little to identify and overcome its manifestations, will be banished. By the use of existing methods such as confirmatory factor analysis and emerging methods of great promise, the study of African American mental health will proceed with greater assurance.

From these advances will come a new generation of research on African American mental health. Key questions will be asked with powerful methods for interpretation and the state of knowledge will advance and the power of our interventions will increase.

REFERENCES

Adoption and Foster Care Analysis and Reporting System (AFCARS). 1999. Unpublished estimates of adoption and foster care. U.S. Department of Health and Human Services.

Alegria, M., and T. McGuire. 2003. Rethinking a universal framework in the psychiatric symptom-disorder relationship. *Journal of Health and Social Behavior* 44:257–74.

Alegria, M., D. J. Perez, and S. Williams. 2003. The role of public policies in reducing mental health status disparities for people of color. *Health Affairs* 22:51–63.

Betancourt, J., A. Green, J. Carillo, and O. Ananeh-Firempong. 2003. Defining cultural competence: A practical framework for addressing racial/ethnic disparities in health and health care. *Public Health Reports* 118:293–302.

Borduin, C. M., B. J. Mann, L. T. Cone, S. W. Henggeler, B. R. Fucci, D. M. Blaske, and R. A. Williams. 1995. Multisystemic treatment of serious juvenile offenders: Long-term prevention of criminality and violence. *Journal of Consulting and Clinical Psychology* 63:569–78.

Broman, C. 1997. Families, unemployment, and well-being. In R. J. Taylor, J. S. Jackson, and L. M. Chatters, eds., *Family life in Black America.* Thousand Oaks, CA: Sage.

Brown, R. T., and S. B. Sexson. 1988. A controlled trial of methylphenidate in Black adolescents. *Clinical Pediatrics* 27:74–81.

Cablas, A. 1999. Treatment outcomes and cost effectiveness of two approaches for minority groups with severe emotional illness detained in juvenile hall: Preliminary results. In J. Willis, C. Liberton, K. Kutash, and R. Friedman, eds., *A system of care for children's mental health: Expanding the research base.* 11th Annual Research Conference Proceedings, Research and Training Center for Children's Mental Health. Florida Mental Health Institute, University of South Florida, Tampa.

Catalano, R. F., D. Dooley, and R. Jackson. 1983. Selecting a time-series strategy. *Psychological Bulletin* 9:506–23.

Catalano, R., L. R. Snowden, and M. Shumway. 2007. Unemployment and coerced treatment: A test of the intolerance hypothesis. *Aggressive Behavior* 33:1–9.

Chow, J., L. R. Snowden, and W. McConnell. 2001. A confirmatory factor analysis of the BASIS-32 in racial and ethnic samples. *Journal of Behavioral Health Services and Research* 28:400–411.

Coleman, J. S. 1988. Social capital in the creation of human capital. *American Journal of Sociology* 94:95–120.

Cross, T. L., B. J. Barzon, K. W. Dennis, and M. R. Isaacs. 1989. Towards a culturally competent system of care. Washington, DC: CASSP Technical Assistance Center.

Cuellar, A. E., L. R. Snowden, and T. Ewing. 2007. Criminal records of persons served in the public mental health system. *Psychiatric Services* 58:114–20.

Cunningham, W. R. 1991. Issues in factorial invariance. In L. M. Collins and J. L. Horn, eds., *Best methods for the analysis of change: Recent advances, unanswered questions, future directions*, 106–13. Washington, DC: American Psychological Association.

Goldstein, J. M., and C. M. Horgan. 1988. Inpatient and outpatient psychiatric services: Substitutes or complements? *Hospital and Community Psychiatry* 39:632–36.

Hargreaves, W. A., M. Shumway, T. W. Hu, and B. Cuffel. 1998. *Cost-outcome methods for mental health.* San Diego: Academic Press.

Hatchett, S. J., and J. S. Jackson. 1993. African American extended kin systems: An assessment. In H. P. McAdoo, ed., *Family ethnicity: Strength in diversity,* 90–108. Newbury Park, CA: Sage.

Herbeck, D. M., J. C. West, I. Ruditis, F. F. Duffy, D. J. Fitek, C. C. Bell, and L. R. Snowden. 2004. Variations in use of second generation antipsychotic medication by race among adult psychiatric patients. *Psychiatric Services* 55:677–84.

Horn, J. 1991. Issues in factorial invariance: Comments. In L. M. Collins and J. L. Horn, eds., *Best methods for the analysis of change: Recent advances, unanswered questions, future directions,* 114–25. Washington, DC: American Psychological Association.

Jenkins, E. J., C. C. Bell, J. Taylor, and L. Walker. 1989. Circumstances of sexual and physical victimization of black psychiatric outpatients. *Journal of the National Medical Association* 81:246–52.

Jones-Webb, R., L. R. Snowden, D. Herd, B. Short, and P. Hannan. 1997. Alcohol-related problems among Black, Hispanic, and White men: The contribution of neighborhood poverty. *Journal of Studies on Alcohol* 58:539–45.

Liginsky, W. A., R. W. Manderscheid, and P. R. Henderson. Clients served in state mental hospitals: Results from a longitudinal database. In R. W. Manderscheid and M. A. Sonnenheim, eds., *Mental health, United States, 1990.* DHHS Publication No. ADM 90-1708. Washington, DC: U.S. Government Printing Office.

Manderscheid, R. W., and S. A. Barrett. 1987. Sources and qualifications of data. In R. W. Manderscheid and S. A. Barrett, eds., *Mental health in the United States, 1987.* DHHS Publication No. ADM 87-1518. Washington, DC: U.S. Government Printing Office.

Marcolin, M. A. 1991. The prognosis of schizophrenia across cultures. *Ethnicity and Disease* 1:99–104.

Massey, R. S., and A. D. Nancy. 1993. *American apartheid: Segregation and the making of the underclass.* Boston: Harvard University Press.

McFate, K., R. Lawson, and W. J. Wilson, eds. 1995. *Poverty, inequality, and the future of social policy.* New York: Russell Sage Foundation.

O'Hare, W. P., K. M. Pollard, T. L. Mann, and M. M. Kent. African Americans in the 1990s. *Population Bulletin 1991* 46, no. 1: 1–40.

Sampson, R. J., S. W. Raudenbush, and P. Earls. 1997. Neighborhoods and violent crime: A multilevel study of collective efficacy. *Science* 277:918–24.

Snow, L. 1993. Walkin' Over Medicine. Boulder: Westview.

Snowden, L. R. 1996. Ethnic minority populations and mental health outcomes. In D. M. Steinwachs, L. M. Flynn, G. S. Norquist, and E. A. Skinner, *Using client information to improve mental health and substance abuse outcomes,* 79–87. New Directions for Mental Health Services, no. 71. San Francisco: Jossey-Bass.

Snowden, L. R. 1998. Racial differences in informal help-seeking for mental health problems. *Journal of Community Psychology* 26:303–13.

Snowden, L. R. 2003. Bias in mental health assessment and intervention: Theory and evidence. *American Journal of Public Health* 93:239–42.

Snowden, L. R., and A. M. Yamada. 2005. Cultural differences in access to care. *Annual Review of Clinical Psychology* 1:19–41.

Statistical Abstract of the United States. 1999. *The National Data Book: U.S. Census Bureau.* October.

Sue, S., D. C. Fujino, L. Hu, D. Takeuchi, and N. Zane. 1991. Community mental health services for ethnic minority groups: A test of the cultural responsiveness hypothesis. *Journal of Consulting and Clinical Psychology* 32:616–24.

U.S. Department of Health and Human Services. 2001. *Mental health: Culture, race, and ethnicity—A supplement to mental health.* A Report of the Surgeon General. Rockville, MD: U.S. Department of Health and Human Services, Office of the Surgeon General.

Williams, D. R., and C. Collins. 1995. Socioeconomic and racial differences in health. *Annual Review of Sociology* 21:349–86.

15 | Using Quantitative Methods to Study the Impact of Television Exposure on the Social and Emotional Development of African American Children and Adolescents

L. Monique Ward

Over the past few decades, television has emerged as a powerful agent of socialization, providing value systems, illustrating group dynamics, and modeling examples of appropriate and inappropriate behavior (Berry 1998; Stroman 1991). Its portrayals have not always been kind to African Americans, however, first excluding them, then stereotyping and segregating them. As a result, concern is frequently expressed about the impact of these portrayals on Black youth. One concern is that a lack of recognition on the screen conveys a lack of respect (Clark 1972); a group's absence from the TV landscape implies that the group and its members are unimportant, inconsequential, and powerless (Graves 1999). Of equal concern is the impact on young viewers of stereotypical portrayals, both subtle and overt, that permeate all aspects of the media (Seiter 1990). How might repeated exposure to images that exclude people like oneself or depict them mostly in negative ways affect young Black viewers' beliefs about themselves, about African Americans, and about other social realities?

Although these concerns have been raised repeatedly over the past three decades (e.g., Berry 1998; Graves 1980; Stroman 1984), little is actually known about television's impact on the self and social conceptions of Black youth. Only a handful of studies have examined the impact of media exposure on Black youths' conceptions of themselves; an equally small number have included Black youth in investigations of general media effects. Because television exposure is expected to have the largest effects on those who watch it the most, and African Americans are among the most frequent viewers, Black youth may be especially at risk for negative media effects. Accordingly, the goal of this chapter is to summarize the current state of the field and to offer several suggestions for future research, addressing both methodological and conceptual concerns.

Methodology Matters: Lessons Learned from Research Linking Media Exposure and Black Self-Concept

According to the dominant arguments, frequent media exposure is expected to result in more negative self-esteem, lower racial self-esteem, and acceptance of stereotypes among Black youth because of both an underrepresentation of African Americans on television and the prevalence of negative and stereotypical portrayals. However, the evidence suggests this may not always be the case (e.g., McDermott and Greenberg 1984; Ward 2004). *Global* negative effects of media exposure on self-esteem have not emerged among Black youth. For example, Stroman (1986) reported that greater TV viewing correlated with a more positive self-concept among Black third- through sixth-grade girls but had no connection for boys. Surveying Black high school students, Ward (2004) found that greater exposure to mainstream programming and stronger identification with White characters was associated with lower self-esteem, while stronger identification with popular Black characters was associated with higher self-esteem. What might these results mean? With data from only a few key studies, drawing conclusions about the impact of media use on the self-concepts of young Black viewers would be premature. However, these findings highlight several factors and issues that may inform future research.

The first issue concerns the nature of Black youths' media diets. A central assumption underlying this field is that since Blacks are underrepresented in the media, heavy exposure necessarily means frequent viewing of mostly White portrayals and models. However, Blacks do not use only mainstream media. There is a large minority media market geared toward African Americans that includes Black-oriented movies, magazines, newspapers, radio stations, and TV programs. Indeed, evidence repeatedly indicates that Blacks gravitate to such media and prefer to watch programs that feature Black characters (e.g., Anderson and Williams 1983; Dates 1980; Liss 1981; O'Connor, Brooks-Gunn, and Graber 2000; Stroman 1986). Therefore, despite the small number of Black comedies and dramas on television, Black children watch them frequently, tend to judge Black characters favorably, and often identify strongly with the portrayals (e.g., Anderson and Williams 1983; Dates 1980; Greenberg 1993; McDermott and Greenberg 1984). Moreover, Black viewers are frequently exposed to African Americans in other genres, such as sports programming and music videos, where Blacks are prominently featured. Indeed, the adulation accorded pop music stars and sports figures in popular culture could provide positive effects on Black self-esteem and racial pride. Thus, the degree to which Black youth are exposed both to Black-oriented media and to genres that heavily feature Blacks is likely to have an impact on the nature of the outcomes. However, it cannot be assumed that all Black-oriented media are free of stereotypes and are inherently positive. There is often an assumption that programs by Blacks will contain fewer stereotypes and more sensitive portrayals (Allen 1998), yet this is not always the case. What happens when the images of Blacks produced by Blacks are negative or stereotypical? Black youth may feel less connected to White characters and their behavior, but they may be especially influenced by Black images coming from Black creators. Accordingly, are stereotypical images presented by Blacks (and therefore accorded a degree of credibility) more potentially harmful than stereotypical images presented by Whites (which may often be dismissed)? Consider, for example, the case of *In Living Color*, the sketch comedy variety program that aired during the early 1990s. Whereas Blacks watched the show more than Whites and reported higher levels of enjoyment, a majority of African American college students (68%) surveyed in one study (Cooks and Orbe 1993) indicated that its characters reinforce negative stereotypes. However, respondents who watched the show regularly were less inclined to find the characters offensive and did not agree that the program perpetuated negative stereotypes. Accordingly, future research must continue to examine the potential impact of both majority and Black-oriented media and should also consider the potential positive and negative effects that could come from each depending on the nature of the content.

A second issue is that effects of media exposure are likely to be selective, occurring only for some Black viewers. The Black audience, like all audiences, is not homogeneous (Allen and Bielby 1979; Bales 1986; Berry 1998), and its members are likely to differ in their reactions to media content and in their vulnerability to its influences based on their preexisting values, belief systems, identities, and demographic attributes. Given that positive associations have been uncovered thus far between media exposure and Black children's self-esteem, might there be some environmental forces working to counteract and buffer "outside" negative influences? Two factors often noted for their beneficial contributions for Black youth are religious involvement and extended family support. Among adolescent samples, religiosity has been associated with reduced involvement in criminal activities (e.g., Donohue and Benson 1995; Johnson et al. 2000), lower levels of alcohol and substance abuse (e.g., Johnson, Larson, De Li, and Jang 2000; Wallace and Williams 1997), and lower levels of voluntary sexual activity and sexual risk-taking (e.g., Donohue and Benson 1995; Murray 1994). Similarly, living with extended family members has been found in some cases to buffer the effects of stress and of stressful life events on problem behaviors (e.g., Dubow, Edwards, and Ippolito 1997; McCabe, Clark, and Barnett 1999). Thus, if these factors operate for Black youth as some kind of buffer against outside negative influences, it is possible they may also ward off negative effects to self-esteem created by media exposure. These suppositions, as well as other factors, need to be investigated directly in future research.

A third issue is that, as critical viewers, African Americans may *not* be as susceptible to the negative influences of stereotypical portrayals as many propose. This position has been argued from several platforms. Some have highlighted the roles of experience and authenticity. Here the notion is that because television is believed to be most influential when firsthand experience or alternative sources of information are lacking (e.g., Himmelweit, Oppenheim, and Vince 1958), for Blacks viewing images of Blacks this is seldom the case. Instead, Black viewers are likely to come to the screen with abundant firsthand experiences of life as a Black American and may subsequently reject media images that contradict their own realities and observations (Milkie 1999). From a different platform, others have emphasized the resilience of African Americans as a people, highlighting their survival against tremendous odds (e.g., Berry 1998; Davis and Gandy 1999). The notion is that because of their unique history in America, African Americans may *not* easily allow outside images to dictate their inner self-concepts. As Davis and Gandy (1999) argue, the standard approach that portrays Black audiences as victims of negative and stereotypic media images underestimates the resilience of African Americans and ignores their capacity to resist media texts. They argue that many African Americans have developed skills in producing oppositional readings to mainstream media content and have learned to extract what is beneficial and ignore what is not. Thus, the overall notion is that Blacks may be especially sensitive and critical toward media representations of their own group and may be *less* susceptible to damage to the self. The extent to which these dynamics apply to youth, versus adults, however, is unknown. Critical research is needed in this area, especially work that examines whether having a strong Black identity or a strong connection to the Black community protects young viewers from stereotypical portrayals in mainstream programming.

Finally, one must evaluate methodological issues, such as the particular measures used or the ages tested, when interpreting the meaning of study results. One concern is the less-than-conventional ways in which self-esteem has been measured in some instances. For example, the five-item dependent variable used by Tan and Tan (1979) was more a measure of racial self-esteem or racial pride than of general self-esteem. Participants were asked to judge whether Blacks or Whites are smarter, nicer, or more dependable and were not asked about their own competencies, which may make labeling this study as a test of the media's contribution to self-esteem inappropriate. Future research will need to employ more standard and more extensive measures of this complex construct. A second concern is the limited selection of ages tested. A broader developmental perspective is needed, in which participants of different ages (e.g., prepubertal children, teens, and college students) are tested in the same study to begin to determine how the nature of these associations changes with age. Finally, there is little work examining the impact of media exposure on Black children's stereotypes about Black people. This is an area worthy of further attention, using both surveys to examine the effects of regular exposure levels and experimental approaches to test the impact of specific images.

Does Frequent Media Exposure Lead to Stereotypical Conceptions of Gender and Male-Female Relations among Black Youth?

A consistent finding across decades of research is that media portrayals offer a narrow and stereotypical view of the sexes and that repeated exposure to these images constrains young viewers' own conceptions about gender and about sexual roles (for review, see Signorielli 2001; Ward and Harrison 2005). More specifically, evidence indicates that frequent exposure to mainstream media portrayals is associated with stronger support for sexist attitudes, stereotyped associations about what the sexes do and how they behave, stronger preferences for traditional occupations and activities, and a greater acceptance of casual and stereotypical attitudes about sexual relationships. Although this issue typically has been tested among predominantly White samples, it can be expected that these outcomes may be especially likely for Black youth, not only because they watch more television, but also because their media diets have been found to be especially high in sexual and sexist content (e.g., Brown et al. 2006).

For example, in their analysis of the television and movie behaviors of 795 Black and White teens, Solderman, Greenberg, and Linsangan (1988) found that Black girls received more total exposure to sex acts on television than did Whites and had a higher diet of *R*-rated movies. Similarly, Greenberg (1993) reported that in comparison to the White teens surveyed, Black teens were exposed to more sexual content in both their prime-time and soap diets, watched more *R*-rated movies, and had a higher ratio of *R*-rated movies in their movie diets. It has also been found that rap and hip-hop music videos, which are particularly popular with Black youth, are especially sexual and sexist. In one study, 26.3% of videos on MTV were found to contain sexual content compared to 60.7% on BET (Black Entertainment Television) (Hansen and Hansen 2000). Similarly, Jones (1997) reported that rap-hip videos contained significantly more images of fondling, simulated intercourse, women and men dancing sexually, and women in hot pants than did all other musical genres. How does frequent exposure to these images shape Black youths' conceptions of femininity, masculinity, and male-female relations?

Data from the few studies that have included Black participants reveal predictable results. O'Bryant and Corder-Bolz (1978) included 23 Black children in their study of whether exposure to stereotypic or counter-stereotypic occupational roles would affect children's own stereotyping of and preferences for those jobs. Over one four-week period, the authors exposed six- to ten-year-olds to a set of commercials that featured women in either traditional roles (e.g., manicurist) or nontraditional roles (e.g., pharmacist). Posttest measures revealed that exposure to *nontraditional* images was found to increase girls' preferences for stereotypically masculine jobs. However, exposure had no effects on girls' stereotyping occupations nor on boys' stereotyping or job preferences. In a sample of 530 fourth and fifth graders that was 64% White and 21% Black, Signorielli and Lears (1992) reported a significant positive correlation both for Whites and for "non-Whites" between amount of television watched and stereotypical conceptions about who should do certain chores; viewing amounts did not link to students' actual behavior, however.

Others have looked more directly at links between media exposure and students' attitudes about sexual relationships. In their study of 60 inner-city Black teens, Johnson et al. (1995) reported that girls exposed to eight sexist, nonviolent rap videos were more accepting of teen dating violence than were girls without such exposure; boys' attitudes were not affected. Similarly, Bryant and Bowman (1992) found that 56.7% of Black female teens who reported watching rap music videos more than two hours per week believed that women's behavior in typical videos is okay; only 23% of girls who watched less than two hours each week agreed. In their two-year longitudinal study of the media habits of 1,600 adolescents, Walsh-Childers and Brown (1993) reported that more frequent viewing of soaps and sitcoms predicted *increased* acceptance of relationship stereotypes among Black teens; among White teens, greater total viewing predicted *decreased* acceptance of relationship stereotypes. Finally, in their study of 156 Black teens, Ward, Hansbrough, and Walker (2005) reported both correlational and experimental links between media exposure and students' stereotypes about gender roles and male-female relations. Frequent exposure both to music videos and to music were each associated with holding more stereotypical notions about the sexes. Furthermore, in an experimental paradigm, students exposed to four stereotypical music videos offered stronger endorsement of sexual stereotypes than did students exposed to neutral videos.

Taken together, these findings suggest that among Black viewers, frequent media exposure is associated with holding more stereotypical beliefs about the sexes and about sexual roles, and that young viewers, girls especially, may be growing desensitized to some of the negative images of women due to this constant exposure. Evidence also suggests that viewing nontraditional images may reduce some of these associations, if only temporarily. Future research needs to continue to examine the contributions of media exposure to Black youths' stereotypes about women and men and to examine how these beliefs affect their conceptions of themselves and their relationships. Which age groups are particularly vulnerable to these stereotypes? How does buying into these stereotypes affect behavior in sexual relationships?

Does Frequent Media Exposure Lead to a Poor Body Image and Body Dissatisfaction among Black Youth?

As a visual medium, television places a heavy emphasis on physical appearance, presenting a steady stream of examples of idealized beauty, femininity, and masculinity. The beauty ideal put forth by the dominant culture upholds and perpetuates Eurocentric perspectives and features. For women this ideal focuses on fair skin, long hair, light or blue eyes, delicate features, and thinness (Perkins 1996) and is applied to women of multiple racial and ethnic backgrounds. Because these features do not represent most Black women, how might repeated exposure to these mainstream ideals affect their body image?

At this point, little empirical evidence exists to address this point. Most existing research examining connections between media exposure and women's body image has tested exclusively on predominantly White samples. In the past decade alone, over 65 such studies have been published (for review, see Ward and Harrison 2004), yielding abundant evidence that frequent exposure to thin-ideal media leads to greater body dissatisfaction, greater weight concerns, internalization of the thin ideal, and disordered eating symptomatology among White girls and women. It is typically assumed that for Black women such exposure may be especially detrimental because of the dominance of the White beauty ideal and the exclusion of Black women from the media. What does the evidence indicate?

Data from focus groups and interviews suggest that Black girls are not necessarily accepting the beauty ideal of mainstream media. In surveys and interviews of Black and White teen girls, Milkie (1999) examined students' interpretations of thin-ideal media and the pressure they felt from such media to be thin. She reported that Anglo girls felt pressure to meet thin media ideals even if they reported disliking the thin ideal themselves, because they believed their peers, exposed to similar media, expected them to be thin. In contrast, African American girls appeared more resistant to this pressure to conform to what they perceived as a largely Anglo body ideal. Similar findings were reported by Duke (2000) in her interviews with Black and White teen girls and by Sekayi (2003) in her survey and subsequent focus groups and interviews with Black female undergraduates. These results indicate that Black girls were largely uninterested in the beauty ideals presented in mainstream teen magazines, dismissing them as irrelevant and as intended for White girls. They believed that thin, long-haired, blonde models conflicted with African American standards of attractiveness and did not really admire or seek out these models to emulate. Indeed, the Black women Sekayi (2003) spoke with tended to define "beauty" using a more African-centered model that included both tangible and intangible characteristics, such as self-confidence, personality, and friendliness.

Support for this notion has also been found in survey and experimental work, which also illustrates that the media's influence on Black girls' body perceptions varies based on the race of the media model and the current body image of the viewer. In an experiment with African

American college students, Makkar and Strube (1995) reported that participants high in self-esteem and Black identity rated themselves as *more* attractive after exposure to images of attractive White women. Thus, there may be a sort of contrast effect for secure women exposed to ideal-body images that are judged personally or culturally irrelevant. Looking at the prime-time viewing diets of Black and White female undergraduates, Schooler et al. (2004) found that among Black women, more frequent viewing in high school of programming with predominantly Black casts was associated with a lower drive for thinness, fewer tendencies toward bulimia, and fewer negative thoughts about the body. Few effects came from their viewing of programming with predominantly White casts. Finally, across two experiments Frisby (2004) found that the mood and body esteem of Black undergraduate women were *not* affected by exposure to magazine ads featuring images of White models. However, exposure to magazine ads featuring African American models did diminish the body esteem of young Black women who had already reported low opinions of their own bodies; Black women with a more positive body image were not affected by the exposure.

But some findings suggest that Black girls and women may not be as resistant to mainstream models and comparisons as some initial investigations have suggested. Botta (2000) surveyed the media use habits and self-evaluations of 145 White and 33 African American adolescent girls. Greater TV viewing predicted increased bulimic symptomatology for White girls but not for Black girls. However, for both groups the more the girls idealized TV images and the more often they compared themselves and their friends to those images, the stronger their drive to be thin and the more dissatisfied they were with their bodies. Among those who idealized TV images the most, Black girls engaged in more disordered behaviors than did the White girls. In addition, in her focus group interviews with 15 Black female undergraduates from New York City, Poran (2006) found the participants to be very aware of and pressured by the mainstream beauty ideals and to feel conflicting pressure from these ideals and Black men's beauty ideal. Although the women could describe more things that they loved than hated about their bodies, they also expressed great confusion, frustration, and anxiety at the rigid standards of beauty that they felt could not be ignored. With these findings, Poran tries to raise awareness of the complexity of how Black women relate to media ideals and of the utility of diverse research approaches. Her concern is that survey measures designed with White women in mind may not capture all of the appearance concerns of Black women and could thus present a misrepresentation and overly positive image.

Overall, the data indicate that many (but not all) Black female viewers reject White beauty ideals presented by the media and compare themselves favorably to and may perhaps be inspired by media images of Black females. For those who do accept White ideals, negative self-evaluations emerge as expected. This small body of findings offers up provocative fuel for future research. One approach would be to broaden future assessments of body evaluations to include women's concerns about facial features, hair length, and skin color, issues that might be more relevant for Black viewers. Current work has focused heavily on weight concerns, which may not be paramount among Black viewers. Future research must also investigate which media figures Black women do identify with and why, and determine if those who identify with slender media personalities such as Halle Berry are more negatively influenced than those who identify with Oprah Winfrey or Queen Latifah, whose bodies are closer to that of the average Black woman.

Does Frequent Media Exposure Lead to Inactivity, Poor Health, and Obesity among Black Youth?

It has been estimated that a quarter of children aged 6–11 are obese in America, defined as being 20% or more heavier than one's ideal weight. Over the past decade, a significant correlation has been reported between greater amounts of TV viewing and obesity among children and adolescents (e.g., Dietz 1990; Robinson 2001). For example, Dietz and Gortmaker (1985) reported that in three national samples of youth aged 12 to 17, significant associations were reported between time spent watching television and the prevalence of obesity, which increased by 2% for each additional hour of television viewed. This connection remained even after controls for prior obesity, region, season, population density, race, SES, and a variety of other family variables. Because both obesity and TV viewing are higher among African Americans, and because being obese increases the risk of many life-threatening diseases including hypertension, heart disease, and diabetes, all of which are more prevalent in Blacks than in Whites, these issues are of great importance.

Several factors are believed to be at work in explaining the link between TV viewing and obesity, including increased exposure to enticing advertising of fattening and unhealthy foods, the inactivity that comes with watching television, and the frequent snacking (often of unhealthy foods) that accompanies viewing. All of these factors are especially pertinent and relevant for African American youth not only because Black youth consume more television than do children of other ethnic groups but also because recent reports indicate that what they view may be especially unhealthy. For example, Harrison (2006) compared the nutritional attributes of television commercials that did and did not feature Black characters. She found that ads with Black characters were more likely to sell convenience foods, especially fast foods, than were ads without Black characters. In their analysis of advertisements in three Black-oriented magazines (*Essence, Ebony,* and *Jet*), Mastin and Campo (2006) found that the majority of ads consistently advertised food high in empty calories and low in nutritional value. Similarly, Tirodkar and Jain (2003) reported that TV shows geared toward African audiences had 60% more food commercials than did shows that attract a general audience. They also reported that 31% of the food commercials on popular Black shows are for sweets and 13% are for soda, compared to 11% and 2% of commercials on programs geared toward a general audience. Thus it appears young viewers of Black prime-time programs are subjected to a disproportionate number of unhealthy food images. This comes at a time when more than 60% of African Americans are overweight, compared to 54% of the general U.S. population.

Research on the physical health consequences of TV viewing for African American youth can also extend to general risk taking, such as drinking alcohol, smoking cigarettes, and smoking marijuana. In their survey of the media habits and risk-taking behaviors of 2,760 teens aged 14 to 16, Klein and colleagues (1993) reported several significant links between these factors. For Black female teens, greater total TV use and greater exposure to rap music predicted more risk taking. For Black males, greater total TV use and greater exposure to sports magazines predicted more risk taking, while greater exposure to TV news and to soul music predicted less risk taking. Whereas these results are correlational only and provide no information about causal relationships, they do indicate that these factors are potentially related. Future research is needed in order to investigate directly the impact of media exposure on weight, obesity, and other health factors. Experimental work is also needed, perhaps investigating which food and drink choices Black children make after exposure to commercials of fattening food or after exposure to programs with heavier characters.

Areas for Future Research

Because of Black youths' affinity for the media coupled with the media's sometimes dismissive and demeaning treatment of African Americans, researchers have continually expressed concern about the media's impact on Black youth. Whereas evidence presented here both supports and questions some of the standard claims, it is difficult to draw firm conclusions with so few findings. Future research is clearly needed. Each of the areas discussed here holds the potential to greatly affect the social and emotional development of Black youth, yet steps cannot be taken to address these effects without accompanying empirical evidence. Building on the excellent ideas offered by other reviews (e.g., Graves 1980; Stroman 1991), we make four suggestions for future research directions.

1. Consider the nature of Black youths' exposure to media, looking at the differential impact of exposure to mainstream versus Black-oriented media.

The findings presented here make it clear that the specific content of Black youths' media diets is important. In addition to assessing their overall exposure to multiple media in multiple genres, we must also examine the proportion and amount of exposure to mainstream versus Black-oriented media, for these distinctions appear to make a difference.

A related issue worthy of attention is the potential impact of underrepresentation and misrepresentation. Given that Blacks are excluded from some programs and are included in others but portrayed mostly in a negative light (e.g., as criminals), it would be informative to examine which situation produces the most detrimental effects on the self-conceptions of young Black viewers. Are Blacks perceived as less important, competent, or powerful when they are absent from television or when they are present yet depicted stereotypically? Experimental research here could follow the lead of the dissertation research of Sherryl Brown Graves (1975, cited in Graves 1980), which examined the impact of positive and negative portrayals of Black cartoon characters on the racial attitudes of Black 6- to 8-year-olds. She found that Black children exposed to a cartoon featuring Black characters expressed more positive attitudes toward Blacks than did a control group who viewed a cartoon with *no* Blacks in it. Additional work is needed along these lines with children of different age groups, with different types of media stimuli (e.g., clips from comedies vs. cartoons vs. reality programs), and with different types of experimental conditions (e.g., excluded vs. token vs. dominant yet stereotypical). Outcome variables could examine Black youths' stereotypes about Blacks, racial pride, and estimates of the numbers of Blacks in positions of power.

2. Examine Black-oriented media, and consider its complexity and heterogeneity.

As further attention is given to the potential impact of mainstream versus Black-oriented media, it becomes clear that Black-oriented media, in itself, is quite complex. Three issues are particularly important. First, Black leads are often presented differently in different genres. In Black situation comedies, the comedic, family situations of African Americans are featured, sometimes taken to the extreme. On talk shows, hosts such as Oprah and Montel Williams are presented as well-spoken, intelligent leaders. The same can be said of Black judges on courtroom reality programs. Sports programming, especially basketball, features Blacks prominently as driven, athletic players and coaches. Given these differences, we cannot assume that exposure to "Black-oriented media" means exposure to only one image of Black people. Within this domain, researchers need to look specifically at the type of content and models typically portrayed; some could be positive and others could be quite negative.

Second, African Americans do not appear only in Black-oriented media. Nearly all of the current prime-time dramas (e.g., *Law and Order, CSI, ER*) feature at least one Black cast member as a player in an integrated work setting. Although such characters might not be the stars of the program, they do offer young viewers information about Black people and about being Black in America, and show Blacks and Whites working and solving problems together. Indeed, in the dissertation work discussed above, Graves (1980) found that of the students exposed to the Black cartoon characters, Black children who had seen the characters in an integrated setting had more positive attitudes toward Blacks than did participants who had seen the Black characters in a segregated setting. Further work is needed, then, on the potential impact of the positive and negative portrayals of African Americans in integrated versus segregated settings.

Finally, images of Blacks may carry more or less influence or cachet depending on the race of the source. For example, it is probable that Black characters in Black films directed by White directors may be perceived as less authentic or influential than Black characters in films written and directed by Black directors such as Spike Lee (e.g., *Do the Right Thing*), John Singleton (e.g., *Boyz in the Hood*), or Gina Prince-by-the-Wood (*Love and Basketball*). The salience and impact of these distinctions need to be examined.

3. Investigate risk and protective factors.

The evidence presented in this chapter also highlights the need to examine individual factors among Black viewers that may make them especially vulnerable or resistant to media influence. As noted earlier, religiosity and a strong extended family structure are protective factors against negative influences and may ward off certain kinds of negative media influences as well. Another important factor to consider is racial pride and racial self-esteem. Viewers coming to the screen with a strong connection to and pride in their Black heritage are drawn more often to Black-oriented media and appear to be less open to accepting negative images of Black people. We need to look further at the protective influence of racial pride, examining whether its influence extends to exposure to sexual and gender stereotypes of Black women and men and to body evaluations, as well.

It would also be informative to assess the extent and impact of any critical viewing training Black youth may have received informally from family members or formally in schools and after-school programs. What role do Black parents play as mediators? Solderman, Greenberg, and Linsangan (1988) reported that Black girls faced more rules and more limits on TV watching and talked more often with their parents about TV content than did White girls. Similarly, Greenberg (1993) reported that Black teens discussed television more with their parents than did White teens. The lessons that Black parents teach their children about media images need to be examined.

4. Develop and extend conceptual models that describe African Americans' media use and its impact.

Given the complexity of media influence as outlined here and in the literature, we need to begin to develop models that incorporate multiple factors and mechanisms. One example is Allen's conceptual models of Black self-concept (1993, 1998). In these models, Allen views the media as a filter through which African Americans obtain information about their group and about its relationship to the dominant society. In his model outlining antecedents of an African American racial belief system for Black children and adolescents, Allen (1993) posits that a set of five social structural variables (religiosity, perceived social class, total family income, education, and Black socialization environment) influence seven areas of communication use and exposure (Black establishment magazine exposure, Black nonestablishment magazine exposure, Black TV public affairs exposure, Black TV entertainment exposure, majority magazine exposure, majority TV public affairs exposure, majority entertainment TV exposure), that then affect six racial beliefs and self-conceptions (Black autonomy, closeness to elites, closeness to mass groups, positive stereotypic beliefs, negative stereotypic beliefs, and self-esteem). Although this model has not yet been tested with children, a related model tested with adults has been validated (Allen 1993; Allen, Dawson, and Brown 1989). In her 1991 review, Stroman offers an informative hypothesized model for understanding television's social impact. According to this model, television exposure → mediating variables (14 child characteristics and 4 environmental characteristics) → positive and negative outcomes. Future research needs to continue to develop and test models of African American media use and its impact.

Conclusion

With their ability to frame, define, amplify, and neglect aspects of the social world, the American media are a potent social and cultural force (Milkie 1999). While only one of many factors shaping the social and emotional development of Black youth, the media are potentially very powerful. This chapter summarizes current findings in four research areas in order to call attention to these potential influences; there are likely many others. Key issues identified are summarized in the box. Although these potential influences have been under-studied over the past three decades, it is hoped that we can reverse this trend over the next thirty years.

Lessons Learned—Summary of Key Issues for Media and Black Youth

The literature on the impact of media exposure on Black youth is primarily shaped by the following questions.
- Does frequent media exposure lead to stereotypical conceptions of gender and male-female relations among Black youth?

- Does frequent media exposure lead to a poor body image and body dissatisfaction among Black youth?
- Does frequent media exposure lead to inactivity and poor health and obesity among Black youth?

Suggestions for future directions for research in this area include the following.

- Consider the nature of Black youths' exposure to media, looking at the differential impact of exposure to mainstream versus Black-oriented media.
- Examine Black-oriented media, and consider its complexity and heterogeneity.
- Investigate risk and protective factors.
- Develop and extend conceptual models that describe African-Americans' media use and its impact.

REFERENCES

Allen, R. 1993. Conceptual models of an African-American belief system: A program of research. In G. Berry and J. K. Asamen, eds., *Children and television: Images in a changing sociocultural world*, 155–76. Newbury Park, CA: Sage.

Allen, R. 1998. Class, communication, and the Black self: A theory outline. In J. K. Asamen and G. L. Berry, eds., *Research paradigms, television, and social behavior*, 153–202. Thousand Oaks, CA: Sage.

Allen, R. L., and W. T. Bielby. 1979. Blacks' attitudes and behaviors toward television. *Communication Research* 6:437–62.

Allen, R. L., M. C. Dawson, and R. E. Brown. 1989. A schema-based approach to modeling an African-American racial belief system. *American Political Science Review* 83:421–41.

Anderson, W. H., Jr., and B. M. Williams. 1983. TV and the Black child: What Black children say about the shows they watch. *Journal of Black Psychology* 9:27–42.

Bales, F. 1986. Television use and confidence in television by Blacks and Whites in 4 selected years. *Journal of Black Studies* 16:283–91.

Berry, G. 1998. Black family life on television and the socialization of the African American child: Images of marginality. *Journal of Comparative Family Studies* 29:233–42.

Botta, R. A. 2000. The mirror of television: A comparison of Black and White adolescents' body image. *Journal of Communication* 50:144–59.

Brown, J. D., K. L'Engle, C. Pardun, G. Guo, K. Kenneavy, and C. Jackson. 2006. Sexy media matter: Exposure to sexual content in music, movies, television, and magazines predicts Black and White adolescents' sexual behavior. *Pediatrics* 117:1018–27.

Bryant, Y., and S. Bowman. 2002. *African American female adolescents and rap music video's image of women: Attitudes and perceptions.* Poster presented at the biennial meeting of the Society for Research on Adolescence, New Orleans.

Clark, C. 1972. Race, identification, and television behavior. In G. Comstock, E. Rubinstein, and J. P. Murray, eds., *Television and social behavior,* vol. 5, *Television's effects: Further exploration,* 120–84. Washington, DC: U.S. Government Printing Office.

Cooks, L. M., and M. P. Orbe. 1993. Beyond the satire: Selective exposure and selective perception in "In Living Color." *Howard Journal of Communication* 4:217–33.

Dates, J. 1980. Race, racial attitudes, and adolescents' perceptions of Black characters. *Journal of Broadcasting* 24:549–60.

Davis, J. L., and O. H. Gandy. 1999. Racial identity and media orientation. *Journal of Black Studies* 29:367–97.

Dietz, W. H. 1990. You are what you eat: What you eat is what you are. *Journal of Adolescent Health Care* 11:76–81.

Dietz, W. H., and S. L. Gortmaker. 1985. Do we fatten our children at the television set? Obesity and television viewing in children and adolescents. *Pediatrics* 75:807–12.

Donahue, M. J., and P. L. Benson. 1995. Religion and the well-being of adolescents. *Journal of Social Issues* 51:145–60.

Dubow, E. F., S. Edwards, and M. F. Ippolito. 1997. Life stressors, neighborhood disadvantage, and resources: A focus on inner-city children's adjustment. *Journal of Clinical Child Psychology* 26:130–44.

Duke, L. 2000. Black in a blonde world: Race and girls' interpretations of the feminine ideal in teen magazines. *Journalism and Mass Communication Quarterly* 77:367–92.

Frisby, C. 2004. Does race matter? Effects of idealized images on African American women's perceptions of body esteem. *Journal of Black Studies* 34:323–47.

Graves, S. B. 1980. Psychological effects of Black portrayals on television. In S. B. Withey and R. P. Abeles, eds., *Television and social behavior: Beyond violence and children,* 259–89. Hillsdale, NJ: Lawrence Erlbaum.

Graves, S. B. 1999. Television and prejudice reduction: When does television as a vicarious experience make a difference? *Journal of Social Issues* 55:707–27.

Greenberg, B. S. 1993. Race differences in television and movie behaviors. In B. S. Greenberg, J. D. Brown, and N. L. Buerkel-Rothfuss, eds., *Media, sex, and the adolescent,* 145–52. Creskill, NJ: Hampton.

Hansen, C. H., and R. D. Hansen. 2000. Music and music videos. In D. Zillmann and P. Vorderer, eds., *Media entertainment: The psychology of its appeal,* 175–96. Mahwah, NJ: Lawrence Erlbaum.

Harrison, K. 2006. Fast and sweet: Nutritional attributes of television food advertisements with and without Black characters. *Howard Journal of Communication* 17:249–64.

Himmelweit, H. T., A. N. Oppenheim, and P. Vince. 1958. *Television and the child.* London: Oxford University Press.

Johnson, B. R., D. B. Larson, S. De Li, and S. J. Jang. 2000. Escaping from the crime of inner cities: Church attendance and religious salience among disadvantaged youth. *Justice Quarterly* 17:377–91.

Johnson, J., M. S. Adams, L. Ashburn, and W. Reed. 1995. Differential gender effects of exposure to rap music on African American adolescents' acceptance of teen dating violence. *Sex Roles* 33:597–605.

Jones, K. 1997. Are rap videos more violent? Style differences and the prevalence of sex and violence in the age of MTV. *Howard Journal of Communication* 8:343–56.

Klein, J. D., J. D. Brown, K. Walsh Childers, J. Oliveri, C. Porter, and C. Dykers. 1993. Adolescents' risky behavior and mass media use. *Pediatrics* 92:24–31.

Liss, M. B. 1981. Children's television selections: A study of indicators of same-race preferences. *Journal of Cross-Cultural Psychology* 12:103–10.

Makkar, J. K., and M. J. Strube. 1995. Black women's self-perceptions of attractiveness following exposure to white versus black beauty standards: The moderating role of racial identity and self-esteem. *Journal of Applied Social Psychology* 25:1547–66.

Mastin, T., and S. Campo. 2006. Conflicting messages: Overweight and obesity advertisements and articles in Black magazines. *Howard Journal of Communication* 17:265–85.

McCabe, K. M., R. Clark, and D. Barnett. 1999. Family protective factors among urban African American youth. *Journal of Clinical Child Psychology* 28:137–50.

McDermott, S. T., and B. S. Greenberg. 1984. Black children's esteem: Parents, peers, and TV. In R. Bostrom, ed., *Communication yearbook* 8:164–77. Beverly Hills, CA: Sage.

Milkie, M. A. 1999. Social comparisons, reflected appraisals, and mass media: The impact of pervasive beauty images on Black and White girls' self-concepts. *Social Psychology Quarterly* 62:190–210.

Murray, V. 1994. Black adolescent females: A comparison of early versus late coital initiators. *Family Relations* 43:342–48.

O'Bryant, S. L., and C. R. Corder-Bolz. 1978. Black children's learning of work roles from television commercials. *Psychological Reports* 42:227–30.

O'Connor, L., J. Brooks-Gunn, and J. Graber. 2000. Black and White girls' racial preferences in media and peer choices and the role of socialization for Black girls. *Journal of Family Psychology* 14:510–21.

Perkins, K. R. 1996. The influence of television images on Black females' self-perceptions of physical attractiveness. *Journal of Black Psychology* 22:453–69.

Poran, M. 2006. The politics of protection: Body image, social pressures, and the misrepresentation of young Black women. *Sex Roles* 55:739–55.

Robinson, T. N. 2001. Television viewing and childhood obesity. *Pediatric Clinics of North America* 48:1017–25.

Schooler, D., L. M. Ward, A. Merriwether, and A. Caruthers. 2004. Who's that girl: Television's role in the body image development of young White and Black women. *Psychology of Women Quarterly* 28:38–47.

Seiter, E. 1990. Different children, different dreams: Racial representation in advertising. *Journal of Communication Inquiry* 14:31–47.

Sekayi, D. 2003. Aesthetic resistance to commercial influences: The impact of the Eurocentric beauty standard on Black college women. *Journal of Negro Education* 72:467–77.

Signorielli, N. 2001. Television's gender role images and contribution to stereotyping: Past, present, future. In D. G. Singer and J. L. Singer, eds., *Handbook of children and the media*, 341–58. Thousand Oaks, CA: Sage.

Signorielli, N., and M. Lears. 1992. Children, television, and conceptions about chores: Attitudes and behaviors. *Sex Roles* 27:157–70.

Solderman, A. K., B. S. Greenberg, and R. Linsangan. 1988. Television and movie behaviors of pregnant and non-pregnant adolescents. *Journal of Adolescent Research* 3:153–70.

Stroman, C. A. 1984. The socialization influence of television on Black children. *Journal of Black Studies* 15:79–100.

Stroman, C. A. 1986. Television viewing and self-concept among Black children. *Journal of Broadcasting and Electronic Media* 30:87–93.

Stroman, C. A. 1991. Television's role in the socialization of African American children and adolescents. *Journal of Negro Education* 60:314–27.

Tan, A., and G. Tan. 1979. Television use and self-esteem of Blacks. *Journal of Communication* 29:129–35.

Tirodkar, M., and A. Jain. 2003. Food messages on African American television shows. *American Journal of Public Health* 93:439–41.

Wallace, J. M., and D. R. Williams. 1997. Religion and adolescent health-compromising behavior. In J. Schulenberg, J. L. Maggs, and K. Hurrelmann, eds., *Health risks and developmental transitions during adolescence*, 444–68. Cambridge: Cambridge University Press.

Walsh-Childers, K., and J. D. Brown. 1993. Adolescents' acceptance of sex-role stereotypes and television viewing. In B. S. Greenberg, J. D. Brown, and N. L. Buerkel-Rothfuss, eds., *Media, sex, and the adolescent*, 117–33. Creskill, NJ: Hampton.

Ward, L. M. 2004. Wading through the stereotypes: Positive and negative associations between media use and black adolescents' conceptions of self. *Developmental Psychology* 40:284–94.

Ward, L. M., E. Hansbrough, and E. Walker. 2005. Contributions of music video exposure to Black adolescents' gender and sexual schemas. *Journal of Adolescent Research* 20:143–66.

Ward, L. M., and K. Harrison. 2005. The impact of media use on girls' beliefs about gender roles, their bodies, and sexual relationships: A research synthesis. In E. Cole and J. H. Daniels, eds., *Featuring females: Feminist analyses of media*, 3–23. Washington, DC: American Psychological Association.

Wilson, M. N. 1989. Child development in the context of the Black extended family. *American Psychologist* 44:380–85.

Wilson, M. N., and T. F. Tolson. 1990. Familial support in the Black community. *Journal of Clinical Child Psychology* 19:347–55.

16 | Regarding Black Audiences: Qualitative Approaches to Studying Black Media Consumption

Catherine Squires and Bambi Haggins

Many scholars and social commentators have turned a critical eye toward representations of African Americans and racial issues across many genres, including news and political advertising (e.g., Dixon and Linz 2000; Entman 2000; Gilens 1999; Mendleberg 2001; Valentino 1999) and sports, advertising, and entertainment media (e.g., Dates and Barlow 1990; Gray 1995; Riggs 1991). These important critiques of content and assessments of media effects reveal an unsatisfying array of Black images in mainstream media with the exception of a few bright spots of innovation and inclusion of Black talent. Similarly, those who study the effects of negative racial representations and deployments of racialized political messages find that White audiences come away with skewed views of African American life and/or malformed opinions that reinforce harmful stereotypes.

However, there has not been as much study of how African Americans themselves interpret or respond to media representations of their racial group. A few recent effects studies have investigated the impact of particular media, like rap music and music videos (e.g., Johnson, Jackson, and Gatto 1995; Ward, Hansbourough, and Walker 2005), and more work in this area is needed. But in addition to experimental research in the effects tradition and content and textual analyses, more audience-centered studies—that is, research that focuses on African American audiences' interactions with and opinions of media texts—are needed to address a range of Black communities' experiences with media.

Qualitative methods, such as ethnographic and cultural-historical research, can lend insight into which cultural practices, rituals, or ideologies guide Black media consumers through what often seems like a minefield of problematic images. Taking a close look at a small, well-defined audience can help us understand the new media environment faced by Black audiences. Herman Gray (2001) advises scholars to reexamine the guiding assumptions about mass media and racial representation. Specifically, as we survey the world of 500 channels, the Internet, niche publications, and cheaper independent digital production, we must recognize that all audiences face a new set of resources and challenges. Thus, racial groups that were ignored or defamed in the era when the Big Three television networks, local newspapers, and radio were the main choices may today interact with the new array of media outlets and opportunities quite differently. And, as advertisers and media producers seek to reach a global, ethnically and racially diverse pool of consumers, we may see changes in the range of texts available to those audiences, as well as changes in how audiences consume media.

In the twenty-first-century media environment, we argue that qualitative audience research, with its emphasis on audience agency and reading practices, can help us better understand how African Americans interact with the 500-channel, digital media landscape. The audience research tradition, although it does not offer the generalizations of survey research or the scientific punch of experiments, does give us depth and detail into a given audience's experiences with media. Focusing on the particular identity and culture of a specific Black audience can elucidate important nuances and exceptions that are not the territory of quantitative methods. This is not to say that quantitative study of the audience is unhelpful; rather, because there has been so little research on Black audiences, the richer, if less generalizable, results of qualitative audience studies may serve as a foundation for future hypotheses and research designs in the quantitative traditions. For example, audience ethnographies may uncover themes and audience concerns that can be converted into frameworks for survey questionnaires.

This chapter summarizes influential works in the growing field of Black audience studies and then turns to the details of a recent study completed by the authors. The study, a comparison of White and Black women's reactions to popular comedies, builds upon key principles and innovations of prior studies and provides an illustration of the promise of audience ethnographies in the rapidly changing media environment.

Qualitative Research with African American Audiences

The forms of qualitative audience research most applicable to our project are those studies that foreground the readings of media texts by "active" audiences—spectators and cultural readers—and the ways in which those readings correspond to the participants' lay theories of identity formation and reception. In order to understand the studies summarized in the tables, one must return to the seminal work that has inflected much of audience study of the past two decades, Stuart Hall's "Encoding/Decoding" (1980). For the Birmingham school of cultural theory, informed by Marxist (and Althusserian) theories of ideology, audience study needed to reflect the nuanced sense of the complexity of television as a text and as a concept. This represented a departure from the communications studies model of "uses and gratifications," a functionalist, sociological model, and borrowed from anthropology an ethnographic approach to audience study, without necessarily adopting the heavily quantitative methodology of the social sciences.

In "Encoding/Decoding," Hall defines the "ways" in which the audience can "read" a televisual text, thereby rejecting the communications studies model of a linear relationship of sender-message-receiver. Hall offers three different models for "readings" and codes used in these readings: (1) the dominant, in which the televisual spectator completely accepts the "dominant" message of the text (as coded) without interrogating either the source of the narrative or the narrative itself; (2) the negotiated, in which the spectator picks and chooses parts of the "dominant" message while rejecting others; and (3) the oppositional, in which the spectator reads "against the grain" and "detotalizes the message in the preferred code in order to retotalize the message within some alternative framework of reference" (Hall 1980, 138). It is in the final category—the "oppositional reading"—where Hall posits the greatest struggle with ideology: "Here the 'politics of signification'—the struggle in discourse—is joined" (138).

Although there are clearly problems with the way in which these categories of reading are stratified, particularly when one considers the possibilities for interpretation in the "picking and choosing" of the negotiated reading, the notion that all reading of media texts is a struggle with ideology is extremely significant. The study of struggle and negotiation with the televisual text, with the embedded ideology, and with identity are integral to audience study. Exemplary early studies influenced by these concepts are summarized in table 16.1. It is notable that these early studies did not deal with racial identity or Black audiences; not until the 1990s did scholarship begin to emerge to address this gap.

The studies presented in table 16.2 describe investigations by researchers committed to exploring the experiences and desires of Black audiences. Most of these studies, as one might expect, are concerned with how Black audiences respond to depictions of Black life in various media, whether it be fictional or "reality"-based media. One of the main

TABLE 16.1.   Influential Qualitative Audience Studies

Titles and Authors	Audience and Method	Theoretical/ Conceptual Frameworks	Analysis Strategy	Main Findings
Ien Ang, *Watching Dallas* (1985)	Readers of a Dutch women's magazine who responded to researcher's call to correspond with *Dallas* fans	Encoding/ decoding	Analysis of written responses of *Dallas* viewers	The audience's negotiation with the text is a complex process that is as much a struggle with individual lived experience as it is a struggle with ideology.
David Morley, *The Nation-wide Audience* (1980)	Open ended group interviews with students, most of whom were White and male.	Encoding/ decoding, ideology/ hegemony	Analysis of interview transcripts	Class position of viewers influenced their reading of "*Nationwide*" and its political meanings.
Janice Radway, "Functions of Romance Reading" (1991)	Ethnographic focus group interviews with female romance novel fans and textual analysis of romance novels	Encoding/ decoding, feminist theory, ideology/ hegemony	Analysis of focus group transcripts	Women readers used the novels not only to "escape" but also to critique the quality of their everyday lives and relationships. Radway discerned a nascent feminist critique in their discussions.
Henry Jenkins, *Textual Poachers* (1992)	Semiethnographic study of fan "communities." Reveals fans to be proactive constructors of an alternative culture using elements poached and reworked from the popular media.	Interpretive community, feminist literary theory, "poaching."	Analysis of fan inter-views and surveys of fan critical/ creative work	Maps fandom as an interpretive and creative community actively appropriating the content of television for its own pleasures and purposes

TABLE 16.2. Selected Research Focused on Black Audiences

Titles and Authors	Audience and Method	Theoretical/ Conceptual Frameworks	Analysis Strategy	Main Findings
Sut Jhally and Justin Lewis, *Enlightened Racism* (1992)	Focus groups with small groups of middle- and working-class, Anglo Americans and African Americans in a large city	Modern racism; hegemony; encoding/ decoding	Comparison of under-standings of *The Cosby Show* by viewers of different racial groups	An indictment of the colorized American Dream of *The Cosby Show*
Jacqueline Bobo, *Black Women as Cultural Readers* (1995)	Focus groups of African American women	Interpretive communities	Analysis of women's discussion of the film *The Color Purple*	Women interwove their own under-standings of the book with the film
Bambi Haggins, "Transforming the Mythos" (1999)	Ethnography and individual interviews	Application of lay theory, encoding/ decoding	Analysis of field notes; transcripts of interviews with participants regarding television, identity, and the American Dream	Negotiated readings done by participants reveal complicated lay theories that parallel cultural and theoretical practices
Robin Means-Coleman, *African American Viewers and the Black Situation Comedy* (2000)	Individual interviews with African American adults	Encoding/ decoding; ideological hegemony based on racial domination, marginaliza-tion, and exclu-sion; polysemic nature of the sitcom	Textual analysis of Black sitcoms and analysis of interviews with partici-pants regard-ing their opinion of Black sitcoms	Analysis reveals the complex negotiation processes involved in Blacks' viewing of Black sitcom texts in a particular sociohistorical moment
C. Squires, "Black Talk Radio" (2000); "Black Audi-ences, Past and Present" (2002)	Ethnography of talk radio shows at a Black-owned radio station	Oppositional consciousness; interpretive communities	Analysis of field notes; transcripts of radio talk shows	Five major themes for a critique of mainstream media and a desire for more Black control of media

themes of this body of research is the effort to recognize diversity within and across Black communities. Scholars of Black audiences have borrowed aspects of ethnographic research in order to recognize diversity within and across Black communities and to look at different subsets of that audience in order to make sense of their experiences with particular media texts. These scholars strive to avoid constructing a monolithic notion of "The Black Audience." These studies provide glimpses of the complex and nuanced readings that take place as segments of the African American audience interact with different media texts and media events.

Notable among these studies is Jacqueline Bobo's groundbreaking work on Black female audiences. Her book *Black Women as Cultural Readers* (1995) applied the idea of interpretive communities to audience research, theorizing that Black women, who share particular experiences and identities, craft unique interpretations of media texts. The work explains how audiences integrate their own life experiences and cultural knowledge into their reading of a media text. For example, even though many African American critics considered Steven Spielberg's adaptation of Alice Walker's novel *The Color Purple* a disaster, the Black women Bobo interviewed had woven their knowledge of Walker's original work and the feelings the novel gave them into their viewing experience (Bobo 1995, chap. 3). These women were able to transfer the emotional involvement experienced in reading and talking about the book with their friends into the movie environment. While their integrative reading practices do not negate the readings of critics who found the film racist and sexist, their alternative reception cautions us to steer away from assuming a homogeneous interpretation of texts across Black communities.

As encoding/decoding and the concept of interpretive communities have been applied in other settings, scholars have revealed both compelling similarities as well as important differences within and across Black communities interacting with various media texts. Many of these studies emphasize the ambivalent, often conflicted relationship African Americans have with media systems that have routinely excluded and/or stereotyped their group; others explore the pleasurable and critical aspects of media consumption, often experienced simultaneously by African American audience members.

Bambi Haggins found that her subjects integrated life experiences into their reception of televisual texts. In the first part of her autoethnographic Homefront study, Haggins's examination of the interplay between the medium of television, the American Dream and racial/national identity formation is framed by multiple "lay theories" of spectatorship gleaned from interviews with a family of African American women (ages ranging from the early thirties to the late sixties) (Haggins 1999a). Haggins occupied dual spaces throughout the interview process—confidante and critic, "sister" and scholar, transcriber and translator—because of her long-standing relationship to the respondents (which was more intimate than the affinity between the respondent and interviewer in either Bobo's or Seiter's study). Thus, in the Homefront study, which was constructed to privilege "lay theory," Haggins was a virtual insider who both empathetically and intellectually understood the history and culture that inflected the women's responses and shared with them both literally and metaphorically a "homefront" (Haggins 2000).

When questioned about their definitions of the American Dream, the respondents spoke directly to processes of "translating" the Dream and "reading" *across the grain* of televisual texts. As the discursive components of their lay theories of televisual spectatorship, their readings (and/or rereadings) of televisual texts reflected what Marie Gillespie, reflecting on Paul Gilroy's work, referred to as the "special role" that the medium plays "in mediating both the racial [and national] identities that are freely chosen and the oppressive effects of racism" (Gillespie 1995, 7).

This segment of the Homefront study acknowledges that these Black women, with a multiplicity of shared affinities and ideological as well as cultural and familial bonds, must also be recognized as individuals, whose readings are inflected by, among other things, the historical moment at which each came of age both emotionally and intellectually. However, while the participants' responses can be interpreted as a family's equivocated acceptance of both the American Dream and television's role in shaping their senses of self, they also reveal their conflicted and conflictual relationship between the mythos, the medium, and, by extension, the African American community.

The second phase of Haggins's Homefront study expanded the boundaries of the homefront from the family to another larger social construct within a community: a public school. Haggins's choice of site for the school component was influenced by the desire to replicate the dual status she had enjoyed in the first phase of the Homefront study.[1] The year of classroom contact (as coteacher/tutor in two required senior social studies classes) afforded Haggins the opportunity to gain partial insider status while conducting in-depth individual interviews with an ethnically, economically, and racially diverse group of self-selected student participants.

Interestingly, the students' negotiated readings *across the grain* of tele-visual texts, picking and choosing the voices that speak to them in the most ancillary ways, mirrored that conflicted and conflictual process of identity formation discerned in the familial component of the study. As exemplified by one African American female respondent's assertion that she loved the WB network teen dramedy *Dawson's Creek* despite ac-knowledging that she knew the "show was for white people," the stu-dents' responses revealed that, in the process of negotiation with the tele-visual text, there is an unspoken acknowledgment of exclusion and/or absence; the identifications are defined not by *what is you* but rather by *how your experience can be reframed* within another's context. The read-ing is not oppositional, rather it is a form of conciliatory resignation for the spectator—taking what is given by the medium and making do by making meaning. This portion of the study also reminds us as scholars to remember that Black audiences continue to consume and interact with media texts not specifically targeted to them, and may interact with said texts with a degree of tension.

While the respondents in the Homefront study commented upon televisual texts from a variety of genres and eras, Robin Means-Coleman (2000) examined Black viewers' relation to contemporary Black situa-tion comedies. This genre, which many critics accuse of recycling harm-ful stereotypes, elicited a range of reactions and opinions from Black au-dience members. Her study employed multiple interviews, reflecting the ethnographer's stance that "the relationship with the participants is col-laborative, intersubjective" (11). The result is that she and the partici-pants were able to dialogue about the sitcoms. These dialogues portray an audience in a "struggle over meanings originating from what is deemed the dominant society, as perpetrated through television, and what those meanings say about Blackness" (Means-Coleman 2000, 13). The interviews reveal varied answers to three basic questions often asked but, save for the first, rarely vigorously explored in Black audience re-search: How are African Americans portrayed? How do African Ameri-cans regard themselves in relation to Black sitcom characters? How do African Americans characterize the relationship between television rep-resentations of Blackness in Black sitcoms and societal perceptions of African Americans and Blackness? In addition to addressing these ques-tions, the interviewees also offered up potential solutions to what were seen as problematic patterns of representation. Solutions often involved an increase in Black-owned or Black-controlled media institutions.

Just as it is important to understand African Americans' relationship with mainstream or dominant media sources, so too must we revisit media owned by and texts produced by and for African Americans. Catherine Squires's (2000, 2002) studies of Black news media audiences combined ethnographic participant-observation, a mail-in survey, and analysis of talk radio transcripts and Black newspaper content to provide an in-depth view of how African Americans utilize Black-owned media as a virtual and physical public sphere. The second study compared the reactions of contemporary and past Black audiences to perceived racism in mainstream media. Utilizing transcripts of Black talk radio programs, letters to Black newspapers, and commentary published in those newspapers, Squires (2002) excavated how active Black audiences sought to directly critique and/or address White media practitioners. Both in direct conversation with White media makers (via talk radio) and through mediated public discussions (via letters to the editor), Black audiences expressed five basic concerns about the impact of mass media on Black collectives.

1. Mainstream media only shows extremes in the Black community, not a continuum of actions and identities. Negative events and actions of Blacks (usually in the lower economic classes) are emphasized.
2. Whites believe stereotypical depictions of Blacks, thus perpetuating harmful racial stereotypes.
3. Differences between Blacks and other ethnic groups are blown out of proportion to incite conflicts and controversy.
4. Media producers and figures must be held accountable for racist texts.
5. Blacks need to create and use their own media to distribute better information and less racial bias in coverage of Black life (Squires 2002).

These studies found that the Black media consumers utilized the Black-owned programming to reinforce a strong, African American–centered "oppositional consciousness"[2] to deal with dominant media depictions of Blackness and what they perceived to be racially charged political events.

Squires's work foregrounds the notion of a Black audience actively engaged in the process of interpreting and reacting to media messages. However, the sector of the audience she investigated was already politically active in their community. Not all audiences will be as politically aware or consume media with that politicized frame of mind, or with the same oppositional framework. Indeed, a recent collection of Black audience studies, *Say It Loud! African-American Audiences, Media, and Identity* (Means-Coleman 2002), reveals a landscape of variety within the Black audience, as well as a host of approaches to Black audiences. Contributions to the book include studies focused on how media impact Black audiences' attitudes about masculinity, how youth process images of Blackness and Black male achievements, and other spotlights on the diverse issues and media choices facing Black communities. As editor Robin Means-Coleman states in her introduction, the book presents new avenues for research as well as a group of new questions to be pursued.

Discussions of Black audiences and their reactions to media texts cannot be complete without considering class, gender, and sexuality. Future work needs to continue to explore how these intersectional identities work in viewing, listening, and reading contexts as Black audience members interact with a host of media in both public and intimate settings. Relatedly, scholars must investigate how these differences work themselves out as Black audiences seize upon ever-increasing opportunities to migrate to new media spaces and capitalize on new media technologies. Black audience interactions with online, satellite, digital, and "underground" media spaces have rarely been explored (Cornwell and Orbe 2002). Work must be initiated on whether and how Black communities use digital media to connect across distance throughout the Diaspora. Scholarship on the global diffusion of Afrocentric music and forms of Black popular culture suggest that Black audiences may be migrating digitally through what Appadurai (1993) calls "mediascapes," connecting with producers and fans of Black popular culture across the Atlantic and Caribbean.

As the media landscape changes with economic and technological trends, the twentieth-century model of maximizing audiences has morphed into a twenty-first-century strategy to cater to multiple demographic slices of the audience, both within and across particular venues. Groups with different racial, ethnic, class, gender, age, and sexual orientations are all being sought, and media producers are trying to find the next big thing to satisfy these different audiences, often across as well as within national boundaries. Thus, media producers scramble to create media texts that sell to a variety of audiences, or, as in the recent case of Viacom's takeover of BET, acquire formulas that work.

One mechanism of addressing an audience ever-splintering along complicated demographic lines is the phenomenon that Haggins characterizes as *mirror sitcoms*. These television programs replicate each other in characters and situation setups, but with "opposite race" casts, wherein "parallel constructions of American life are created—often in Black and White." Exemplary of this trend are the dyads *The Cosby Show/Family Ties* and *Friends/Living Single,* mirror sitcoms from the 1980s and 1990s, respectively. One can argue that "mirror sitcoms" are variations of what Herman Gray refers to as "separate but equal discourses" (1994). Their narratives "situate Black characters in domestically centered Black worlds and circumstances that essentially parallel those of whites. Like their white counterparts, these shows . . . maintain a commitment to the universal acceptance into the transparent 'normative' middle class" (87).

A recent mirror sitcom dyad is formed by HBO's acclaimed hit *Sex and the City* (*SATC*) and the Warner Brothers (now CW) network's *Girlfriends* (*GF*). These shows are clearly products of the niched, narrowcasted postnetwork era; they are also reflective of the narrative and aesthetic divide between network programming and that of premium cable. These twin shows, targeted at female audiences of different racial groups, are productive texts to explore the ways in which specific members of Black audiences respond to and understand their role in the evolving media landscape.

Our recent study attempted to tease out the pleasures and pedagogies involved in young single women's readings of the two series, inspired by the methodological frameworks discussed above. Utilizing a participant pool of Black women and White women (ages 18–26), focus groups of four to six women (Black women only, White women only, and a group with both White women and women of color) were formed. Each group met once a week for a period of four weeks. Like Jhally and Lewis (1992), we wanted to use the mechanism of comparison to see how race plays out on screen for differently raced audience members; however, we are also attuned to the importance of cross-cutting identities, such as gender and class, which can complicate readings of texts that are so clearly raced and gendered. Thus, multiple, rather than single, conversations with these women provided the opportunity to engage in a collaborative effort with the participants. This approach facilitated nuanced discussions about their interactions with and understandings of these televisual texts. Over the course of the month of weekly meetings, the women became more candid with each other and with us. Thus, the analyses of the data from these focus groups provided a deeper understanding of the women's reactions not only to the racial mirroring but also to the processes of reading these texts for both aesthetic pleasures and ideological directives, particularly as they related to the respondents' notions of "realism."

In the first article generated from the focus group data, "What A Girl Wants: 'Realism,' Identification, and Pleasure in *Girlfriends* and *Sex and The City*" (Haggins and Squires 2006), we focused on how specific notions of realism were mobilized by the respondents of the Black-only and White-only groups to speak to issues of gender through the doubled lens of race and class. Aesthetic, industrial, and generic conventions (comedy with melodrama in *SATC* vs. conventional sitcom in *GF*) shape the narrative trajectories of these two series. *SATC*, which aired its series finale in 2004, has passed into the realm of the DVD and syndication in network and basic cable form while *Girlfriends*, one of the few Black sitcoms to find a coveted space in the CW's Monday "Black block," continues. As a prime-time network sitcom, the UPN (now CW) series *Girlfriends* could be neither as bawdy nor, we argue, as angst ridden as its HBO counterpart.

In order to give participants entrée into these series at roughly the same point in narrative development, they were shown episodes from the second season of each series. Our belief was that these episodes were early enough in the series' life to be reflective of the show's initial zeitgeist and late enough for the characters to have established both their voices and their shtick. Undoubtedly the fact that, in the popular press (and, arguably, mainstream popular culture), *Girlfriends* was nicknamed "*Sex and the City* in Black" reveals a privileging of White culture that is only partially based on notions of "quality television." The groups' different reactions go beyond questions of broadcast TV versus premium cable, three camera versus single camera, conventional sitcom versus comedy with melodrama, and Black cast versus White cast. As signified by the participants' responses, their "reading" processes and the possibility for identification across lines of race and class continue to be problematic as these polysemic televisual texts reinscribe issues of class and race in ways that are simultaneously reductive and complex.

The focus group discussions followed screenings of *SATC*'s "The Freak Show" (airdate June 20, 1999) and *GF*'s "I Have a Dream House" (airdate January 21, 2002) foregrounded the differences in the "perceived" agenda of each series by Black and White audiences. The storyline of the *SATC* episode focuses on Carrie bemoaning the dating pool's similarity to a covert "freak show" and her comeuppance upon realizing her own freakiness. The storyline of *GF* depicts Joan lobbying her White male boss to recognize Martin Luther King, Jr. Day. The boss makes explicit racial and sexual jokes and inappropriate remarks throughout the show.

Interestingly, the notions of realism became closely associated with women at work and at play for both focus groups. Despite a lack of attention to the characters' source of endless income, White respondents claimed that *SATC* was more "realistic" than *GF*. White respondents asserted that *SATC* was a show where each episode was built around a theme, like "freaky dates," so that the workplace was not a necessary element of each character's life. Only one woman in the White group disagreed; she asserted that *GF* was more realistic because the characters' work lives and class position were closer to her own. While most members of the White groups acknowledged that a freelance writer could hardly afford the clothes, shoes, and apartment Carrie Bradshaw enjoys on the series, they did not say it detracted from the realism of the themes or their identification with the experiences of the characters. They also noted, as did the African American group, that the New York of *SATC* was decidedly "upper crust," as one respondent put it, and largely devoid of people of color.

The theories spun by the White group on how the issue of race or even a person of color might be worked into the show provided insight on how the "issue" could be dealt with.

WR1: . . . I can see Carrie like havin' a whole episode about, like—her first line would be something like "MLK Day and why don't we celebrate it?" or like "why don't we . . ."—you know. I don't think that type of issue would take away from the success of the show *we* have already.

WR2: . . . it would have to have some sort of sexual twist to it [*she laughs*].

WR1: Like Samantha's dating a black guy or—[*many people laugh and assent*]. And he's trying to bring awareness to the women [*she laughs along with group*].

While the final remarks were made facetiously, it is interesting that they did not imagine the *SATC* women being politically involved in an issue. One wonders if the idea of making a political stand on race or sexual harassment in the workplace is seen as something that these respondents felt that they would either not need to do or would not even consider doing.

When later asked to elaborate upon why they found *SATC* "realistic," a number of White respondents focused on their disidentification with *GF*.

WR1: Well, I mean, for these episodes that we just watched, I think all of us can relate to dating someone that's a little scary, but like, I don't know, the stuff in GF, me personally, like fighting for MLK that would be weird because I'm white [*laughs*].

One could argue that there were many more ways to identify with Joan's protests of her boss's refusal to honor MLK Day. The White male boss clearly harassed Joan and other women, and the dilemma of how a woman can find a way to speak out against a male employer is certainly an experience many women of all colors confront in their careers. However, for this respondent (and given the silence of the group, other participants as well) Joan's experience was primarily a *racial* one, not a career or gendered incident.

Unsurprisingly, Black respondents did not share the White respondents' view of Joan's situation. The scenes depicting Joan's conflict with her White boss were seen as having been played broadly, but also to resonate with real-life experiences; they insisted that confrontations with racist and sexist White male employers happen in the real world. Unlike the White group, they discussed how one might prosecute a claim institutionally and were upset that the laugh track seemed to support the "humor" in the boss's lame jokes about subscribing to *Jet* as a substitute for honoring MLK.

Moderator 1: So do you think that boss-employee relationship is realistic?
BR1: Actually I think it is realistic. Like, I think it does happen. Maybe not to that extreme, but I really do think that does happen.
BR2: I don't think to that extreme either, because with the Jet and those comments and um, "I'm down with your peeps," comments like that she could have taken to some higher authority if there is one (people assent) 'cause those are like—I don't know if that's like a racial—it's something, you know what I mean—that you shouldn't do. It's inappropriate basically. So I think she should have said something about that, you know what I mean? I don't think that kind of joking should go on, the race jokes.

Whereas differences in production style and the absence of minorities were discussed in both groups, Black women introduced and explored these topics in a radically different way. First, they, like the women in the White group, also noted that *SATC* did not center on the work lives of its main characters, while *GF* did. They theorized this was due in part to the need to provide audiences with more positive portrayals of Black people in high-end professions.

BR1: [The SATC characters'] jobs seem more laid back [*others assent*]. I mean, Miranda is a lawyer but she, for the most part, she always has time to do whatever it is they're doing. . . .

BR2: I think GF wants to show the audience that a black woman is capable of. . . . they want to emphasize blacks are smart and they have the ability of reaching a high corporate level.

BR3: I think that a lot of this—this is an assumption. I'm not going on factual evidence. But I think a lot of times black shows have the purpose of, kind of like promoting positive, you know, things about black life. . . . So maybe there's not a need for that in SATC. We don't need to know about their career, you know what I mean?

As cultural theorists and media scholars, we would hope that both White and Black groups would be able to see the situation like the Black women did, and have all of them hypothesize about institutional ways Joan could have gotten support to confront her boss, or say definitively that his actions and statements were racist, and that asking an employee for help "hooking up" with her friend was at best borderline sexual harassment. Instead, the White women seemed to find it funny that the White boss was attracted to a Black woman and missed the inappropriateness of his jokes and his attempts to enlist Joan in his seduction efforts. It appears that the overarching narrative within *Girlfriends* was only partially discernible for the White women, and the allegedly racialized issue (MLK day) provided an impediment to identification regarding women in the workplace. To the White women the *Girlfriends* episode was about MLK Day not about workplace harassment, and they saw the boss's bigotry rather than his sexism. The Black respondents saw both.

The Black respondents contended that an additional imperative/burden on Black-themed shows is to promote "positive" images of Blackness while also playing into the historical stereotypes of Black women as "born-workers" and White women as more delicate members of the leisure class. Neither the historical nor the contemporary aspects of these assertions were noted by the White discussants. As one Black respondent said, people are used to seeing White people with money, so *SATC* does not have to explain why these women have money to buy the clothes and eat at the fancy restaurants.

Lessons Learned

- Researchers must steer away from assumptions of homogeneous interpretation of media across Black communities.
- Black audiences consume and interact with media texts even when they are not specifically targeted at them, often with a degree of tension.
- Data collected from focus groups provide a deeper understanding of women's reactions to televisual texts.
- The focus group approach facilitated nuanced discussions about participants' interactions with and understandings of televisual texts.
- Multiple, rather than single, conversations provide an opportunity to engage in a collaborative effort with participants.

Conclusions and New Directions

Certainly the variations in the narrative and stylistic conventions of two single-women comedies impact the processes of identification with the women of *SATC* for both groups and the White groups's disidentification with *Girlfriends;* however, one can also discern how the process of what de Certeau (1984) described as "making do" continues to inflect the spectatorial practices and pleasures of the Black focus group participants in ways that simply do not occur to their White counterparts. While the White respondents were drawn into "realistic" experiences of dating (thematic rather than plot driven) in *SATC,* the particular issue-driven aspect of the *GF* narrative failed to resonate. Black women see themselves in both series or, in the case of *SATC,* desire to see themselves, aspiring to something that is often just out of reach for Black women on television and in mainstream popular culture: The representations of often unfulfilled aspirations for leisure (connected to economic privilege) and respect (awarded rather than necessarily fought for in the professional realm) and to be feminine and considered a feminine woman with sexual agency without falling into the stereotype of the hypersexualized Black woman, the tragic mulatta, or the desexualized caretaker.

While there are many ways that *Girlfriends* is clearly an imperfect text, as is *SATC,* the readings by and resonances for these respondents, both Black and White, call to mind Mimi White's (1992) assertion about the ideological function of television: "As a site of textual activity, television is the locus of the intersection and coexistence of varying narratives, genres, appeals, and modes of address. Viewers consent to watch, and submit to its array of appeals, in exchange for the text and the *possibility* of identifying particular meanings, mobilizing the voices that seem to speak 'to them'" (191). For many of these female respondents, the promise of that possibility remains at least partially unfulfilled. It is our hope that the research described above will open new avenues for understanding Black audiences as well as increase audience awareness and empowerment.

NOTES

1. The time at William L. Blair High in Pasadena, California, was the return of the native for Haggins, who had attended the high school during the era when conflicts over Court-ordered desegregation (the "Pasadena Plan") were inflecting the school and community culture (both positively and negatively).
2. The term *oppositional consciousness* is taken from Aldon Morris (1992).

REFERENCES

Ang, I. 1985. *Watching Dallas: Soap opera and the melodramatic imagination.* London: Routledge.

Ang, I. 1991. *Desperately seeking the audience.* London: Routledge.

Ang, I. 1996. *Living room wars: Rethinking audiences for a post-modern world.* London: Routledge.

Bobo, J. 1995. *Black women as cultural readers.* New York: Columbia University Press.

Bourdieu, P. 1984. *Distinction: A social critique of judgment and taste.* Cambridge: Harvard University Press.

Dates, J., and W. Barlow, eds. 1990. *Split image: African Americans in the media.* Washington, DC: Howard University Press.

de Certeau, M. 1984. *The practice of everyday life.* Berkeley: University of California Press.

Dixon, T., and D. Linz. 2000. Overrepresentation and underrepresentation of

African Americans and Latinos as lawbreakers on television news. *Journal of Communication* 50:131–54.

Frutkin, A. J. 2006. For diversity's sake: Will African-American comedies find a home on CW? *Mediaweek* 16, no. 5: 6.

Gilens, M. 1999. *Why Americans hate welfare: Race, media, and the politics of anti-poverty policy.* Chicago: University of Chicago Press.

Gillespie, M. 1995. *Television, ethnicity, and cultural change.* London: Routledge.

Gray, H. 1994. Response to Justin Lewis and Sut Jhally. *American Quarterly*, March 1994.

Gray, H. 1995. *Watching race: Television and the struggle for "Blackness."* Minneapolis: University of Minnesota Press.

Gray, H. 2001. Desiring the network and network desire. *Critical Studies in Media Communication* 18, no. 1: 103–8.

Haggins, B. 1999a. Transforming the mythos: Homefront viewers rethink the American Dream. *Emergences: Journal for the Study of Media and Composite Cultures* 9, no. 1: 117–30.

Haggins, B. 1999b. There's no place like home: African American identity, the situation comedy, and the American Dream. *Velvet Light Trap*, 43:23–34.

Haggins, B. 2000. The American Dream . . . by any means necessary: Lay theories from urban suburbia. PhD dissertation, University of California, Los Angeles.

Hall, S. 1980. Encoding/decoding. In S. Hall et al., eds., *Culture, media, language,* 128–38. London: Hutchinson.

Jenkins, H. 1992. *Textual poachers: Television fans and participatory culture.* London: Routledge.

Jhally, S., and J. Lewis. 1992. *Enlightened racism: The Cosby Show, audiences, and the myth of the American Dream.* Boulder: Westview Press.

Johnson, J. D., L. A. Jackson, and L. Gatto. 1995. Violent attitudes and deferred academic aspirations: Deleterious effects of exposure to rap music. *Basic and Applied Social Psychology* 16, no. 1–2: 27–41.

Katz, E., T. Liebes, and L. Berko. 1994. On commuting between television fiction and real life. In N. Browne, ed., *American television: New directions in history and theory.* Langhorne, PA: Harwood Academic.

Means-Coleman, R. R. 2000. *African American viewers and the Black situation comedy.* New York: Garland.

Means-Coleman, R. R., ed. 2002. *Say it loud! African American audiences, media, and identity.* New York: Routledge.

Morley, D. 1980. *The "Nationwide" audience: Structure and decoding.* London: British Film Institute.

Morley, D. 1992. *Television audiences and cultural studies.* London: Routledge.

Morley, D. 1996. *Family television: Cultural power and domestic leisure.* London: Comedia.

Morris, A. 1992. Political consciousness and collective action. In A. Morris and C. McClurg Mueller, eds., *Frontiers in social movement theory,* 351–73. New Haven: Yale University Press.

Radway, J. 1991. Interpretive communities and variable literature: The functions of romance reading. In C. Mukerj and M. Schudson, eds., *Rethinking popular culture: Contemporary perspectives in cultural studies,* 465–86. Berkeley: University of California Press.

Riggs, M. 1991. *Color adjustment.* Film. San Francisco: California Newsreel.

Seiter, E. 1995. *Television and new media audiences.* Oxford: Oxford University Press.

Squires, C. 2000. Black talk radio: Defining community needs and identity. *Harvard International Journal of Press/Politics* 5, no. 2.

Squires, C. 2002. Black audiences, past and present common sense media critics. In R. Means-Coleman, ed., *Say it loud! African American audiences, media, and identity,* 45–76. New York: Routledge.

Valentino, N. 1999. Crime news and the priming of racial attitudes during evaluations of the president. *Public Opinion Quarterly* 63:293–321.

Ward, L. M., E. Hansborough, and E. Walker. 2005. Contributions of music video exposure to Black adolescents' gender and sexual schemas. *Journal of Adolescent Research* 20, no. 2: 143–66.

Webster, J., and P. Phalen. 1997. *The mass audience: Rediscovering the dominant model.* Mahwah, NJ: Erlbaum.

White, M. 1992. Ideological analysis and television. In R. C. Allen, ed., *Channels of discourse, reassembled,* 191. 2nd ed. Chapel Hill: University of North California Press.

Contributors

Dr. Jewell F. Brazelton is Professor in the Department of Behavior Sciences and General Studies at American Baptist College. Her research considers the challenging issue of disclosure of childhood sexual abuse for a cohort of African American women ages 40–55, focusing on how the childhood trauma has affected the social functioning and well-being of these women as they execute their many midlife roles, including parenting and caring for aging relatives.

Dr. Cleopatra Howard Caldwell's research interests involve the mental health risks and opportunities involved in early childbearing, perspectives of multiple family members who have been affected by the birth of a baby to a teenage mother, and black churches as community-based institutional support systems. She is an associate professor in the Department of Health Behavior and Health Education at the University of Michigan. Some of her recent publications include "Social Networks: Community-Based Institutional Supports for Black Women," in N. J. Burgess and E. Brown's *African American Women: An Ecological Perspective* (2000), and "Culturally-Competent Research Methods in African American Communities: An Update," in R. Jones's *Advances in African American Psychology* (1999).

Dr. Letha A. Chadiha is associate professor in the School of Social Work at the University of Michigan. Her current research focuses on the mental health, social roles, and service use of African American women caregivers assisting African American older adults and the recruitment and retention of ethnically diverse older adults in health-related research.

Dr. William A. Darity Jr. is Arts and Sciences Professor of Public Policy, African and African-American Studies and Economics at Duke University. His current projects include skin shade and labor market outcomes; caste and race; job tenure versus work experience; editing the *International Encyclopedia of the Social Sciences,* stratification economics; in-

equality by race, class, and ethnicity; North-South theories of development and trade; social psychology and unemployment exposure; reparations; schooling and the racial achievement gap; and financial crises in
developing countries.

Dr. Bambi Haggins is an Associate Professor in Film & Media Studies at
Arizona State University. Her research explores representations of class,
ethnicity, gender, race, and region in American fim and television. Her
first book, *Laughing Mad: The Black Comic Persona in Post Soul America*
(2007), won the prestigious The Katherine Singer Kovacs Book Award
for outstanding book of the year from the Society for Cinema and Media
Studies. Her publications include articles in *Emergences, Flow,
Framework,* and *Ms.* as well as essays in *The Essential HBO Reader* (2007)
and *Satire TV* (2009). She is currently working on a project dealing with
the cultural history of American television, identity, and the American
Dream.

Dr. Darrick Hamilton is an associate professor of economics and urban
policy at The New School, a faculty research fellow at the Schwartz Center for Economic Policy Analysis, an affiliate scholar at the Center for
American Progress, and a research affiliate at the Research Network on
Racial and Ethnic Inequality at Duke University. He is a key contributor
in the emerging economic subfield of stratification economics. His work
focuses on the causes, consequences, and remedies of racial and ethnic
inequality in economic and health outcomes, which includes an examination of the intersection of identity, racism, colorism, and socioeconomic outcomes.

Dr. Michelle Harris is an associate professor and Graduate Program Coordinator in the Department of Sociology and Social Work at Northern
Arizona University. In 2002 she was Co-Principal Investigator of The
Study of the Family in Jamaica, a survey research project that gathered
data on a number of topics including family life and the mental and
physical health of Jamaican adults. Most recently, she conducted a survey
of Indigenous identity formation in New South Wales, Australia (2007),
and was the founder of the Working Group on Emergent Indigenous
Identities (2010) that is comprised of a multinational/multidisciplinary
group of scholars who explore identity construction and performance
among indigenous peoples around the world. Her scholarly and teaching
interests focus on mental health, specifically psychological distress and
well-being in adult populations, perception of discrimination among

minority Americans, immigrant acculturation and well-being, critical race theory, and identity development among adults.

Dr. Julia F. Hastings is assistant professor in the Schools of Public Health and Social Welfare at the University at Albany, SUNY. Globally, her research interests cover health and mental health disparities among ethnic minority populations, African American mental health, welfare participation dynamics, and ethnic minority women's health issues. Her research projects focus on the interrelationships between race, mental health outcomes, health conditions, risk and protective factors, and poverty. Dr. Hastings has published on culturally competent research methods within African American communities, welfare participation, depression, and body weight. She received her MSW from the University of Washington and PhD from the University of California, Los Angeles. Her postdoctoral training occurred at the University of Michigan in the Program for Research on Black Americans at the Institute for Social Research; the School of Public Policy; and the School of Social Work. She also completed a certification in epidemiology from the Department of Epidemiology at the University of Michigan's School of Public Health.

Dr. Andrea G. Hunter is an Associate Professor in the Department of Human Development and Family Studies at the University of North Carolina, Greensboro. Her research focuses on variations in the context, structure, and social organization of families and social networks and their impact on roles, behavior, and well-being across the life span; constructions of gender and the ways in which gender shapes family roles and the life course; African American family history; the life course and social change; and intellectual traditions in Black Family Studies. Underlying this work is an emphasis on the influences of race, gender, social class, and culture on family life and well-being and on intellectual thought. Dr. Hunter is published in a variety of national and international academic journals in the areas of family studies; child development, developmental psychology, and youth studies; aging; gender and African American studies; social and family history; and social work.

James S. Jackson is the Daniel Katz Distinguished University Professor of Psychology, professor of Health Behavior and Health Education, School of Public Health, and Director of the Institute for Social Research, all at the University of Michigan. His research focuses on issues of racial and ethnic influences on life course development, attitude change, reciprocity, social support, and coping and health among blacks in the Diaspora.

He is past director of the Center for Afroamerican and African Studies and past national president of the Black Students Psychological Association and Association of Black Psychologists. He is the recipient of the Distinguished Career Contributions to Research Award, Society for the Psychological Study of Ethnic Minority Issues, American Psychological Association, and recently received the James McKeen Cattell Fellow Award for Distinguished Career Contributions in Applied Psychology from the Association for Psychological Sciences. He is an elected member of the Institute of Medicine of the National Academies of Sciences. He serves on several boards for the National Research Council and the National Academies of Science and is a founding member of the Aging Society Research Network of the MacArthur Foundation.

Dr. Deborah J. Johnson is professor of Human Development and Family Studies at Michigan State University. Her research is on status-based, race, and culturally related development, parental socialization, and parent-child relations in early and middle childhood. In particular, how parental messages and context influence the racial coping responses of children has been the focus of her work. Much of her work has been in the area of racial/ethnic identity development and racial socialization in varying contexts, including child care principally among African American and other ethnic children and families, but also internationally with Zimbabwean youth. She continues with her international interests exploring these issues among Sudanese refugee youth and indigenous youth of Western Australia. Of 45 published articles and chapters, several recent publications focus on disentangling race, poverty, and culture; theory development in the area of racial-ethnic socialization; and research methods in cultural communities. She is a co-editor (with Slaughter-Defoe, Arrington, and Stevenson) of a recent volume entitled *Black Educational Choice in a Climate of School Reform: Consequences for K–12 Student Learning and Development* (2011) and lead editor on the book (with Agbenyiga and Hitchcock) *Vulnerable Children: Global Challenges in Education, Health, Well-Being, and Child Rights* (forthcoming).

Dr. Heidi T. Kromrei is an epidemiologist with Henry Ford Health Systems in Detroit, Michigan. Her research interests include performance management and improvement and strategic planning for research organizations. She completed her Master of Arts Degree in Performance Improvement and Instructional Design with the University of Michigan–Dearborn and is currently a PhD student enrolled in the Administrative and Organizational Studies Division, Department of Instructional Technology, at Wayne State University's School of Education.

Dr. Amanda E. Lewis is an Associate Professor in the Department of Sociology at Emory University and a co-leader of the university's Race and Difference Initiative. Her research focuses on how race shapes educational opportunities and on how our ideas about race get negotiated in everyday life. She also has written extensively about the role of white people as racial actors in American society. She received her BA in educational studies from Brown University, her MA in education from the University of California at Berkeley, and her PhD in Sociology from the University of Michigan. Her previous work includes *Race in the Schoolyard: Negotiating the Color-Line in Classrooms and Communities* (Rutgers University Press, 2003), an edited volume (with Maria Krysan), *The Changing Terrain of Race and Ethnicity* (Russell Sage, 2004), and *Challenging Racism in Higher Education: Promoting Justice* (with Mark Chesler and Jim Crowfoot—Rowman and Littlefield Press, 2005). Her research has also appeared in a number of academic journals, including *Sociological Theory, American Educational Research Journal, American Behavioral Scientist, Race and Society,* and *Anthropology and Education Quarterly.* She is currently at work on a new book (with John Diamond) titled *Despite the Best Intentions: Why Racial Inequality Persists in Good Schools* (Oxford, forthcoming).

Dr. Nikeea Copeland Linder is an assistant professor in the Department of General Pediatrics and Adolescent Medicine at the Johns Hopkins University School of Medicine. Her research focuses on the impact of psychosocial stressors on the mental health and health risk behaviors of youth. She is particularly interested in community violence exposure as a source of stress in the lives of youth and the role of parental and cultural factors in fostering resilience despite chronic exposure. In addition, she has conducted research on the protective role of ethnic identity and religion among populations exposed to chronic stress. She conducted research in Soweto as a Fogarty International Research Trainee.

Dr. Jennifer Mueller is an associate professor at the University of Wisconsin–Milwaukee. She is the Program Chair for the Early Childhood Teacher Education Program. Her research interests include teacher education policy, pedagogy, programming, curriculum, and practice related to preparation of teachers for equitable teaching practice in urban, multicultural, and diverse settings. Her most recent writing focuses on how identity (marked by race, social class, gender, and sexual orientation) frames and influences the ways that teacher education students engage with and take up multicultural teacher preparation. She and her colleagues at UW-M were recently awarded a multiyear grant from the Department of Education Office of Language Acquisition to enhance the capacity of local educators of young children to engage in effective teaching practices with English Language Learners in order to maximize school success. Dr. Mueller earned her BS in elementary education from the University of Wisconsin–Madison and was a practicing classroom teacher for several years. She completed her MA in Educational Foundations and Policy and her PhD in Teacher Education at the University of Michigan.

Dr. Dolores G. Norton is the Samuel Deutsch Professor Emerita in the School of Social Service Administration (SSA) at the University of Chicago. Her areas of special interest include early child development and ecology, human development and diversity, early linguistic interaction and temporal development related to school achievement, and family support practice and programs. Professor Norton has published on early linguistic interaction and school achievement; diversity, early socialization, and temporal development; and black family life patterns. Her 20-year longitudinal research, "Children at Risk: The Infant and Child Development Project," investigates patterns of parent/child interaction related to developmental outcomes, especially school achievement, of high-risk inner city African American children and their families. She has helped to shape more effective supports for these children through her work with the California Department of Education Preschool Learning Guidelines, the Family Focus Advisory Board, the Zero to Three, and the U.S. Administration for Children, Youth, and Families Advisory Board on Early Head Start. She is a member of the advisory boards of the Urban Teacher Education Program at the University of Chicago, the Bryn Mawr Graduate School of Social Work and Social Research, and the Revere Community School.

Dr. Carla O'Connor is Arthur F. Thurnau Professor and Associate Professor of Education at the University of Michigan. Her disciplinary emphasis is sociology of education, and she has expertise in the areas of African American achievement, urban education, and ethnographic methods. Her work includes examinations of how Black identity is differentially constructed across multiple contexts and influences educational outcomes; how Black people's perceptions of opportunity vary within and across social space and shape academic orientation; and how Black educational resilience and vulnerability are structured by social, institutional, and historical forces. Dr. O'Connor's work has been published in the *American Educational Research Journal, Educational Researcher, Sociology of Education,* and *Ethnic and Racial Studies.* She coedited (with Erin McNamara Horvat) the book *Beyond Acting White: Reframing the Debate on Black Student Achievement.* She currently serves as codirector of the NSF-sponsored Center for the Study of Black Youth in Context. Dr. O'Connor received her PhD in Education from the University of Chicago. She also holds an MA in Education from the University of Chicago and a BA in English from Wesleyan University.

Dr. Terri L. Orbuch is a professor of sociology at Oakland University and a research professor at the University of Michigan, Institute for Social Research and Institute for Research on Women and Gender. She is the project director of a long-term study on marriage and divorce (1986–present) funded by the National Institutes of Health. She has published several articles on marriage and divorce, dating and sexuality, parent-child relationships, accounts and storytelling, and the effects of divorce on children. Dr. Orbuch's work has been published in *Social Forces, Journal of Marriage and the Family, Family Relations, Psychological Science,* and *Social Psychology Quarterly.* Her latest books are *5 Simple Steps to Take Your Marriage from Good to Great* (Delacorte Press, 2009) and *Finding Love Again: 6 Simple Steps to a New and Happy Relationship* (Sourcebooks, 2012).

Dr. Sherrill L. Sellers is an associate professor in the Department of Family Studies and Social Work at Miami University in Oxford, OH, and an Adjunct Faculty Associate at the Institute for Social Research, University of Michigan. Her research program centers on the examination of the impact of social inequalities on mental and physical health and in social institutions. Dr. Sellers seeks to understand the intersections of race, class, and gender, specifically the pathways, processes, and mechanism by which these social dimensions are translated into differential outcomes. Her most recent research investigates physicians' understanding of human genetic variation and the role of race in clinical decision making. She has published extensively using both quantitative and qualitative research methods, including articles in *Gender & Society, Ethnicity & Disease, American Journal of Public Health,* and the *Journal of Health and So-*

cial Behavior. Dr. Sellers has also authored numerous book chapters on social and cultural factors that affect physical and mental health of ethnic minorities. Dr. Sellers's professional objective is to increase the provision of culturally and linguistically appropriate services to underserved populations.

Dr. Lonnie R. Snowden is a professor at the University of California at Berkeley. His research interests include organization and financing of health/mental health service systems with a focus on access and effectiveness of care to minority and underserved populations. His current research is on minority access to mental health treatment and culturally focused outreach; treatment effectiveness and quality of care to minorities; and emergency care for minority adults and children.

Dr. Catherine Squires is the inaugural Cowles Professor of Journalism, Diversity, and Equality at the University of Minnesota. Squires's first book, *Dispatches from the Color Line,* analyzes news coverage of controversies surrounding people of multiracial descent. Other work has been published in journals such as *International Journal of Press/Politics, Rhetoric and Public Affairs,* and *Critical Studies in Media Communication.* She has chapters in the books *Counterpublics and the State* (SUNY, 2001), *Say It Loud! African American Audiences, Media, and Identity* (Routledge, 2002), and *African American Communication and Identities: Essential Readings* (Sage, 2004). Her most recent book, *African Americans and the Media,* was published by Polity Press in November 2009.

Ms. Julie Sweetman is a research associate at the Program for Research on Black Americans at the University of Michigan Institute for Social Research. She received her BA in Psychology (2001) and her MS in Survey Methodology (2006) from the University of Michigan. She has extensive experience as the data manager for the National Survey of American Life and is an expert on the use of complex sample survey data.

Ms. Myriam Torres, MS in statistics, is a former Senior Research Associate for the Program for Research on Black Americans (PRBA) at the Institute for Social Research at the University of Michigan. She has over 25 years of experience in all aspects of survey research, including planning, development, fieldwork, data collection, management, documentation, and analysis. Her responsibilities included maintaining the integrity and quality of PRBA data as well as training national scholars in the use of PRBA data sets.

Dr. Joseph Veroff (deceased) was a professor emeritus of psychology at the University of Michigan and a Research Scientist Emeritus, Institute for Social Research.

Dr. Jacquelyn Vincson is a part time lecturer in social work at the University of Illinois Chicago. Her research focuses on early childhood education and high-risk children and families in collaboration with Dolores G. Norton. She is a consultant for the Department of Family and Social Services in Chicago, IL, and works with local early childhood programs to improve child language and literacy outcomes. She also conducts program evaluations for the Teen Parenting Service Network and other human service organizations.

Dr. L. Monique Ward is a professor at the University of Michigan in the Department of Psychology. Her research interests center on children's and adolescents' developing conceptions of both gender and sexuality and on the contribution of these notions to their social and sexual decision making. She is particularly interested in how children interpret and use the messages they receive about male-female relations from the media. To what extent do media portrayals shape adolescents' attitudes and expectations about dating and sexual relationships, which in turn inform their sexual decision making? In a second line of research, she examines how adolescents incorporate sexual communication from their parents with input from other sources. Her work also explores the intersections between gender ideologies, body image, race, and sexuality and explores the dynamics of sexual socialization and sexual development among African American women.

Dr. Melissa Joan Wilhelm is a child development specialist and accomplished researcher. Her professional expertise and work concentrate within the areas of early childhood program development, program evaluation, child outcome assessment, preschool and primary school teacher education, and social emotional assessment of young children. She has worked extensively with Chicago Public Schools to develop strength-based early intervention strategies for children described as "at risk," served as a research associate identifying risk and protective factors for young children at the University of Oxford in Oxford, England, and worked as a therapist in a residential program for young children with emotional and behavioral disabilities. Through her work with the Center for Early Childhood Research at the University of Chicago, Melissa has developed teaching strategies to assess the impact of various environmental factors on academic achievement and currently serves on a number of steering committees and boards for educational programs in the Chicago region.

Dr. Colwick M. Wilson received his PhD in sociology from the University of Michigan. He was Department Chair for Counseling and Family Sciences at Loma Linda University and is currently an associate professor in the University of Michigan School of Nursing. His interests include quantitative and qualitative methodologies, health of Caribbean immigrant families, families in the Anglophone Caribbean, and the influence of family factors on chronic illness.

Monica L. Wolford, MA, is a survey statistician and methodologist with the federal government currently working with the National Center for Health Statistics. Her research interests are longitudinal nonresponse, race and gender issues in survey response, and survey design modes.

Index